sleep with no worries

To Judy,
Hoping you enjoy our story!
Dave & Anne

DAVE AND ANNE BLACK

Trafford
PUBLISHING

Order this book online at www.trafford.com/07-1837
or email orders@trafford.com

Most Trafford titles are also available at major online book retailers.

Note for Librarians: A cataloguing record for this book is available from Library
and Archives Canada at www.collectionscanada.ca/amicus/index-e.html

Printed in Victoria, BC, Canada.

ISBN: 978-1-4251-4377-0

We at Trafford believe that it is the responsibility of us all, as both individuals
and corporations, to make choices that are environmentally and socially sound.
You, in turn, are supporting this responsible conduct each time you purchase a
Trafford book, or make use of our publishing services. To find out how you are
helping, please visit www.trafford.com/responsiblepublishing.html

Our mission is to efficiently provide the world's finest, most comprehensive
book publishing service, enabling every author to experience success.
To find out how to publish your book, your way, and have it available
worldwide, visit us online at www.trafford.com/10510

Trafford
PUBLISHING

www.trafford.com

North America & international
toll-free: 1 888 232 4444 (USA & Canada)
phone: 250 383 6864 ♦ fax: 250 383 6804
email: info@trafford.com

The United Kingdom & Europe
phone: +44 (0)1865 722 113 ♦ local rate: 0845 230 9601
facsimile: +44 (0)1865 722 868 ♦ email: info.uk@trafford.com

10 9 8 7 6 5 4 3 2 1

For Haxhi, Nazife and Dani Brajshori,
who took us on an incredible journey.

As a Canadian,
you must uphold the principles
of democracy, freedom and compassion
which are the foundation
of a strong and united Canada.

From the Canadian Certificate of Citizenship, awarded March 8, 2004 to Nezir, Nazife and Dani Brajshori, nearly five years after their arrival in Canada as refugees from Kosovo.

Foreword

This is a true story, about real people, written in the form of a novel. Some names have been changed to protect the privacy of individuals. All the main characters including the refugee family, their close friends, and the sponsors are identified by their real names.

All the events in this book actually happened. The order of events has been adjusted slightly, to facilitate the flow of the narrative.

In writing this book, the authors attempted to place events within an accurate historical, cultural, political and religious context. However, they make no claim to expertise in any of these areas, and apologize for any errors which may have crept into the text. They ask readers to remember that this is a story of events seen through their eyes and the eyes of the refugees they sponsored, and so in the end involves a rather subjective interpretation of the world.

Acknowledgments

Thank you Nezir, Nazife and Dani for allowing us to write your story. We are indebted to Theresa, Don, Rose-Aline, Claire and Anne M. for joining us and making this sponsorship possible. Thank you Mr. Chrétien for your feedback and encouragement. We wish to thank all our friends for their advice, for their unwavering support and for reading our manuscript. A particular note of thanks in this regard to Catherine Proctor, Mary Black, Jeannette Limoges, Valerie and Lee McDonald, Bob Serré, Valérie Albert, Agnes Westran, Bob Black, Joan Boles, Theresa and Don Myrick, Rose-Aline Belcourt, Claire Knudson, Anne Moore, and Val Willis.

We would also like to thank the many Albanians who helped us experience their warm hospitality firsthand, for their help with translations and for helping us understand some of the cultural differences. We are especially grateful to Shano and Nusret Bejkosalaj, Hava and Rrahman Viniqui, Ismail and Rukije Latifi, and Avdi and Maria Brajshori.

Lastly, our thanks to you, Suzanne Desrochers, for making this all possible. Without your patience, your help, your encouragement, and your wisdom, we would never have got to first base, and this book would not exist.

One

BECOMING SPONSORS

It was a sunny March day in the little French village of Meslay. The kind of day you dream about all winter, if you live in Canada.

Anne and I were in France to seek out our ancestral homelands, the countryside and villages where our ancestors worked and played over three hundred years ago. We had rented a *gîte* just outside the village, and had been gently roused that morning by the sound of swallows flying back and forth to a nest somewhere under the eaves. We had lingered over our breakfast of croissants, orange juice, and *café au lait*, enjoying the sunshine and the bouquet of daffodils set out by our landlady the day before to welcome us to the *gîte*. Now we were headed into the village to pick up a baguette, cheese and *pâté* for the picnic we would have later on. We were filled with even more than the usual anticipation, as this was to be our first drive through the historic province of *Perche*, nestled in the hills just east of Normandy. It was here that one of our ancestors, Jules Trottier, had plied his trade of *charpentier de gros oeuvres*. We were not quite sure what this meant, but thought he may have had a hand in building some of the old bridges and stone churches you still see in almost every village.

We swung into the village square. It was almost noon. People scurried this way and that, carrying plastic bags of groceries, cut flowers, pastry boxes, or baguettes. This was the normal pre-dinner flurry of activity, and we knew the shoppers were already picturing themselves at home, relaxing over a substantial meal, perhaps followed by a nap. There was another, more practical reason for the rush in the square. All the shops would close promptly at 12:00, so that the merchants could also enjoy the time-honoured custom of *déjeuner en famille*. The shops would reopen around 2:00.

We joined the shoppers, heading for the main grocery store. I had already grasped the door handle, and we were about to go in, when we saw a small notice in the form of a letter, taped carefully to the door's glass panel. "*À tous nos chers clients*," it read, "For those of you who would like to help the refugees in Kosovo, we invite you to prepare a basket of personal necessities for a Kosovar family in the refugee camps of Macedonia and Albania. We suggest your basket contain the following items: hand soap, disposable razors, deodorant, dish soap, dish towels, tooth paste. ... " The list went on, but our eyes were drawn to the ending: "*S'il vous plaît*, leave your baskets at the front of the store with the cashier. The Post Office has donated boxes and will pack them and arrange for shipment. Several national trucking companies have donated trucks and drivers, and will transport and deliver the boxes to the refugee camps, where they will be distributed by international aid workers. *Merci pour vôtre gentillesse, Le Gérant*."

Like everyone else, we knew about the war in Kosovo from the television reports every evening. The bombing in Serbia had started off almost casually, a few days before, and the reporters on the spot in Belgrade had delivered eager commentary as the bombs exploded behind them, almost as though they were covering a sporting event. But suddenly the war had taken a nasty turn, as Slobodan Milosevic stepped up his campaign of ethnic cleansing. We knew that thousands of Albanian Kosovars had been driven from their homes and their villages burned. We knew that convoys of refugees were streaming into the neighbouring countries of Albania, Montenegro, and Macedonia. Refugee camps were springing up overnight, and the people needed food, clothing, and medical attention. Already, countries were responding, and France was not to be left out.

What struck us most about the notice on the grocery store door was the way the French government and business were co-operating to bring the huge problem of humanitarian response down to the level of sleep with no worries

individuals going about their daily affairs. How easy it was for all of us to participate. We even had a list of products required. All we had to do was fill a basket as we went about our shopping, and drop it off with the cashier. We filled our basket, placed it with the two dozen baskets already waiting at the front of the store, and then, forgetting Kosovo, set out eagerly for our drive through *Perche*.

As we glided by pastures full of dairy cows, fields ploughed and waiting to be sown, and cosy centuries-old farmsteads fashioned from local stone, we tried to picture Jules Trottier building one of these houses in 1646. That was to be his last year in France. We drove into a *grande allée* of magnificent plane trees, joining high above us in an arch over the road, turned right into the old village of Igé, wound our way down narrow streets into the tiny village square, and stopped in front of a modest seventeenth century church. Jules may well have helped to build this, we thought.

Jules had left France of his own free will, looking for a better life for his family. An entrepreneur, and known to be talented and resourceful, he negotiated a seven-year contract to operate the agricultural holdings of the *Seigneury de Portneuf,* on the St. Lawrence River just west of Quebec City. So as not to prejudice his contract, he had neglected to make any mention of his family to his employer. We can only imagine the Seigneur's surprise and annoyance, when, on the day his ship was to set sail, Jules appeared with a pregnant wife and four children in tow. As it was too late to annul the contract, the Seigneur could only accept the inevitable, and the whole family set off for Canada. Jean-Baptiste, his son, was born during the crossing, and baptized in Quebec City.

We were still musing about the courage, energy, and audacity of Jules when we arrived back at our *gîte* around six o'clock that afternoon. By the time we had our *apéritif* and prepared our supper, it was time for the news, which the French normally enjoyed, *en principe*, along with their evening meal. I flicked on the television, and we sat down to eat.

The lead story featured the Kosovar refugees. Today it was a column of hundreds, maybe thousands, crossing the border into Albania. Some were crowded onto wagons, pulled mostly by tractors or, occasionally, by horses. Others were on foot, pushing wheelbarrows or pulling little

13

carts, piled high with suitcases, plastic bags, little children, or elderly relatives too weak to walk. There were women and children, and a few old men, but almost no men of fighting age. These we assumed had either been killed, or disappeared into the hills to join the Kosovo Liberation Army, or, as it was now commonly known, the KLA.

The endless procession made its way slowly past the cameraman. There was little interaction, and even less conversation, among the participants in this forlorn convoy. Their clothing was simple, unpretentious, and utilitarian: long dresses and heavy sweaters, jeans or coveralls, jackets or heavy three piece suits. Heads bowed, shoulders drooping, the human forms shuffled past, bearing unseen burdens. Occasionally, a face would rise toward the camera, revealing tangled hair and deep brown eyes. Eyes fixed on the camera, but not seeing it, emotionless and empty. No recognition, no reaction. Human forms still moving, carrying on, more acted on than acting, living out their fate.

I felt a deep regret well up inside me, and averted my eyes. It did not help. Here we were, about to enjoy *escallope de veau, sauce de morilles à la crème, pommes de terres vapeur,* and *haricots verts,* along with a *vin blanc de La Loire,* and there were all these people, not far away, who probably had not had a proper meal for days, and did not know where they were going to sleep that night. I looked around the room at the red tile floor, roughcast plaster walls over stone, hand-hewn oak beams above us, and comfortable homey furniture. Ours was probably not unlike the homes many of these people had relaxed in only a day or two before, much as we were now, except theirs had now been vandalized and burned. Momentarily, it was too much for us, and we turned off the TV.

Our pilgrimage to ancestral villages provided welcome counterpoint over the next few days to war in Kosovo. We set out early one cool, blustery morning to drive to Falaise, in Normandy, home to another ancestor, Alice Marie DuPont. Falaise had been almost totally razed during the Second World War, as the retreating Nazis were caught by a pincer of Allied forces in the Battle of the Falaise Gap. One of the few medieval structures that was not destroyed, the chateau in which William the Conqueror was born, still hovers like a protective sentinel over the town. The town itself is totally rebuilt, a prosperous, modern market centre, standing witness to how people, working together, overcame the disaster, devastation, and apparent hopelessness of war.

The next day we voyaged even farther west, into the old province of *Bretagne*. There, near Ploermel, we sought out the village of Roc Brien, seventeenth century home to another branch of the family, the Briens. The Brien ancestors had escaped to Canada in 1676, in the midst of a violent Breton rebellion against King Louis XIV. As we wandered the quiet gravel lanes of Roc Brien, and later as we sipped tisane and sampled local pastries at a tea house in Ploermel, we began to see Kosovo's troubles in a broader perspective. All of history, and not the least our own, had been filled with war, uprisings, and massive population movements, not always voluntary. And yet life went on for these immigrants and for those they left behind, and eventually better times prevailed, both in old country and new. Hopefully, too, the Kosovars would ultimately face better times.

Before leaving northern France, we were delighted to be invited to the home of an old friend, Robert, now retired and living in Le Mans. The smell of spring filled the room as we sat down amongst huge floral bouquets in Robert's apartment. Before long, our conversation turned to current events, and then to Kosovo. "You know," Robert was saying, "Jacques Chirac tried to play the role of peacemaker, earlier this year. *En fait*, France was cosponsor with Britain of the Rambouillet Conference in February. Mr. Chirac had compared the Albanian-Serb antagonism to the historic Franco-German hostility, which had led to three wars between 1870 and 1945, but was now resolved. *C'était un message de l'espoir.* What's more, the Chateau at Rambouillet had been attacked three times by the English over the years, but France and Britain were now co-hosting the Conference in that very same chateau."

"The symbolism seems compelling," I offered. "But why did the peace talks fail?"

"Ah," he reflected, "It was a typical negotiation, with the diplomats pressing for resolution, and eventually proposing a compromise. In the end, it was all for nothing. After much hesitation, the Albanian Kosovars accepted the compromise deal, which would have seen NATO troops deployed in Kosovo, Serbian soldiers gradually withdrawn, and institutions to protect the rights of the minority Serbs. The

Serbs, however, refused to sign, and Serbian President Milosevic was adamant, right to the end. *Une vrai tragédie.*"

We continued our discussion over coffee and cognac. Robert had been reading about Balkan history and was in a reflective mood, happy to share his knowledge. I asked him what was really going on in Kosovo.

"Well, you know, this is not the first time Serbs and Albanians have clashed. For hundreds of years, each group has been trying to claim Kosovo as their own, to the exclusion of the other. There is a long history of resentment, hatred, and bloodshed. And the beliefs are very deeply held. Children are brought up on legends of heroic deeds and hateful acts of vengeance, and learn songs glorifying ethnic righteousness and revenge."

"So the Albanians have not always been the underdog?" I asked.

"*Pas du tout.* The Serbs were in the ascendancy during the middle ages, but when the Ottoman Turks drove them out of Kosovo in the fourteenth century, the Albanians moved into the vacuum that had been created. So for hundreds of years the Albanians occupied Kosovo. They were under Turkish rule, but seemed to have considerable local control. By the beginning of the nineteenth century, however, Serbia started to make a comeback. In the 1870's the Serbs began to push the Turks southward, burning Albanian villages as they went. Finally, just before the First World War, the Serbs drove the Turks all the way back to Istanbul. Serbia took over Kosovo. After the First World War, Albanian rebel resistance was violently repressed. Serb migrants flowed into Kosovo, and thousands of Albanians fled, many going to Turkey."

Robert leaned forward in his chair and reached for the bottle of cognac. He topped up all our glasses and then leaned back, sipping slowly, contemplating. I was still curious, and hoped he would carry on. "So in the twentieth century Kosovo has belonged to the Serbs?" I questioned.

"You could say that. Although there were moments during the First and Second World Wars when the invading Austrian and German armies provided cover for the Albanians to extract a measure of revenge. During the Second World War, many Kosovar Albanians collaborated with the Germans, and thousands of Serbs were killed or expelled.

However, when the War ended, Tito declared marshal law, wiped out Albanian resistance, and then formally annexed Kosovo to Serbia.

"Actually, the arrival of Tito was a mixed blessing for the Albanians. After an initial period of repression, Tito allowed a certain amount of self-determination for the Albanians. He was a master of the art of compromise, and somehow got all the Balkan ethnic groups to live together peacefully in a single state, Yugoslavia. The Albanians even got their own university, and Albanian communists controlled the local government and the police."

"So Kosovo was peaceful for a time," I interjected. "But it's not very peaceful now. What happened? What is at the root of the current war?"

"After Tito died, there was a gradual deterioration in the relationship of Serbs and Albanians in Kosovo. Serbs outside Kosovo began to fret about the decline of Serb population in Kosovo. Milosevic used these concerns to whip up Serbian nationalism, and engineered an end to Kosovo's autonomous status. Albanians began to experience increased repression. By the early 1990's, Albanians could not buy houses or land from Serbs. Thousands of Albanians in public sector, civil service or managerial jobs were dismissed. The police force was purged of Albanians, doctors and medical staff were dismissed, and the police took over radio and television stations and shut down the Albanian newspaper. The Serbian curriculum was introduced into the schools, and Albanian books were banned."

"So I guess all that harassment finally led to Albanian resistance," I offered.

"*C'est vrai*," Robert confirmed, "but look where it has led. All this violence! There has to be a better way –," his voice trailed off. The atmosphere in the room had become heavy. We were all silent for a while as we pondered the hopelessness of the situation. Then Robert filled our glasses one last time, and we turned to more cheerful topics.

Two days later we thanked the hosts at our *gîte*, said goodbye, and set off in a cool drizzle for Provence. Most people we knew crossed from northern to southern France in a single day of driving on the *autoroute*. We liked to split it in two, stopping overnight in one of the many family-run hotels that dot the countryside, offering personal service and gourmet meals. That night we stayed at the Auberge

Saint-Romain in Anse, on the edge of Beaujolais country just north of Lyon. Kosovo could not have been farther from our minds. The next day as we headed south, the land began to change. Tidy hedges and manicured borders of pansies and forget-me-nots gave way to a careless clutter of vegetation – forsythia, rosemary, lilacs, courtyard fences hung with wisteria, cherry trees in bloom, and massive pines. Industrial towns with ordered rows of brick townhouses gave way to little villages of dusty beige villas clinging to hilltops, interspersed with broad valleys of dormant grapevines, gnarled and weathered, gripping tenaciously to their wire supports. Olive groves began to appear. We were in Provence.

Coming into Provence was, for Anne and me, like coming home. Ever since we had lived there, eight years earlier, we felt a special affinity for this countryside of vineyards, orchards and olive groves, punctuated by limestone cliffs and forested mountains. We had been touched by the warmth with which we had been made welcome, by the locals' willingness to share with newcomers, and by the strength of family ties. We felt at home with their love of the outdoors, their preoccupation with good food, and their universal disrespect for the *mistral*, that cold wind from the north, which regularly and unpredictably spoiled an otherwise perfect climate. We had adopted without hesitation the habits of shopping at farmers' markets, stopping at outdoor cafés for a coffee or *jus d'orange pressé*, and carrying home a fresh baguette and a bottle of *vin rosé de provence* for the evening meal. In short, we had been thoroughly spoiled.

We were invited to dinner at the village home of a retired couple who had been among the first to befriend us eight years earlier. Pierre had been a heating contractor, and Juliette a homemaker, raising three sons. We turned sharply through the gate in a massive stone wall, drove down a slight incline, and parked under an olive tree. Beside us, the first roses of the season bloomed against a southern wall. Further up, as we mounted a staircase, mauve wisteria cascaded down the hand-hewn stones. We were greeted at the front door like long-lost children, sharing the traditional French *bise*. Juliette spoke excitedly, her red hair bouncing in response to her gestures, and the song-like cadence of her speech belying her city of origin, Marseilles, a few kilometres to the south. Pierre, a Provençal by choice from an early age, spoke with an accent from the North. He had been brought up in Orleans, just south of Paris.

We were ushered into the sun room for pre-dinner drinks. Pierre poured us all a pastis, while Juliette took us to the windows, knowing how much we enjoyed the view. We were overlooking a broad valley, with vineyards in the foreground that blended into wheat fields and disappeared into pine forest and jagged, rocky hills in the distance. In the afternoon sun it was a subdued mixture of browns, greens, and blues, but I knew that later on it would be transformed into an impressionist's palette of oranges, pinks, mauves and purples as the setting sun worked its magic. My eye was drawn to the west, where the massive arched viaduct of the TGV, *train de grand vitesse*, cut a swooping swath across the end of the valley. A ribbon of asphalt emerged from under the viaduct, the *autoroute La Provençal*, bisecting the valley into two neat halves. Opposing streams of traffic, miniaturized by distance, crawled in slow motion up and down the valley, like convoys of beetles. Far to the south, through a gap in the hills, the *Étang de Berre* shimmered in the sunshine, hinting at the broad expanse of sea that lay beyond.

As we caught up on news of friends and family, we hardly noticed the time pass. It was time to eat. While Juliette busied herself in the kitchen, Pierre poured more pastis, and discussion turned to politics as we sipped, munching on tiny, salted crackers and roasted nuts. Then we were called into the dining room. Juliette emerged from the kitchen, and dishes followed one after the other, in carefully choreographed succession, each with an enhancing wine. Close to three hours later, meal over, we retired into the living room. Pierre disappeared into the kitchen this time, to prepare a *tisane* from a handful of fresh herbs from the garden. Juliette turned on the TV.

Our minds snapped back to the reality of the war in Kosovo. The ethnic cleansing of Albanians in Kosovo was continuing, the bombing of Serbia intensifying. A journalist was standing in mud in the middle of a refugee camp in Macedonia. Behind her was row on row of military tents. The camera shifted to an airport, and a plane arriving. Aid was arriving, she was saying, from France, Germany, and other European countries. The camera shifted again, to aid workers at the back of a truck, handing out boxes to refugees who formed a long line stretching out of camera range. The cameraman zeroed in on the activity at the back of the truck. We could not believe our eyes. There they were, piles and piles of boxes from *La Poste* in France. Perhaps the very same boxes we helped prepare the week before in northern France. One box for every family. "*Ces pauvres gens,*" Juliette was saying. "It is so good that we can help them a little. They need all the prayers and support we can give."

By the time we arrived back in Ottawa it was early May, and as we entered Ottawa along the parkway the show of daffodils provided conclusive proof, even to sceptics, that spring had arrived. Downtown, battalions of tulips in beds along the canal, having waited patiently all winter under three feet of snow, poked their spiky leaves toward the welcoming sun. In ten days they would erupt in geometric patterns of brilliant colour, and the Tulip Festival would bring thousands of people from near and far, pouring out of their houses and hotels to stroll among the flowers in celebration of spring.

In no time at all we were back into our normal routine, renewing contact with friends and family, preparing an album on our visit to ancestral homelands, and enjoying our early morning runs along the river and our daily walks to the Market. We had both opted for early retirement a few years earlier, choosing the luxury of time over material goods, a decision which neither of us had regretted for an instant. We lived in a condominium apartment downtown, not ten minutes walk from Parliament Hill, and had thereby conveniently sidestepped the usual chores of home and garden maintenance. In fact, having jettisoned both the work world and the responsibilities of home ownership, we found ourselves that spring with very little of any dimension to distract us from enjoying ourselves.

Television coverage of the war in Kosovo had followed us to Canada. However, it was vastly different from what we had become used to in France. Not that the course of the war was any different. The exodus of refugees continued; the bombing, if anything, was more intense. But somehow the war seemed more impersonal, less real. Most of the reporting was in technical or military jargon: number of bombing sorties flown, targets hit, or tanks destroyed. We would be treated to displays of bombing acumen on the television screen, and regaled by visions of "smart bombs" going down chimneys and causing great havoc to the Serbian "war machine." The war began to resemble some gigantic video game, with the good guys seeming to score all the hits, but the bad guys somehow holding on.

Occasionally, some mention would be made of the humanitarian plight of what was estimated at close to a million Albanian Kosovar refugees now outside Kosovo in camps, and hundreds of thousands more on the run inside. But usually such references were in the context of some bombing error made by NATO planes, like the terrible tragedy at Djakovica where NATO planes mistook a column of refugees for a column of enemy soldiers. Otherwise, the refugees had largely faded from sight.

We knew that Canada and other countries, including Australia, Britain, France, Germany and the United States, had agreed to evacuate thousands of Albanian Kosovar refugees from the overcrowded refugee camps. This was partly a humanitarian gesture, and partly a geopolitical necessity, as Macedonia had borne the brunt of the refugee influx, and could not accommodate the ones already there in healthful conditions, let alone the thousands more who were arriving every day. Besides, the influx of Albanians into Macedonia threatened to throw the equilibrium between the country's Slavic majority and Albanian minority into serious imbalance, possibly touching off another war. In fact, we had heard a commentator saying on TV that Milosevic was hoping for just such an eventuality, calculating that his chances would be improved if war started to spill from one country to another throughout the Balkan region.

We listened with interest when we heard that Canada had agreed to take in 10,000 refugees, and that some had already started to arrive. They would be resettled across the country, particularly in cities where there were already a few people able to speak Albanian and where the government could find sponsors to help them integrate into the Canadian way of life. We were particularly intrigued with the concept of sponsorship, because we saw it as a way that individual Canadians could contribute, in a very personal way, to solving the humanitarian disaster brought on by war.

One evening, we heard an official on a TV talk show describing the need for new sponsors. Sponsors would be expected to find accommodation for their refugee family, to help them master the day-to-day practicalities of such things as shopping, public transport, doctors, dentists and banking, and to provide a friendly shoulder for the family to lean on while they adapted to their new land. The government would provide basic apartment furnishings and a stipend to cover food and rent for two years, or until the family members of working age found jobs. The official gave a 1-800 number for all those with an interest in becoming sponsors, and Anne copied it down eagerly.

After the show, I could see that Anne was becoming excited. "What do you think," she asked, "of us becoming sponsors? Now that we are retired we have the time, and this could be our small way of helping to alleviate all the suffering that is going on. Besides, it would be fun."

Anne was right. We did have the time, and like her, I felt a need to be more directly involved. "Excellent idea," I replied. "Let's get on it right away."

The next morning Anne called the number, and found herself talking to a Citizenship and Immigration officer somewhere in Alberta. She promised to send us an information package, and explained how sponsorship would work. All sponsors had to be part of an official sponsorship group. Groups could be either affiliated with organizations that already had an umbrella Sponsorship Agreement in place (mainly churches and charities), or ad hoc Groups of Five, made up of five or more individuals prepared to commit themselves to two years of sponsorship. Every destination community would have a local co-ordinator who would provide information to sponsors and organize the selection and arrival of refugee families. Ottawa was a destination, and we would have to talk to the co-ordinator for details.

The next day we went to work to set up a Group of Five. We needed three more members. Ideally these should be persons we knew well and could work with comfortably, and who would have time and energy to commit to a two-year project. Immediately, our thoughts turned to Theresa, Anne's sister and a recently retired teacher, and her husband, Don, also recently retired from his job as a cartographer with the Canadian government. They were both enthusiastic, but asked how much time would be required. Quite a bit at first but after that probably not too much, we responded naively, recounting the experience of another friend who had sponsored a Vietnamese family, and whose responsibilities had dwindled rapidly after a few months as the family became fully independent.

We needed one more member. Anne talked the project up with several friends. Everyone was interested, and Rose-Aline, another recently retired teacher, immediately said yes. Two others, Claire, a part-time teacher, and Anne M., a full time teacher, agreed to participate informally, without being official signatories. We were ecstatic. We had our group!

Several days had passed since we had called the 1-800 Kosovar Hot Line, we still had not received our information kit, and we were now well into the month of June. We were going away on holiday to visit my mother in Saskatchewan in just four days, on June 12, and would not be back until the 24th. We began to get concerned about the time. Our formal application to become a Group of Five still had to be sent in, processed and accepted. Having come this far, we did not want to miss the boat.

Anne looked back in her papers. She had the street address of the Ottawa co-ordinator, but no phone number. It was on the same street as us, apparently not too far from our apartment. Ten minutes later, we had found the address, not half a block away. We knocked on the door.

We were at the back door of an old three storey red brick house, nestled between Christ Church Cathedral and the Office of the Bishop, an imposing Victorian mansion on a cliff overlooking the Ottawa River. There were racks of canoes behind the house, and a sign beside the door warning of falling snow and ice. We both looked up instinctively, although with a temperature of 28 degrees Celsius, our brains were telling us that the risk was less than small. There was no answer, so we knocked again.

I tried the handle, and the door eased open, letting us into a small room that had probably once been a kitchen, but was now lined with shelves containing books and stacks of paper. A photocopier stood in one corner, and a small desk, covered in papers and sporting a half-full coffee cup, sat against one wall. There was no one to be seen. We walked down the corridor toward the front of the building, sticking our heads into unoccupied offices as we went, and, finding no one, headed up the stairs.

We knocked on the first closed door. "Come in," a friendly voice immediately shot back. The door opened into a large room which had probably been the master bedroom. A huge desk filled the centre of the room. Papers covered the entire surface and spilled over the edges. Our eyes were drawn to the young woman seated at the desk, whose wide grin spread up into the sparkle of dark eyes, to lose itself somewhere under a cascade of tiny black braids that washed over her forehead. "My name is Malaika," she offered. "I am the assistant co-ordinator for the Kosovar Refugee Program. Can I help you?"

We explained who we were and why we had come. "Oh," she replied, "you are our first visitors. I'm so glad to meet you. Please come in, and I will get all the particulars."

Malaika wrote down our name and phone number, and handed us an application for a Group of Five. We noticed a space on the first page where we were to fill out the company or charity to whom we were affiliated. We had none. "No problem," Malaika told us. "What the government wants is to know that you are serious and committed. If you could send them something about yourselves, like a curriculum vitae, that would be good."

Malaika explained excitedly that there were four hundred Albanian Kosovar refugees coming to Ottawa, and that the government needed at least sixty sponsoring groups. Our application had to go to head-quarters, but she expected it to be accepted. Why didn't we come to an information meeting being held at the Regional Citizenship and Immigration Office the next day? We would be updated on developments, and someone would be speaking about Albanian culture.

We went home filled with energy and immediately called the other sponsors. Then we showed up the next day for the meeting.

There were over a hundred people in the auditorium, which we were told also doubled as the courtroom for immigration hearings. Maybe that explained the fancy wood trim and solid oak lecterns at the front of the room, and the elaborate anteroom with furnishings a few notches above standard government issue. The room filled with the hum of conversation as people compared notes on the anticipated deluge of new refugees that everyone was keen to help. Then all was quiet as Carolyn, the Co-ordinator for the Kosovar Refugee Program, introduced herself and Malaika, and then pointed out a number of other people in the room with important roles, including John and Edith, two Citizenship and Immigration officers, and Sylvia, a volunteer from the United Church with a long history of helping refugees and being a sponsor.

We were updated on developments. NATO had officially suspended bombing that very day. Milosevic had capitulated. The Russians were in Prishtina and the British were on their way. A buzz of excited relief engulfed the room. Then we all started to wonder what it meant for the refugees. Were they still coming? "Not to worry about your sponsorships," broke in Carolyn, anticipating our questions. "We still need all of you. There are over 5,000 refugees already in Canada at various Canadian Forces Bases. Except for a few who may now decide to go home, all of them will be settled here in Canada."

Carolyn explained how the matching of sponsors and refugees would take place. First, the sponsors had to create their sponsorship groups – in our case, a Group of Five. Second, Citizenship and Immigration would suggest a match between each sponsoring group and an appropriate refugee family. Then it would be up to the sponsors to find a place for the refugee family to live. Finally, Citizenship and Immigration would provide furniture, and arrange for the refugees to arrive.

There would be quite a bit of work when the refugees first arrived. Sponsors were expected to welcome the newcomers, make them feel at home, help them learn about buses, schools, shopping, banking, doctors and dentists, and generally be on call every day for about six weeks to troubleshoot and help in case of emergency. After that, the refugees would be increasingly self sufficient, and our role would gradually taper off into one of friendship and occasional contact.

It seemed straightforward and Carolyn made it sound easy and rather fun. I could feel the atmosphere in the room lighten as we collectively relaxed, and started to picture ourselves with our families.

Carolyn moved on to the highlight of the evening, a description of the Albanian cultural background of the new arrivals. Shano, a distinguished-looking blond woman, gave us the details. Shano, herself originally from Albania but in Canada now for many years, explained that the Albanian Kosovars were almost all Muslim. There were differences between the younger, urban Kosovars, some of whom spoke English and were quite Westernized, and the older, rural Kosovars who spoke only Albanian and still lived the traditional way of life. Traditional Albanian culture was patriarchal. The father was the family leader, the oldest son was second in command, and he took over when the father died. There was tremendous respect for age; the eldest was always served first. Guests took priority over hosts. Even if guests arrived uninvited, they would always be greeted at the door with a smile, invited in, welcomed personally one by one, and then immediately offered a drink. Guests always brought a gift. Guests were seated in the place of honour, and when it was time to eat, the host would always serve the most sumptuous meal possible, even if it meant he had to borrow to afford it. Overnight guests always got the best bed, even if it meant the host had to sleep on the floor. Many of the older refugees would still follow these traditional customs, Shano explained, and she hoped our role as sponsors would be easier, and our own lives enriched, if we knew where they were coming from.

We went home that night stimulated and all psyched up to meet our future refugee family and maybe experience some of the traditional Albanian culture first hand. The next day we hurried to finish off our application to become sponsors, and fired it off to Citizenship and Immigration headquarters. Then we breathed a sigh of relief, and took off on the evening plane for our vacation in Saskatchewan.

two

GETTING READY

When we arrived home after our trip, Ottawa was in a heat wave. Even walking the half block to the Refugee Co-ordinator's office was enough to make us wilt. We wanted to see where things stood. As we approached the office, we could hear conversation, and when we arrived at the door, two heads looked up. Malaika, recognizing us, broke out into a broad smile, and was just about to greet us when Carolyn pre-empted her.

"Hello. Who are you?" Carolyn tried to put on a welcoming expression, but she could not hide the note of stress that had crept into her voice. She was still bent over the table and she had not put down the papers that filled both hands.

We explained who we were, and that we had come hoping to get confirmation that our group had been accepted as sponsors. We wanted to find out how we were to proceed, now that we were back in town and keen to get to work. Carolyn relaxed a little as she put down her papers, but it was obvious we were interrupting. "How did you find us?" she asked. "We did not give our address to anyone, and we were not expecting visitors. We have so much work to do."

I mumbled something about getting the address from the Kosovo Hot Line, and apologized for disturbing them. We could see that they were in the middle of a gigantic process of organizing all the information on the Ottawa sponsors, as there were papers everywhere now, even on the floor. Carolyn moved behind the desk, rummaged through some papers, and picked out a list. "Yes," she confirmed, at last giving us a genuine smile, "your group has been accepted. We should be able to tell you in a few days who your family will be."

Our faces broke into grins. Malaika, who had been quietly observing, took this as an opportunity to break in. "You can start now to get a feel for the rental market. You won't be able to actually rent until you know how many are in your family, but at least you will know what is available. The market is very tight right now. It is best to start looking right away."

We knew that Malaika would not be able to talk for long before she would have to get back to work. She was speaking fast. There was no housing committee to co-ordinate rental opportunities. Every sponsor group was on its own. We could contact Trung or Celia at the Reception House for rental ideas and they could also tell us what parts of the city had lots of Serbs and would therefore be prudent to avoid. Also, we could contact Dana, who could give us access to a warehouse of used household items that had been collected for the refugees by some downtown community associations. The government would be giving basic furniture to every family, but things like kitchen and electrical appliances were not included. Specifically, sponsors should look for curtains, a television, and a vacuum, none of which were included on the government's list of essentials.

Malaika jotted down some telephone numbers on a slip of paper and handed it to us. There was no time for follow-up questions. The two women had already started back to work. We quickly said goodbye, and eased our way out the door.

We immediately contacted the other sponsors and decided on a strategy. A date was set for all the sponsors to visit the warehouse in search of useful household items. In the meantime, everyone would keep his eyes and ears open for possible rental leads, and Anne and I would do a thorough search of the newspaper rental ads.

As we worked our way through the ads, our apprehension began to build. There were not a lot of apartments available. The economy had been booming, and lots of people had been arriving in the city. On the other hand, no new apartment buildings had been constructed for years. The vacancy rate had dropped to less than one third of one percent. Furthermore, of the apartments available, most were out of our price range. Very ordinary one bedroom apartments seemed to start around $600 per month plus utilities, and the nicer ones were more. We knew that a refugee couple would be allowed about $500 per month for rent, including utilities. A family of three would be allowed between $500 and $600. But two bedroom apartments seemed to start around $700 per month, and most were $800 or more. No matter how we did the math, we seemed to be at least $100 short. Even if we found something within our price range, it did not automatically follow that we would be able to rent it. Landlords were of course noncommittal over the phone, but we noticed a change in attitude when we mentioned that we were calling on behalf of refugees on a government stipend. Apartments which at first seemed available would become mysteriously less and less available as our particular circumstances became more precise.

Anne phoned for a whole day without finding anything within our budget. We decided to take another tack. We would cruise the streets of downtown Ottawa, looking for "for rent" signs. This would also allow us to assess the various residential districts in relation to schools, public transportation, and shopping, especially grocery stores, which we knew would be an essential.

We had decided in consultation with the other sponsors to give preference to downtown areas. We had been told that most refugees preferred, if possible, to live downtown. Downtown Ottawa was very ethnically diverse, and we could understand that many refugees would feel more comfortable there. Downtown was also reasonably accessible to all the sponsors, who lived in various areas of the city.

We spent another whole day driving around looking for rental signs. There were very few. We began to understand what Malaika meant when she said the market was tight. We dropped into several of the larger apartment rental offices to see if anything was available. Each time we got out of the car, we were hit with a wall of heat, and we could feel the little beads of perspiration form under our arms. The story at each office was predictable and disappointing. There were no apartments available, or if there were, they were out of our price range.

We went home that night tired and discouraged. After only two days of looking, we were not ready to give up, but we had seen or heard nothing to suggest our quest was anything but hopeless.

Getting together the next day with the other sponsors, to go through the warehouse of household items, gave us a welcome break from apartment hunting. Dana had given us the key and the code for the security system, and we followed each other to a rather obscure brick building on the edge of a riverside park. There was a sign outside saying "City Parks Maintenance Office," but the building looked deserted and the yard was anything but maintained. What had once been a lawn was overgrown with weeds, but even the weeds had withered and were turning brown in the unforgiving heat. We stepped gingerly over a dead crow as we walked up the path to the front door. I opened the door and punched the security code into the keypad on the wall to turn off the burglar alarm. The sponsors all trooped in behind me.

There was hardly anywhere to stand. All around us, and in every room we could see, were the remains of what looked like a gigantic, unsuccessful yard sale. Boxes were piled in haphazard, unsystematic jumbles, their contents sticking crazily out their tops or hanging precariously over their sides. Some larger pieces of furniture had been deposited unceremoniously here and there, and had in turn been covered in boxes and loose items: lamp shades, old picture frames, televisions, toasters, curtains, bags of clothing, toys, and pieces of disassembled yard furniture. A contingent of old bicycles had been thrown one against the other on one side of one of the rooms, and a heap of old vacuum cleaners had been carelessly relegated to a corner.

To most people, the scene we surveyed would have been just a mess of dusty, useless trash, to be hauled away to the dump at the next convenient opportunity. To us, it was a treasure trove, and we bristled with energy as we set about, perspiration dripping from our faces, to unearth buried riches. I concentrated on choosing and testing the best vacuum, while Anne and Don sought out kitchen equipment and utensils, and Theresa and Rose-Aline rummaged through curtains, clothing, and linens. In no time at all we had filled the back of Don's van, and the trunks and back seats of two other cars. We reset the security system, brushed the dust off our clothes, and took off in a convoy towards Rose-Aline's, where our treasures would be stored until our family's arrival.

When we arrived back home, the little light on our voice mail service was flashing. It was Malaika. Her voice was eager. Our group had been matched with an elderly couple, Nezir and Nazife Brajshori. They were currently living at Camp Borden, near Barrie, Ontario, and would be coming to Ottawa very soon.

The message ended abruptly, but it was the answer we had been waiting for. We were ecstatic. Anne immediately phoned the other sponsors to give them the good news. Then we rushed over to the Refugee Co-ordinator's office. We needed more information.

Malaika and Carolyn, obviously still feeling the pressure of their work, were both looking a little harried. Malaika showed us the printout on our couple. Nezir, 68, spoke Albanian, Serbo-Croatian, Arabic, and a little Latin. His wife, Nazife, spoke only Albanian. Neither knew any English. There were no other details. We started to ask questions: "When will they be arriving in Ottawa, and when will we be told? What can we give to a prospective landlord to prove that the Brajshoris are in a government program and that the government will be paying the rent? Will the government give us the first and last month's rent that the landlord will be expecting immediately, before giving us an apartment? Who is going to pay to ensure that the electricity and phone are hooked up before the Brajshoris arrive? Will they have any money for food and other necessities when they arrive in Ottawa?"

Carolyn came over to join us, and Malaika started taking notes. These were all questions that had to be answered, they told us, and they were happy to get advance notice, so they could look into these issues before other sponsors started to call. For now, they advised, we should try to find an apartment, since everything else depended on the refugees having a place to live when they arrived. Malaika gave us the phone number of the person in Toronto, Peter, who was making the financial arrangements for the Camp Borden refugees. We could get information directly from him if we needed it fast, although normally we should be coming to them with our questions. We promised not to abuse their contact, and hurried out the door.

We went into high gear. Everything depended on our finding a suitable apartment at the right price and we knew it would not be easy. Anne telephoned all the prospects we could find and made appointments to view each apartment.

The first appointment was on Cooper Street, a tree-lined avenue of century-old mansions, with occasional bland high-rises sitting like ugly ducklings amongst the stately Victorian houses. Our appointment, at 10:00AM, was to view two apartments in the most imposing house on the block, whose huge Doric columns recalled more genteel times. Now the building was subdivided into seven or eight apartments. Other potential renters began to arrive. Apparently this was not a private showing. At least, by standing under the portico, we did not have to wait in the blazing sun. By 10:15 there were three groups of students and ourselves, all milling around. We struck up a conversation with a young couple. They were hoping to find an apartment now, prior to the big influx of students in September. Yes, they confirmed, they had already been looking for a while, and there wasn't much around that was affordable. Maybe this would be their lucky day. We wished them luck, but inside we were hoping the luck would be ours.

Finally at about 10:20 the rental agent appeared. Without any introductions or other formalities, she unlocked the front door and we all filed in after her like sheep. The hall inside was dark, but it smelled of new wax and we could see that the original wood trim and mouldings were still in place. My spirits rose a little. The first apartment was toward the back of the building, on the ground floor. The agent opened a door to reveal a small studio, even darker than the hall. Our spirits sagged. Several of the students screwed up their faces in disgust and did not even bother going in. We were curious. There was a large window, so why was it so dark? We went over to the window to investigate. Outside, not more than a metre away, was the dour red brick wall of the neighbouring building. No sunshine would ever enter this room. We turned to study the kitchenette, clumsily extruding from a converted clothes closet. There was only a hot plate—no stove, no counter, and only one forlorn cupboard over a decrepit sink. We went into the bathroom and our deception grew as we took in the rusty toilet bowl, dripping tap, and scarred porcelain. "How much is this apartment?" I asked the agent as I beat a hasty retreat. "Four hundred and fifty dollars, but that includes utilities." It was the first time the agent had spoken. In fact, she had not even gone inside the apartment. Obviously, she felt no need to promote her wares. I felt even more depressed.

No one seemed interested in the studio. We all clambered up a huge staircase to the second floor. The agent seemed keen to show off her premium offering of the day, a "more interesting" one bedroom apartment with balcony. We were the last to enter the apartment. The narrow entry hallway led straight past the bedroom. Obviously, the apartment was still inhabited. We tried to look past the cluttered mess of blankets, books and clothing to picture the room as it might be with a tidy double bed, dresser and lace curtains, the kind that Europeans often favour. Even thus transfigured, it would still be small. We moved on to a crowded, dilapidated kitchen. The refrigerator standing by the entry looked old and somewhat suspect, so I opened the door, only to be greeted by a missing vegetable crisper, rusty shelving, and a freezer door hanging crazily from a single hinge and revealing a minuscule freezer clogged with frost.

By this time the main contingent had already passed into the final room, a living area with a curious false fireplace and wood-trimmed mantle, made inviting in comparison to the rest of the apartment by the sunshine which poured in a glass door and abutting windows. The door led to a tiny metal balcony harbouring two large red geraniums in green plastic pots. I peered out, and noticed that the balcony served double duty as a landing for a metal fire escape that disappeared down the back of the building. I turned around. The two students who had been first up the stairs and first to crowd into the entrance hallway were busy finalizing a deal with the rental agent in one corner of the room. The apartment, at $640 including utilities, was already rented!

We were both feeling disheartened as we left the building and walked towards our car. If our experience on Cooper Street was any indication of the current market – run down, overpriced apartments renting like hot cakes – we were doomed to failure.

The other risk that began to bother us was that we might, out of frustration or haste, take an apartment that was inappropriate for Mr. and Mrs. Brajshori. We were absolutely determined to put our refugee family in a decent home. How were we to avoid lowering our standards out of frustration, and taking something inappropriate? We concluded that our rule of thumb would be to ask ourselves if we would be prepared, if necessary, to live in the apartment ourselves. If the answer was "no" for us, then it would be "no" for the Brajshoris as well.

Our next stop was somewhat outside the city's core, on Donald Street. We knew most central areas rented at a premium over the suburbs, so maybe we would find better value farther out. The apartment we were going to inspect rented for $500 including utilities, so was within our budget. We guessed it would be equivalent to a $600 apartment downtown.

We stopped in front of a new-looking single family house clad in white aluminum siding, with an attached garage. A stern looking man wearing a white dress shirt but no tie invited us in. We found ourselves in the front hall opening up to a pleasantly furnished living room. "The apartment is downstairs," he said bluntly, as he saw us eyeing his living room. It dawned on us that we were in this man's house, and that we were going to be shown a basement apartment.

The proprietor ushered us down a flight of stairs to the basement. My heart sank, as I took in the single hanging light bulb, the narrow corridor and the dirty tile floor. Ahead was the furnace room, but it was "out of bounds," except for him. "The stairs are one way only," he advised. To the right, empty except for a bed standing on its side, stood a small, windowless room without a closet, whose only potentially redeeming quality was that it had recently been painted bright red. "The closet is in the hall," our rather matter-of-fact guide was saying. As we went back down the hall we took note of the closet, a narrow alcove covered by a limp curtain that may have been grey but was more likely a dirty blue. The bathroom next to it was small and windowless, and smelled of damp.

Our host had already moved on to the living room, and by the time we entered two more bare light bulbs had been turned on in support of the hint of natural light filtering through two minuscule windows. He had stopped and turned, but was silent, letting us absorb the details for ourselves. A run down kitchenette with drooping cupboards dominated one wall. My eyes lighted on the ancient stove, a curious and almost equal combination of rust and dirt. I swivelled, sidestepped a sagging sofa, and stepped over an overturned floor lamp, trying to ascertain whether these were the furnishings, or just the junk the former tenants had not bothered to cart away. "The new tenants can keep the furniture if they want," offered the landlord, "or they can throw it out. Come on. I'll show you their private entry."

We backtracked part way down the hall, through another door, and up a narrow stairway, emerging at ground level in the garage. We surveyed the scene for a moment, overwhelmed by the impressive quantity of old tools, tires, fuel drums, boxes, bicycles and lawn furniture that someone had managed to squeeze in. As we moved toward the front door, carefully navigating between a greasy engine block and a snow blower, I enquired whether the garage would be cleared to make a proper entrance for the new tenants. "Oh no," came the reply, totally incredulous. "It stays like this. I need somewhere to store my things."

We were back on the sidewalk in front of the house, so it was easy for us to say our thanks and quickly slip away.

There were two more apartments to see that day, and three the next. They were all dumps, and all too expensive. We dragged ourselves home, fatigued by the heat, stumbling over our own feet, clothing damp with perspiration and clinging to our bodies. We felt defeated, and not knowing what to do. We phoned the other sponsors and commiserated. They had not found anything either. Perhaps it was not meant to be.

The next day, Sunday, was Canada Day, the anniversary of Confederation. Downtown Ottawa erupted in celebration. The heat and incessant sunshine conspired to turn it into a beach party, as people dressed down to shorts, cut-offs, and bathing attire. We went to the noon show on Parliament Hill, watched the buskers juggle and eat fire on the Mall, and listened to music in the park. Try as we might, however, we could not get our refugee family out of our mind. We reviewed all our options and tried to think of a strategy that would lead us to a suitable apartment.

The next morning we woke up rested and refreshed. Optimism crowded out all our doubts. Anne eagerly recounted how her nephew's girl friend had found, some years earlier, a reasonably priced one bedroom apartment in a high-rise in Lowertown, not far from the

Market and the University of Ottawa. We should look at that building. Perhaps we would find what we were looking for.

Anne phoned the management company responsible for the building, and was put on the line with Tom. He would meet us at the front door of the building at 11:00AM We went early so we could check out the neighbourhood. It was on Clarence Avenue, a quiet dead-end street with a bus service just around the corner. Rows of tidy townhouses filled the neighbourhood, and young children played in the front yards. The town houses had been built by the City, and we assumed most of them were subsidized for low-income families. There were older single family houses, too, and we knew these were not subsidized. We counted three corner stores, and noticed a public school a block away. A huge Loblaws grocery store was just down the street, perhaps five or six minutes away on foot, and a bank, pharmacy, and bakery were also close by. The Market was a little farther, but still reachable on foot, in perhaps a fifteen minute walk.

Tom – a big, jovial man with a permanent smile – showed up right on time. We explained who we were and why we were looking for an apartment. We rode together in a worn out, hesitant elevator to the top floor. The hallway was a bit narrow and one of the walls had been damaged by water, perhaps from a leak in the roof. At least it was clean. We stopped in front of apartment 701 and Tom knocked. "He is moving out some time this week I think," Tom was saying, "but he asked me to rent the apartment as soon as I can. Otherwise he will be responsible for the rent until the end of the month."

There was no answer, so Tom unlocked the door. We all entered and stood for a moment in a roomy entrance hall. I noted, with some satisfaction, a large clothes closet by the front door. It looked like the current tenant had already left, more or less. The large living/dining room was empty, and the shining parquet floor reflected brilliant sunshine streaming in through the windows. Not a single nail hole marred the freshly painted walls. "I guess he moved out already," Tom mused. Then, as if to answer my unspoken question, he went on: "We redecorated this apartment completely just before the tenant moved in last May. I guess he didn't hang any pictures or put up curtains. He must have found another place."

We checked out the balcony, with its fine view over Lowertown, and then moved into the bedroom. A single mattress covered by a sheet, a red blanket, two pillows, an alarm clock and a beer bottle sprawled across the freshly varnished parquet floor. A sliding door to a large closet lay open, revealing a few hanging clothes. "I guess he's still sleeping here," Tom said simply. As we left the room, we sneaked a peek at a large linen closet, and then poked our heads into the bathroom. The top of the toilet tank had been replaced with a piece of plywood painted white to match the toilet, and on which the current tenant had set out soap, razor, tooth brush and a box of tissues. My eye followed a sloppy streak of mouldy caulking across the top of the sink, for which there was no vanity, and settled on an amateurish patch and gaping hole in the wallboard beside the tub. Probably water damage, I speculated. The tub itself was full of tiny splotches of rust, like a bad case of the measles. Oh well, I thought, as I ran the taps and flushed the toilet, at least everything works.

The kitchen was too small for a table, but was equipped with a huge pass-through, cleverly designed to double as a counter. The fridge, almost brand new, was large, with a roomy freezer. The stove looked older, and a bit greasy, but there were lots of cupboards. There was a large stainless steel sink and arborite counter. Anne and I looked at each other, and her eyes flashed back a smile. She did not have to say anything; I knew that she was pleased. We moved back into the sun-filled living area. "How much is the rent?" I asked, with just a little apprehension showing in my voice.

"It's $525," replied Tom, noticing my apprehension and trying to soften the blow. "Unfortunately that doesn't include electricity. But hot water is included. I hope it's not too much for your couple?"

"It's a little over budget, but maybe they could manage it," I responded. "We'll have to check to see how much the utilities are. When can they move in?"

"As soon as the current tenant leaves definitively. I could contact him and ask him if July 15 is OK. I expect he will be more than happy, since that will save him two weeks' rent."

I could see that Anne was formulating a plan. "If we take it for the 15th, would we be able to come in beforehand, clean things up, put up curtains, and get it ready for them?" She queried.

"I don't see why not," came the response. "As long as the tenant has gone."

We thanked Tom and promised to get back to him as soon as we could. We rushed home, discussing the pros and cons as we went. The pros were in the overwhelming majority. The apartment clearly passed our test of being a place that we would be able to live in ourselves, if tough times struck. We telephoned Ottawa Hydro to get a reading on the average monthly electricity bill, which turned out to be only $20 to $25. Our couple could just afford it. They would have to use about $35 a month from their food allowance to cover their rent, and we worried about the hardship that might cause. But it seemed a necessary compromise under the circumstances. We would find ways to help them out if it became necessary. We decided to take the apartment.

Anne checked with Malaika to see whether July 15 would be a good date to start the lease. Then she called Tom right away, to confirm that we would take the apartment. "Good," said Tom. "Come in tomorrow and we'll sign the papers. Your family can sign the lease when they arrive."

The morning's events had lifted a huge weight from our shoulders, and as we went home for lunch not even the oppressive heat could dampen the spring in our steps. We phoned all the sponsors to give them the good news. Then Anne composed a letter to Mr. and Mrs. Brajshori to tell them who we were, that we were eagerly waiting to meet them on their arrival, and that their apartment would be ready and waiting for them. She traced out a sketch of the apartment and appended it to the letter. Then she contacted the Canadian Forces Base in Borden to ensure we sent it to the right address and that someone would be able to read and translate it to the Brajshoris when it arrived.

That evening Carolyn chaired a meeting at the Regional Citizenship and Immigration Office to update all the sponsors on developments. When we arrived the room was full and abuzz with chatter as people swapped stories on their families and apartment searches. We were pleased to see that the agenda covered all the questions that we had raised with Carolyn and Malaika. The Ottawa contingent of refugees would be arriving over a two-week period. Our family would be on the first bus to arrive, on July 16. Their furniture would be programmed to arrive at their apartment the day before, and sponsors had to plan to be at the apartment all day long to receive deliveries that would be coming in several different trucks at different and unscheduled times. We were to pick up linens and kitchen utensils on the same day from the Reception House near the Market. The refugees would be given a cheque in Borden to cover their food and incidental expenses for the first month. The sponsors should arrange to take them to open a bank account. The refugees would also be bringing sealed envelopes containing their preliminary medical histories. It was up to us to find them a doctor and take them, with their files, for the more detailed medical examinations and tests required of all new immigrants. There was a final word of practical advice. When the refugees arrived by bus in Ottawa, they would have a lot of luggage, as a result of gifts of clothing and other items such as bicycles they had received at Camp Borden. The sponsors should arrange for an adequate number of cars and vans to meet them at the bus stop, to ensure there would be room for all this luggage.

In a meeting of our Group of Five the next day, Anne and I undertook to get the apartment ready for its new tenants. We would start the very next morning, and arranged to meet the superintendent, Jim, who had agreed to help us.

At 9:00AM on the dot we lumbered up the sidewalk to the apartment building, heavily laden with mops, pails, soap, rags and brushes, a vacuum, and a toolbox full of every imaginable item that could serve in giving our apartment a thorough once-over. Jim met us at the front door. A tall young man with crew cut hair and a smile in his eyes, he whistled to himself as he helped load our equipment into the elevator, and we rode up together. The three of us walked round the apartment, itemizing the things that had to be done. Jim quickly agreed with all our suggestions, chatting casually as we walked around. He had only just begun his job as superintendent, work he had never done before, but his father had been a superintendent in Timmins, his home town. Some of his father's skills had probably rubbed off on him, he speculated. Anyway, it didn't look too complicated. For the time being, he was moonlighting, working a full shift as a cook's assistant in a restaurant in the Market. Maybe in time this would prove to be too much, but for now it was OK. We were his first new tenants, and he would be happy to help us out in any way he could.

By the time we finished our walk-around, Jim had agreed to re-paint the metalwork on the balcony, where paint was peeling off in huge strips. He also agreed to order a replacement porcelain top for the toilet tank, replace the caulking around the bathroom sink and repair the hole in the bathroom wall. He would find a ceiling light fixture to replace one that was broken, see if he could fix a binding balcony door that was difficult to open, and look into replacing the worn vinyl tile in the entrance and kitchen. We would concentrate on cleaning. It seemed like an excellent division of labour to us, and we immediately got to work as soon as Jim had disappeared down the hall.

In no time at all Jim was back with the replacement ceiling light fixture. We thanked him and commented on his efficiency as we took possession of the fixture. Then we happily got back to work.

We had started on the kitchen. The stove, which had looked a little greasy on first sight, was caked in layer upon layer of hardened cooking oil and fat. The counter, which we thought was grey, turned out after many scrubbings to be a patterned beige. The kitchen cupboards had become a depository for whatever grease had missed the stove, and the cabinet door knobs, which we had assumed to be smooth black plastic, turned out to be finely filigreed brass. We worked right through lunch time, and suddenly noticed how hot and tired we had become.

We opened the windows and balcony door, then propped open the apartment door. A hot breeze immediately began to waft through the apartment, not cooling us as we had hoped, but better than nothing as at least the air was now moving. We were lucky to find a fan in the warehouse, we thought. The Brajshoris were going to need it. We had a sandwich lunch sitting on the floor. Then, although the kitchen was not even half finished, we tried to motivate ourselves by going to work on the bathroom fixtures. We scrubbed and scrubbed, but the rust was not coming off. Finally we gave up in frustration, and spent the rest of the afternoon cleaning kitchen cupboards.

Jim greeted us with a cheery hello the next morning. We asked him if he would be coming to work in our apartment and he said no, he had an urgent paint job to get another apartment ready. He would try to get to ours the next day.

We finished cleaning the kitchen, put up curtain rods, and disposed of the rust in the bathroom using heavy duty cleaner and scouring pads. There were still a lot of jobs left, but many of them were the ones Jim had said he would do. We left for home that afternoon feeling that we were at last beginning to get somewhere.

Our illusion of progress began to unravel the following morning when Jim reported that no toilet tops existed anywhere in town that would fit our antique toilet, and then made some apologetic noises that he would not be able to help us that day either. We were beginning to wonder why everyone else's apartment was a higher priority than ours. We told him that if he would bring us the paint, we would look after the balcony ourselves. He happily agreed.

Theresa and Don came over to help us wash the windows and scrub the aluminum window tracks. With clean tracks, the windows opened and closed like a charm. We put up the curtains and all stood back to admire the first really visible sign of progress in three days of cleaning.

Anne woke up the next morning with an unusually sharp pain in her right arm, so I took her to the clinic. The first question the doctor asked when she came into the examining room was "Have you been doing any cleaning lately?" Anne left with instructions for a set of exercises, and a referral to the physiotherapist.

She was not to be stopped. We went back to the apartment, and while I sanded down the balcony railing and divider, and applied a coat of primer, Anne alternated between cleaning closets with her left hand, and exercising her right one by lifting it ever so slowly as high as she could reach.

As the days wore on, Anne gradually regained the use of her right arm. We gave up completely on Jim, resigned to do everything we could ourselves. We replaced the caulking in the bathroom, touched up the enamel in the bathtub, and filled the hole in the bathroom wall with a waterproof cement compound. Anne borrowed an industrial floor cleaning machine from Jim and we scrubbed our grey tiles in the entrance and kitchen, gradually revealing a worn but attractive white and beige design.

The apartment was almost ready when we got a voice mail message from Malaika saying the Brajshoris would not be coming to Ottawa. They had decided to accept the option provided by the government, now that the war was over, to go back to Kosovo at the government's expense. Our hearts sank. We already felt attached to them, and knowing we were working to give them a decent home had been a huge motivation for us.

No cause for concern, Malaika told us when we dropped over to visit her. They would get someone else for the apartment. Sure enough, a little later we received a phone call asking if we could fit a crib and a double bed together in the bedroom. They had a young couple and a baby needing sponsors. We rushed over to measure, and then unfortunately had to call right back to say no, there was no way of squeezing in a crib. They would have to find another couple.

We worked hard to finish off the apartment and ensure we had everything ready to receive a refugee couple, but our hearts were not in it. We had been scrubbing for seven days, and had a lot of laughs, saying how naive and gullible we were to do all the work that the landlord should have done. It did not seem funny any more, now that we were without our elderly couple to put in our pristine apartment.

A couple of days passed, and we were just getting over our disappointment when the phone rang again. They changed their mind again, Malaika reported, the Brajshoris are coming to Ottawa after all, and would be arriving on the 16th as originally planned.

We felt our spirits soar, but there was no time to lose. It was already the 13th. Our group sprang into action. Rose-Aline and Claire researched Albanian food preferences and bought a large order of Albanian cultural favourites – beef, chicken, rice, peppers, onions, olives, cabbage, flour, olive oil, and yoghurt – along with a number of staples for the kitchen. Anne M. picked up a full range of cleaning supplies to stock their broom closet, and confirmed the telephone connection to ensure it would be hooked up when they arrived. Theresa and Don picked up the items we had in storage in Rose-Aline's garage, and brought over a television that a neighbour had donated. Anne and I looked after last minute administrative details. We delivered the government cheque for the first and last months' rent to the landlord, had extra keys made, and transferred the Ottawa Hydro account to the Brajshoris' name. Then we verified with Peter in Toronto that the Brajshoris would be carrying with them the promised government cheque for living expenses, and that subsequent cheques would be sent to the Brajshoris' new address in Ottawa. We spoke to a local banker, preparing the ground in advance for us to take the Brajshoris to the bank to open an account a few days after their arrival. There were a hundred and one things to do, and somehow they all got done.

All the sponsors assembled at the apartment the morning of the 15th to await the furniture and help to turn the apartment into an inviting home. It was only 9:00 o'clock, but the morning sun announced another scorching hot day. Theresa and Don left for the Reception House to pick up the linens and kitchen utensils. Then the kitchen table and chairs arrived. We could not believe our eyes. It was a standard office table and office chairs, the kind you see in church basements or public clinics. The folding table legs were so cumbersome the chairs would not even slide under the table. How would anyone ever sit down for dinner? The apartment was starting to look more like an office then a place to live.

Before long the sofa, armchair, lamp and coffee table arrived. The lamp was a deep pink and clashed uncontrollably with our blue curtains. The sofa would not fit in the elevator, and even though it was quite light, the delivery men refused to carry it up the stairs on the pretext that they would probably not be able to get it through the door of the apartment. At Anne's insistence that we needed at least some living-room furniture, they brought up the armchair – an ugly brownish green with great gull wing arms. A little later the double bed arrived, so poorly padded, remarked one of the sponsors, that you could feel the springs in your back. A basic white five drawer dresser accompanied the bed. At least all the furniture sent by the government was new.

We suddenly realized that all the furniture we were going to get had already arrived. I had a sinking feeling and I could see from Anne's expression that she shared it. The apartment looked terrible, half furnished, unmatched and unfinished.

Our faces were long with disappointment. We had been working so hard for so long, and now the day before the refugees' arrival we

43

had an apartment that seemed hardly liveable. We huddled around in a powwow. I remembered my mother's old saying, "You can't make a silk purse out of a sow's ear," but at least we had to try. We all came up with ideas of how we could co-ordinate the colours and give the apartment the finishing touches that would turn it into a welcoming home. Anne got on the phone and made arrangements for a smaller sofa to be sent, but was told it could only be delivered in two or three days. What were we to do in the mean time? Anne M. offered to donate a beige armchair she had been storing in her garage, and she and I drove out to her place and brought it back. At least Mr. and Mrs. Brajshori would each have a proper place to sit in the living room when they arrived. Theresa went home and found a table cloth in pink, blue and off-white that transformed our office table into a kitchen table and pulled together the miss-mash of disparate colours in the room. She also found a bedspread and bed skirt, and worked an equally remarkable transformation on the bedroom. Anne went to the Market to buy fresh flowers for the coffee table. Claire brought in a container of green ivy. Don was unhappy with the fuzzy television reception we were getting without cable service, so rushed out to buy new rabbit ears. By the time we had installed a modern looking clock and a few pictures on the walls, a small mirror in a pink plastic frame by the bathroom, and a larger formal mirror at the entrance to the living room, the apartment began to have a homey, ready-to-live-in look.

It was 9:00PM We all dropped into crumpled postures around the living room to survey our work. Our faces had that tired but contented look you sometimes see in a locker room after a particularly tough match that has just been won in overtime. We had been there for twelve hours. We took one last look at the apartment. It was tidy and inviting. We were ready for the special event we had looked forward to with anticipation for so long. The Brajshoris would be arriving tomorrow by bus from Camp Borden. Tomorrow was our big day.

three

FIRST DAYS

We woke up slowly on July 16, our bodies protesting our every move and our eyes heavy with sleep. Preparing the apartment the previous day had been physically tiring, but apparently not tiring enough to send us off to sleep when we had finally gone to bed, and we had lain awake for some time thinking of our refugee couple and the adventure awaiting us.

By the time we sat down for breakfast, we were infused with new energy. Today was the day we would meet Nezir and Nazife Brajshori. It was our responsibility to prepare enough food for the Brajshoris so that they would not have to cook on the day of their arrival. We went to the Market for a fresh baguette, and then prepared a Greek salad with tomatoes, cucumbers, onions, black olives and feta cheese, and a supper dish of chicken with red and green peppers. We had our own lunch and took the prepared food over to the Brajshoris' apartment where we stowed it safely in the fridge. Then we headed to the Glebe Collegiate, the designated meeting place where the bus would drop off the new arrivals.

We were the first to arrive. The heat in the parking lot in front of the collegiate was unbearable, so we sought refuge under the arch of the front door. Don was the second to arrive, followed by others, and soon the group was too big for the shaded arch and spilled out into the parking lot. Little knots of people formed here and there in the lot to chat and exchange experiences. We met Nancy, a young sponsor with a new baby, who along with colleagues in the World University Service of Canada and other service groups had formed five Groups of Five. They were planning to get their groups together in a week or ten days for a picnic, so the Kosovar Albanians could have a social outing together. Anne asked her if we could bring our senior couple, since they had no family in Ottawa, and she readily agreed. Then we met Leka, an Albanian crop duster who had himself recently arrived from Kosovo and had come to the parking lot to help with translation. Leka spoke almost perfect English. Much of Pec, his home town in Kosovo, had been totally destroyed in the war. Sylvia, the sponsor we had met at the first briefing meeting, came over to say hello, and introduced us to the other sponsors from her church. Then Edith, one of the Citizenship and Immigration officers, came over to talk to us.

Edith handed out her business card to everyone in our little group, explaining that she worked on the Citizenship and Immigration team responsible for the Kosovar Refugee Program. I noticed there was no phone number on her card, only an address. "There is no phone number on the card," I observed. "How can we get in touch with you?"

"Oh," she responded, taking back the card. "let me write it in." She did the same for the other sponsors, then turned back to me. "We were told by headquarters not to put phone numbers on our business cards," she confided. "We used to have them there, but we were getting too many calls. We didn't have time to do any work."

I asked her somewhat boldly whether contact from sponsors could be considered part of their work. "I know, I always give my number," was her instant reply. "I am happy to get your calls."

We heard the rumble of a diesel engine from the street, and all our heads turned in unison to see the bus pulling into the parking lot. Curious faces stared out at us and we stared back. The bus came to a stop. The door opened and an older gentleman was the first to come out. He held out his hand to help several other men down the stairs, then started to chat in very animated fashion, touching and then hugging each man in turn. We realized they were saying goodbye to each other.

"Maybe the elderly gentleman is the organizer, or perhaps the translator who accompanied the refugees from Borden," Anne commented.

"Yes, perhaps," I responded. "He seems to be in charge."

We watched while the elderly gentleman organized the refugees as they came off the bus. He was tall, and solidly built. He wore a rumpled dark blue suit over a tan coloured wool vest and his white shirt was buttoned at the collar. A neatly trimmed grey beard not more than half an inch long covered his chin, worked its way up both sides of his weathered face and disappeared under a finely woven cotton skull cap, the kind you associate with devout Muslim men. His large hands were constantly in motion, beckoning people this way and that, touching them on the arm or the shoulder, shaking hands, or vigorously chopping at the air with a finger as he made a point. I could hear Anne whispering softly beside me, "Gee, I hope we get somebody like that."

We were so intent on what was happening by the door of the bus that we had not noticed that we were now in a kind of a reception line. All the refugees were passing by us, saying hello, smiling, and shaking our hands as they went. We smiled and said hello in return. There were a lot of families with children, and a few older people. An older lady was making her way down the line toward us, and I sensed Anne was wondering the same thing as I was: Could this be our Mrs. Brajshori? A white silk head scarf outlined an expressionless face, and fell neatly in two long points down the front of a beige raincoat done up right to the top. She must be roasting, I thought, as she came along, pausing to shake hands mechanically with each sponsor, but not looking up. She was clutching a tightly tied white plastic grocery bag in her left hand. She shook our hands and moved on, without seeing us. All the refugees were wearing name tags, but hers was turned over, so we had no way of knowing who she was. Soon all the people had come off the bus, and the older lady in the beige coat had come to the end of the receiving line and was looking lost. "That must be Mrs. Brajshori," Anne stated. "I'm going over to get her."

By the time Anne reached the older lady, Edith was there too. From where I stood, I could see Anne talking to Edith, and then Edith turned the lady's name tag over. I saw Anne break into a big smile and start talking warmly to the lady while shaking her hand again. She had found Mrs. Brajshori. Anne took her arm, and started to lead her back towards the front of the bus.

Most of the sponsors had by now located their families and had gathered them together in little bunches around the parking lot to give them a more proper, personal welcome. Don and I had not seen Mr. Brajshori yet, and we were beginning to wonder where he might be. I looked back to the front of the bus and saw the elderly gentleman talking to a relaxed looking man in a short sleeved shirt. Then I heard the man speak to someone else in English, and I realized he must be one of the translators. I approached him and asked if he had seen Mr. Brajshori.

"Are you his sponsor?" the man queried, and I nodded agreement. "This is Mr. Brajshori, right here," he went on, touching the elderly gentleman's sleeve. "He has been looking for you."

By this time Anne and Mrs. Brajshori had returned. Anne introduced herself to the translator, and then told the Brajshoris we were happy to meet them and had been waiting for a long time to see them. The translator repeated this in Albanian to Mr. and Mrs. Brajshori. Mr. Brajshori's features exploded into a huge smile, his eyes sparkling. "This is a face I will never forget," he said through the translator, looking Anne right in the eye. Then he gave her a huge, rather crushing bear hug. Releasing her, he looked into his pockets. Pulling out the letter Anne had written them a few days earlier, he explained how much it meant to them to have sponsors waiting for them here in Ottawa. He was effusive in his gratitude, saying that they did not speak English, were old and needed help, and could only thank Allah because they had nothing and there was no way they could ever repay our kindness.

Anne spoke through the interpreter as Don and I looked on. She told the Brajshoris that two sponsors would come every day for the first little while, to check on them and see if they needed anything. Then she said we would like to take them to the bank on Monday, in three days time, to open their account. Mr. Brajshori nodded agreement. "Come anytime," he said. "You are always welcome. And going to the bank on Monday is fine."

Suddenly Shano, the Canadian who had told us about Albanian culture at the first meeting of sponsors, came into our circle. I had not realized she was in the parking lot. She started an animated discussion with Mr. Brajshori that went on for several minutes. Then she turned to us and said, "Mr. and Mrs. Brajshori are very traditional Albanians. I am sure you will enjoy helping them and getting to know them. My husband and I will telephone them and visit them from time to time, and we will let you know if they need anything. One thing they may be asking for is a Turkish coffee maker. They will be wanting to serve their guests coffee in the traditional way. My husband and I will take them to the mosque in a few days, as they will probably want to go regularly every Friday."

We thanked Shano for her offer to keep in touch with the Brajshoris, and told her how pleased we were to be able to meet her personally. We hoped we would be able to see her again.

We began to notice a new kind of commotion around us. The refugee families were gathering up their luggage and loading it into the sponsors' cars. It was time to go. Mr. Brajshori showed Don which bags were his. There were five of them, and two were big, heavy-looking duffle bags like the bags hockey players use to carry their equipment. Don started to carry the smaller bags to his van. Mr. Brajshori picked up a duffle bag in each hand and without showing the least strain carried them across the lot to the waiting van. He must be in good shape, I thought, or else those bags are lighter than they look. I walked over to the van and bent over casually to pick up one of the duffle bags to load it onto the van floor. It did not budge. I had to grab it with both hands and literally heave it up to the van. It weighed a ton.

We were almost ready to go, with the luggage in the van and Nezir and Nazife Brajshori in our car, when Leka came over. He wanted to say goodbye to the Brajshoris. There was a prolonged discussion. The sincerity and feeling in Leka's voice were unmistakable. He turned to us. "They are a wonderful couple. Give me a call if you need someone to translate." He scribbled down his phone number and passed it to Anne.

We drove off, Anne in front with me and Nezir and Nazife in the back seat, Nazife still wearing the beige raincoat that she had refused to take off. At least the car was air conditioned. Nezir started to laugh. He caught Anne's attention and motioned towards Nazife. She was sleeping. Nezir pretended to sleep himself, but could not help himself and broke out laughing again. It was a big joke. He explained that they had been on the bus since 8:00 in the morning—an eight hour trip. It was normal to be tired.

In a few minutes we arrived in front of their apartment building on Clarence Street. We pulled up behind a large van into which a group of people of Chinese origin were loading furniture. They stopped to watch us as we got out of the car. Nezir and Nazife immediately went over to them and started to shake their hands and say hello. For a split second they all had a quizzical look on their faces, but they quickly caught on and all smiled, shook hands and said hello as the Brajshoris made the rounds. "They are brand new Canadians," we said, "refugees from Kosovo."

"Welcome to Canada," came the refrain. "We hope you like it here," they all repeated, as the Brajshoris finished their handshakes.

Theresa and Rose-Aline came down from the apartment to greet the Brajshoris and help them with their luggage. Nazife was intrigued by the elevator, but hesitated to get in. I noticed she was still clutching the white plastic bag, which she had been holding in the crook of her left arm in the car and did not seem to want to let out of her sight. Rose-Aline left Nazife in the lobby and took some of the luggage upstairs. In a few minutes it was time for the Brajshoris to get in the elevator. Nazife looked apprehensively at the open door and refused to budge. Finally Nezir said something to her, and she got in.

Nezir was observing how the elevator worked, and took note of which floor we were going to. Then he looked closely at the number on the apartment door. "*Shtatë zero një*," he verbalized, pointing in turn to each of the numbers.

"That's right," I encouraged, "seven-o-one."

"*Shtatë zero një*," he repeated. He seemed determined not to forget. This man is a real survivor, I thought.

Nezir walked into the apartment and went straight to the balcony. Nazife went to the bathroom and splashed water on her face, then came into the living room. Nezir was just coming back from the balcony. "*Mirë!*" he exclaimed, and then as if to emphasize, repeated. "*Mirë mirë!*" We were not sure what this meant, but it was obviously positive. We could see from their expressions that they both liked the apartment, and were beginning to relax.

The other sponsors said goodbye and left. We stayed on for a few moments to show them the prepared food, try to answer any questions they might have about the apartment, and reassure them that everything would be all right.

Nezir motioned for Anne and me to sit in the two comfortable armchairs. Nazife gave him her white plastic bag, and he pulled out two bottles of coke, a small white coffee cup, and two dirty plastic glasses. Anne saw that he was not happy with the used plastic glasses, and took him into the kitchen where she opened the cupboard full of clean glass tumblers. His eyes widened. "*Mirë!*" he exclaimed, taking four of the tumblers and coming back into the living room. We were directed back to the armchairs, and he and Nazife sat on the kitchen chairs. Nezir poured four glasses of coke and handed us ours. "*Pije,*" he instructed. "*Pije.*" We drank the coke.

We suddenly realized that we had just experienced our first dose of Albanian hospitality. Nazife had protected that coke through thick and thin so that they would have something to give to their sponsors when they arrived in Ottawa. They were now our hosts, and we their guests. It dawned on us that the little apartment that we had been thinking of possessively as "our apartment" now belonged to the Brajshoris. The transformation had occurred the minute they had walked in the door, but we were only realizing it now.

Nazife went into the bedroom and came back with two little boxes. She took a lady's wristwatch from one and gave it to Anne. Nezir took a man's watch from the other and gave it to me. We surmised that they were giving us their own watches, that had probably been given to them as a gift by someone at Camp Borden. We hoped the diffidence we felt did not show on our faces as we both expressed pleasure and graciously accepted. There was no way we could turn down a gift from the heart that was obviously so important to them. We felt very honoured.

We showed them where the food was, and explained that Rose-Aline and Anne M. would come to visit them tomorrow. We gave them two sets of keys to the apartment on key chains featuring red and yellow maple leaves, bought specially for the occasion. Then we said goodbye, shaking their hands in normal Canadian fashion. This did not seem to satisfy them. Nazife gave Anne a hug. Nezir hugged Anne, too, and then gave me the traditional greeting used by men, our two heads gently touching, first on one side, then the other. They accompanied us to the elevator door. As soon as the elevator door closed behind us, we took deep breaths, grinned, and simultaneously started to talk. We could hardly contain our pleasure and excitement as we drove away.

We woke up the next morning wondering how our couple was adapting. Were they all right? Did they need anything? We were like two doting parents. According to the schedule we had agreed with the other sponsors, we were not to see them again until Monday, two days away. Finally we could not help ourselves. We would go to the Middle East Store and buy them the Turkish coffee maker Shano had told us about in the parking lot the day before. That way they would be able to serve Turkish coffee to their guests, and we would have a pretext to see how they were.

Neither one of us had any idea what a Turkish coffee pot was. We had good memories of a trip to Greece many years before, when we had both become pleasantly addicted to the syrupy black liquid called Greek coffee, served in tiny cups. Someone had told us at the time that it was similar to Turkish coffee. So we were not too surprised when the saleslady at the Middle East Store pointed out a series of tiny stainless steel pots with long handles, big enough respectively to hold two, four, or six tiny cupfuls. We picked the four cup version, along with a set of six tiny cups and saucers and six tiny spoons. We also bought a pound of strong-looking house brand coffee. We were ready for our impromptu visit to the Brajshoris.

We rang the apartment from the front door of the building, and Anne M. let us in. She and Rose-Aline were in the middle of their planned visit for the day. Nezir and Nazife came to greet us at the door to their apartment. Nezir embraced Anne in a massive bear hug, then grasped me by the shoulders and repeated the side to side head touching of the day before. Nazife hugged Anne, but when I went to hug her she instinctively pulled back. She was obviously not expecting a hug from me. I offered my hand instead, which she readily grasped.

Anne presented them with our gift. Nezir's eyes widened, and his mouth formed an exaggerated circle. "*Oooh!*" he exclaimed, "*kafe, kafe.*" The items were extracted one by one from the bag, each one eliciting some new exclamation and sounds of gratitude from our host. Shano had been right. They were obviously pleased. The various items were deposited in the kitchen, and then the greetings we had received on entering the apartment were repeated, this time, we assumed, to thank us for the gift.

Nezir led us into the living room, where Anne M. And Rose-Aline were already seated. "*Ungju, ungju,*" he repeated, motioning to us to sit down. Meanwhile Nazife, who had disappeared into the kitchen, reappeared with two glasses of coke which she set on the table in front of us.

"We had a good laugh when we arrived this morning," Anne M. told us. "We rang them from downstairs and Nezir answered the phone, but he must have thought it was a phone call. He just kept talking and talking. Then we realized he didn't know how to open the door. So we had to follow someone else into the building. Nezir and Nazife seemed very happy to see us, and gave us the same welcome they just gave you. After we got settled, we tried to teach them how to press '9' on the telephone to open the downstairs door when someone calls on the intercom. We don't know if they caught on."

While the sponsors considered the intercom issue, Nezir had got up and was now motioning for me to join him in the kitchen. He pointed to the stove, making little clicking sounds and pretending to turn knobs this way and that. He was asking me how to operate the stove. Of course, I thought, they probably used a gas stove in Kosovo. An electric stove would be a novelty. Then he pointed to the coffee. He wanted to make coffee for his guests.

I quickly went over the operating fundamentals of the stove, and then watched while Nezir prepared the coffee. Noticing my interest, he put on a show, talking all the while in Albanian in professorial tones. Using one of the little coffee spoons, he carefully measured out four spoonfuls of coffee. "*Një, dy, tre, katër,*" he intoned, as he placed each spoonful carefully into the pot. Then he did the same with the sugar, flourishing each spoonful before deftly dumping it in with the coffee. Rather a lot of sugar, I thought to myself, as I lost count after about the tenth spoon. Then he poured four cupfuls of water into the little pot, and placed it on the hot element. Holding the pot's long handle, he gently agitated it back and forth, humming a catchy little tune. After what seemed a long time, the coffee began to steam and then to bubble, gently at first and then vigorously, foam filling the space that was left in the top of the pot. Nezir let out an exclamation of satisfaction, and removed the pot from the element. The coffee was ready.

We savoured our coffee, thick and syrupy like the Greek coffee we had remembered. Then Anne and I said our goodbyes and left Rose-Aline and Anne M. to finish their visit. After all, it was their day!

On Sunday evening, Shano called. She and Nusret, her husband, had visited the Brajshoris Saturday evening. They had talked and talked. It must have been therapeutic for the Brajshoris, who told Shano and Nusret all about their expulsion from Kosovo, their sojourn as refugees in Macedonia, and their trip to Canada. They also talked about their family. They had four sons in Germany and one daughter in Kosovo.

Shano recounted how pleased Nezir had been to discover that there was a small mosque in an apartment just down the hall from their apartment. A Somalian man had come to tell him about the time of prayers. Nezir said to Shano, "Doesn't God work in wondrous ways? He has seen that we have a good place to live and food to eat, and now we have a place to pray." Nazife said that she felt alone, that she had always been surrounded by her children. Nezir responded, "What do you mean, alone? We have all these wonderful people visiting us."

Shano also told us that Nusret would come to the bank with us on Monday to translate. We were delighted. This would make their meeting with Patrick, the banker, that much easier.

Right after Shano hung up, Rose-Aline called. She and Claire had visited the Brajshoris earlier that day. They really wanted to speak to their sons, so Rose-Aline had gone to get them a calling card. That was the method we had decided to have them use for overseas phone calls, since phone cards had to be paid by cash in advance. That way, they would avoid running up huge bills that they could not afford on their Bell Canada account. After dialling and dialling, Rose-Aline had finally got through to one of the sons in Germany. It was a moment of joy for the Brajshoris to finally speak to one of their children, after being so long with no news. Nazife was shaking when she got off the phone. We could only imagine how good it would feel for the family members in Germany, too, to know that their parents were all right.

Monday was the day for the bank. I had already arranged an appointment with Patrick, the Assistant Manager, to open their account. Patrick knew that the Brajshoris were refugees, and he had told me what documents to bring. The appointment was at 11:00AM We had arranged to meet Nusret at 10:45 at the Brajshoris' apartment, and would walk together to the bank. We reckoned the walk to the bank would take five minutes, ten at the most.

We were welcomed at the Brajshoris' door with the usual greetings. Nazife had drinks poured for everybody before we even entered the room. Nezir motioned for us to sit down, and started to chat. He seemed to want to entertain us. We sat down, then vainly tried to explain that we had an appointment with the banker in ten minutes, and had to leave right away. Nezir looked perplexed. Why were we so agitated? The banker could wait. What was our problem? It was better to socialize first.

Nusret arrived. Thank goodness, I thought, Nusret can explain in Albanian that we do not have time for drinks. Nusret laughed when we explained our predicament. "They don't understand the concept of having an appointment," he told us. "When they want to see someone, they just show up and wait." Nusret spoke to Nezir. Nezir stood up immediately, and helped us gather together the proper identification papers and the government cheque he needed to deposit. We were already well behind schedule, so I phoned Patrick to let him know we would be a little late. Then we all trooped off together to the bank.

We were twenty minutes late. Patrick was understanding and extremely nice. He greeted all of us with a smile and a friendly handshake, and ushered us into his office. We could hardly squeeze in. There was a large desk where Patrick would be seated, and two comfortable guest chairs. Anne guided Nazife into the first chair and motioned to Nezir to take the second. She stood behind Nazife, Nusret stood between Patrick's desk and a stylish ash bookcase, and I stood in the doorway. When Nazife saw that Nusret was standing, she got up to give him her chair. Nusret politely refused her offer, commenting in an aside to us that Kosovar women always give up their chairs if a man is standing. Then Nusret explained to Nazife that the chairs were for the customers, and, pointing to a woman sitting at a desk in the outer office, said it was normal in Canada for women to sit while men stood. Nazife smiled meekly and sat back down.

Patrick had all the forms ready and filled them out quickly on his computer while we all looked on. Then it was time for the signatures. Nezir signed first, in three places, in a painstakingly crafted flowing script. Then it was Nazife's turn. Nezir handed her the pen, but she looked down and refused to take it, murmuring a demure denial. "She says she can't write," Nusret explained. "She never had the opportunity to go to school."

"That's OK," Patrick replied in an understanding tone. "She can simply make a mark."

Nusret relayed Patrick's comment to Nezir, who in turn explained gently to Nazife what to do. Nazife, hesitant, took the pen awkwardly in her hand and started to make little writing motions in the space for her first signature. "*Hajde, hajde, hajde,*" Nezir made soft encouraging noises until the scribble was long enough to look like a signature, then finished with an abrupt, "*Hah!*" Then Nezir pointed to the second space, and started the process again, "*Hajde, hajde, hajde…Hah!*" A smile crept across Nazife's face. She was beginning to have fun. There was one more signature. Then Nezir proudly presented all the signatures to Patrick.

Patrick perused them briefly. "They are all different," he observed nonchalantly. "But that's all right. These are fine."

"You're a business woman now," Anne commended Nazife. Nusret immediately translated. Nazife looked up shyly, breaking into a soft, gentle laugh that was so pleasant to hear.

Nezir received instructions from Nusret on depositing his monthly cheque, and pocketed his bank book. The meeting was over. Patrick stood up behind his desk, congratulated each of them in turn, and shook their hands. For Nezir, this was not enough to convey his full sense of gratitude. He bounded around the desk and embraced Patrick in a big bear hug. "*Faleminderit, faleminderit,*" he repeated several times.

That means "thank you" Nusret translated. "He is very grateful for your help," he said to Patrick. "He is probably not used to having a bank to manage his money. The Albanians in Kosovo could not trust the bank there. They kept their money in locked boxes in their homes."

"We'll be pleased to help him," Patrick responded. "That's what we are here for. The staff at the counter will help him when he comes in."

And with that, we emerged single file out of Patrick's office and marched triumphantly across the main hall and out the door. The Brajshoris looked very pleased.

We stood on the street for a moment to determine our plans. We wanted to take advantage of our first official visit with our couple to show them Loblaws, the large supermarket near their apartment, and then to have them as guests for lunch at our apartment. Nusret agreed to come too.

We were grateful for Nusret's presence, since it meant we could communicate more easily with the Brajshoris. He was also helping us understand Albanian customs. Nusret had left Albania at the age of seventeen in the wake of the Second World War, fleeing to Italy with his father. His father had fallen ill and died several weeks later, leaving Nusret alone to make his own way in the world. He had somehow found his way as an immigrant to Canada, where he had developed an interesting and profitable career as a restaurateur. Now he was retired and able to devote time and energy to helping the Kosovars newly arrived in Canada.

We walked a block down the street from the bank and came to the traffic lights at the corner. Across the street was Loblaws. An excellent opportunity to explain how the pedestrian crossing signals worked, I thought. Luckily the signals were pictorial—a little white walking man for "walk," and a red hand with fingers spread for "wait." The Brajshoris paid attention, nodding, while Nusret explained. Then we entered Loblaws through the automatic doors. Another pause, while Nusret explained their operation. More nods. How fortunate that Nusret is with us, we thought.

We entered the fruit and vegetable department. The Brajshoris stopped in front of a huge display of red and green peppers, Nezir talking excitedly. We asked what he was saying. "He is saying, 'Look at all the peppers!'" Nusret replied. "They are finding the quantity and quality of the produce here very overwhelming."

We made our way around the store, picking up a few special items that Nazife wanted for her cooking, such as fresh spinach, cucumbers, and paprika. "She puts the paprika in her soups," Nusret explained. Then we went through the check-out. "Money, money!" Nezir exclaimed, trying out a new word as he paid. The clerk smiled and gave him a few cents in change, which he promptly handed back to her. "He's giving you a tip," Nusret explained to the clerk, laughing and taking the money back, which he deposited in Nezir's hands while explaining the proper Canadian protocol. So many little things to learn.

We walked back to our car for the journey to our apartment. When we arrived I sat down with Nusret and the Brajshoris, while Anne prepared the lunch, all soft foods as neither Nezir or Nazife had very many teeth. It was not long before Nezir popped up again, seeming to want to leave the room. "It is time for his noon prayers," Nusret told us. "But first he has to wash. Can you show him where the washroom is? And can you show him a room where he can pray, and let him know which way is East? He has to face Mecca when he prays."

I did all this, then came back to the living room. Five minutes went by, and then we heard the most wonderful, melodious call emanating from down the hall. An enchanting, lilting song filled the room, slow, measured and respectful. Nezir was doing the Muslim call to prayer. We all stopped talking. I felt myself relax as the music pulsed through the air in rhythmic waves. "He has a beautiful voice," Nusret opined. We all agreed.

Prayers over, Nezir rejoined us and we sat down to lunch at the dining-room table. Anne served asparagus quiche, salad, tomatoes, and Italian bread. The Brajshoris seemed to enjoy the meal, especially the tomatoes and the bread. When we had all finished eating, Nezir started to tell the story of their expulsion from Kosovo.

"At first the bombing was in the distance," Nezir began his description. "We stood on our balcony and watched. The bombs would land, and there would be a puff of black smoke and then the explosion."

Nezir indicated the collapsing buildings by making little exploding noises with his tongue and wiggled his fingers showing everything coming down.

"We knew from Albanian television that NATO was bombing the

Serb army positions, so we were cheering them on. NATO was there to help us."

Nezir emphasized his point by making more exploding noises and then chuckling to himself at the idea of the Serbian positions going up in smoke.

"After a few days it came nearer, and we hid in the basement. We didn't know what to expect. We were afraid of the Serb militia, wondering what they might do. We had heard that the militias were going into Albanian villages, forcing the people out of their homes, stealing their money, shooting some of them, and telling the others to leave Kosovo. They told the villagers which road to take, and watched them go. Then they would burn the empty village. There would be nothing left."

He made a sweeping motion in front of him to demonstrate the totality of it all, and his eyes narrowed. I looked at Nazife. Her head was down and her eyes looked sad.

"We had been in the basement for what seemed like an eternity when there was a huge commotion on the street outside. There was a lot of shouting and some shooting. Then one of our neighbours who had stayed upstairs came to tell us that we had to go. The soldiers had given everyone in our building ten minutes to get out. We rushed up to our apartment and tried to pack a few things. We could not take much, because we had to carry whatever we took. I grabbed my Koran and two prayer mats, and two brass coffee grinders our father had given my brother and me when I was four years old. We threw in some blankets and a few warm clothes, and a bit of food. We had no time to think. We left everything behind."

Nezir looked up and made a broad arc with his hand, glancing momentarily at everything in the room, as if to illustrate what they had abandoned. Nazife was still looking down, but I thought I could see a tear on her cheek. I felt badly for them, but I reasoned they probably had to talk about it. Anyway there was nothing we could do, because Nezir had got up a head of steam and was ploughing on.

"When we got down to the street with our two bags, I saw that Nazife was still wearing her slippers. We were afraid to go back, because there was a soldier with a gun at the entrance to the building, but Nazife needed her shoes. We decided that she would go back for them. The guard let her go back to our apartment. She came right out again, wearing her shoes.

"We walked down the middle of the street, with other people around us, all leaving their homes. No one knew where to go. Some of the militia had told us we had to get out of Prishtina. We decided to head down the hill towards the train station. Then an old friend, a Serb I had worked with in construction, spotted me in the crowd and came up to me. 'Don't go down there,' he cautioned. 'The militia are picking people up in dump trucks and taking them to the stadium. You will be trapped. You would be better to go by the back route, along the railway tracks. You can follow the tracks to the station. Maybe you will get lucky and find a train.'"

Nezir paused just long enough for Nusret to make the translation, and then started up again. This time his speech was punctuated with noises of vehicles, shouting and the sounds of gunfire. Then he crouched down in his chair and pointed upwards, as though he was hiding from something up above. His voice resumed, faster and louder now, and tinged with anger. He made a shooting motion, shook his head slowly in disbelief, and then fell silent. For a moment, the only sounds were the soft sobs that Nazife could no longer suppress.

I looked at Nusret, expecting him to translate, but Nusret was silent. His eyes were watery. "I never thought I would go through this again," he whispered. There was pain in his voice. "I just never thought." Then he fell silent.

Nezir broke the silence by carrying on with his story. He was more composed now, his tone more matter of fact. From his body language, I could picture him and Nazife creeping along, trying to stay out of sight, and then finally arriving somewhere. He paused again, and Nusret resumed the translation.

"We followed the tracks to the railway station. We were really lucky. We managed to squeeze into the last train out of Prishtina, heading south for Macedonia. People were everywhere, even standing between the cars, and some young boys were on the roof.

"The train was very slow. It started and stopped and then started again. Finally it stopped for good. I looked out, but I could see nothing. Only the forest. Then some Serb soldiers came through the train, telling us we had to get off and walk, that the border with Macedonia was not far. As we got off the soldiers questioned everybody, and took their passports. They were saying, 'You won't be needing this any more.' We started to walk. We were on a muddy road. Sometimes the mud was over the tops of our shoes, but we just had to keep going. We were very tired. In a while we came to a fence and an army checkpoint. It was the border with Macedonia. After another long wait, they let us through. We spent the first night in the forest. The next morning we set out again and after walking a long time we came to a village."

Nazife stopped sobbing, and at first I thought she had composed herself. But then I looked at her eyes and saw the same blank stare we had seen on the faces of the refugees on television, back in France. Nezir was paying no attention. He was in full flight and we knew he would not stop until his story was finished.

"We went to the village square. There were quite a lot of us, so we were crowded. We huddled under our blankets and tried to keep warm. It started to rain. We found a piece of plastic sheeting and pulled it up over our heads. We shared our food, and then when ours ran out, other people shared theirs with us.

"By the end of the second day we had all run out of food. Some United Nations workers came by in a truck. When word got out that they had food, everyone crowded around, pushing and shoving. I told Nazife that we would stay to the side, that it was dangerous for us to go into the crowd. Then the UN workers were knocked down, and the police waded in to beat the crowd back. It was mayhem. We just sat there and waited. Finally, after the commotion had died down, a policeman noticed us sitting there and brought some bread and water over to us.

"We stayed in the market for over three days. It was cold. Someone saw that Nazife and I had nothing to drink out of, and they gave us a white coffee cup. We still have that cup. Some people started to drift away. Maybe some had relatives in Macedonia, but we had nowhere to go."

Nezir paused ever so briefly, just long enough for me to realize the cup he was talking about was the same cup they had pulled out of the bag with the coke and plastic glasses on their first day in Ottawa.

"Then, on the fourth morning, a young couple who lived on the square came to speak to us. They said they would take us to Skopje, where they had relatives who would take us in for a few days. They went away, but soon came back in a car. They told us to wrap ourselves in blankets in the back seat, and to moan and pretend we were sick if anyone stopped the car. They would say that they were taking us to the hospital. That way we could get past the army checkpoints on the way to Skopje.

"Their relatives looked after us for two weeks. We regained our strength. We knew we could not stay, so when we heard that some countries were taking refugees, we decided to try our luck. We wanted to go to Germany, to be with our sons. Our hosts took us to a big refugee camp where several countries were recruiting. We were put in a big tent with eight other refugees, but at least we had a bed and food to eat. The tent had no floor. One night a snake came into the tent and bit one of the women, but she did not die.

"There was a big board in the camp where countries accepting refugees put up their notices. The first thing we found out was that Germany had closed their stand. They were accepting no more refugees. We were devastated. Where would we go? What country would accept us?

"It turned out that there were other countries still accepting refugees, including Sweden, Canada, Switzerland, Portugal and Turkey. Which should we choose? I already knew about Canada, that Canada was a democratic country. When I was in the army, they sent me to Austria for training, and I met a Canadian there who told me about Canada, that Canadians were free and had democratic government. So we chose Canada, even though we knew it was far away.

"We put our names on a list and in about three weeks we had an interview with some Canadians. We told them we were from Prishtina and that we were all alone, and that we wanted to go to Canada because it was a democratic country. They told us to come back with our bags the next morning at 8:00AM, and that we would be taken to Canada right away.

"The next morning they put us on a bus and soon we were at an airport. We were told to wait. The Canadians went away and left us with the Macedonian authorities. I became suspicious. How could we be sure we were being sent to Canada? I got up and went to look at the airplane. It was an Air Canada plane, with a big red maple leaf on the tail. We felt reassured. But Nazife was getting more and more nervous. She was afraid of airplanes. I told the woman at the gate, and soon another woman came to us and gave Nazife a pill. After about twenty minutes, Nazife was calm again. Then she got very sleepy. I had to help her walk to the plane.

"We landed in Germany, and then took off again for Canada. We were on the plane for eleven or twelve hours. Nazife slept most of the way. When it was time to pray, I asked the attendant which way was East. She told me East was behind us, so I prayed facing the back of the plane.

"We landed at Trenton. There were people there to greet us. They were in a line. They shook our hands and said, 'Welcome to Canada.' Then they took us into a large room full of cots and said we could sleep. We slept for a long time.

"The next day they took us on buses to Camp Borden. When we arrived there they wanted us to wash our hair. I just took off my cap and pointed to my bare scalp, laughing. There was no hair to wash. They just waved me by.

"They took us to see the doctor, too. The doctor who examined me seemed surprised to see an old man in such good shape. He was saying, 'Very good, very, very good.' Then he went and brought back three other doctors. They were all examining me, and nodding, and talking. I don't know what they were saying.

"We stayed at Borden for two months. Then they told us they had found sponsors for us in Ottawa. And now we are here. We are so grateful to our sponsors. We can never repay them for their kindness. But God will see their good deeds, and they will be repaid in heaven."

Nezir raised his eyes as if in supplication to God. His story was finished, and now he was at peace. I looked at Nazife. She seemed more relaxed now, and her eyes, while still sad, looked back in focus. Nusret took a few deep breaths and started to relax, too. Repeating Nezir's story had been hard on him. He had not told us everything that Nezir had said. Perhaps it brought back suppressed memories of the Second World War and his own flight from Albania many years earlier.

We left the table. Nazife started to look for something. She looked around the dining room, peered into the kitchen, and assessed the living room from top to bottom. She asked Anne a question and Nusret translated. "She is concerned about the cold winters we have in Canada, and would like to know how you heat the apartment," Nusret repeated. "She can't find any stove or heater." Anne pointed to the vents in the ceiling, explaining how the heating and air conditioning worked. Then she remembered that a neighbour had given us a wonderful warm woman's winter coat to give to Nazife. We were saving it for the arrival of winter, but now Anne was having second thoughts. "I think I'll give it to her now," Anne whispered to me in an aside. "She may be worrying about how they will get through our cold winters without proper winter clothing." She fetched the coat from deep inside the closet and asked Nazife to try it on. It fit perfectly and looked great on her. The smile and expression on Nezir's and Nazife's faces were ones we will never forget. He was thrilled and made a big deal by pretending to try the coat on himself.

It was getting late, and time to take the Brajshoris home. We all said goodbye to Nusret, and Anne and I drove the Brajshoris back to their apartment.

For two days we waited while the other sponsors looked after our couple. We were regaled with stories about Nezir and Nazife going to the Market and coming home with huge bags of cucumbers and potatoes, and about walks in the park where they said hello to perfect strangers and engaged them in long, animated conversations. All the while the weather remained hot and sticky, and we wondered how they were getting along in their apartment where they had a fan but no air conditioning. Then it was our turn again, and we arrived at their place, documents in hand, ready to take them to sign their lease.

By this time their sofa had arrived, so they now had living-room seating for five. We were warmly greeted as usual at the door, and led into a smoke-filled room. A young gentleman in his twenties, seated on the sofa, got up immediately to introduce himself, revealing to advantage a tailored white gown that did up tightly around his neck and fell almost to his stockinged feet. His name was Ahmed, from Ethiopia, and he had been in Canada for six years. He wore the same little white skull cap as Nezir, but of a different style, more like a pill-box. Seeing that Nezir was new in the building, he had come to see how he could help, and had been invited in for a coke. Everyone but Nazife sat down, and soon we, too, had a glass of coke, while Nazife hovered in the background. Ahmed took a long puff on his cigarette, exhaled and smiled at Nezir, but spoke to us, "He is a good man. All the brothers like him," he confided. "Nezir comes to prayer five times a day in the mosque across the hall. He is a very religious man."

Ahmed paused for a moment, and we all looked at Nezir, as if to confirm the truth of this statement. Nezir was quietly enjoying his cigarette, letting the other man speak. Holding a Turkish cigarette-holder deftly between his thumb and two fingers, he inhaled and exhaled almost imperceptibly, making the act of smoking as natural as breath itself. The cigarette holder, finely carved from what looked like amber, gave him a distinguished, old world look. Ahmed went on.

"The brothers will take him to the main mosque tomorrow. Friday is the Muslim holy day."

We asked if Nazife would go, too.

"No," he responded, "probably not, since women usually pray at home. Women are allowed in mosques to pray, but are always physically separate from the men, in a balcony or behind a curtain."

Our curiosity getting the better of us, we asked about the significance of the white skullcaps.

"The cap means he has been to Mecca, as I have," Ahmed explained. "Only people who have been on a pilgrimage to Mecca may wear the cap. It confers on them the religious title of Hajji. Those with the title of Hajji are allowed to lead the people in prayer."

"I noticed that you address Nezir as Hajji," I said to Ahmed. "And Nazife calls him Hajji, too. Is that his name?"

"No, it's his title, not his name," Ahmed cleared up the mystery. "Some people who have been to Mecca like to be called by their title. You can call him by his name or by his title, as you wish."

From that moment forward, we began to address Nezir by his title. It seemed natural that so religious a man be called by his religious title.

We were enjoying our discussion with Ahmed, but time was moving on and we had an appointment with the landlord to sign the lease.

We said goodbye, and headed off with our two charges to the landlord's office in Westboro, a fifteen minute drive. We parked and walked to the front door. The outside temperature was so hot that stepping into the marble foyer of the landlord's office building provided welcome relief. Nazife was by now used to elevators, and visibly enjoyed the ride up to the second floor. The receptionist asked us to sit down while she paged the agent who would look after the lease.

A smiling dark-haired young lady soon emerged, carrying a sheaf of papers. Her name was Christine, she informed us, shaking our hands in turn. She was pleased to have the Brajshoris as tenants, and had all the papers ready. All she had to do was take them through the papers and have them sign.

Christine ushered us into a private office, and explained all the papers in detail. It was exactly as we had negotiated with Tom. The lease was for one year, and the Brajshoris would have the option after one year of renewing the lease, or staying there on a monthly basis. We asked if they could pay their rent by automatic bank debit. Yes, she told us, that would be fine, but there was another paper that would have to be signed. She would have to go back to her office to get it. Christine got up and left the room, closing the door behind her.

Hajji, who had been listening intently without understanding a thing, looked at us with mischief in his eye. Was she going away to call the police, he gestured, who would come and take them away? He crossed his hands, pretending to be locked in hand cuffs, and then pretended to turn a key in a lock, laughing heartily to make sure we knew it was all in jest.

Christine came back with the papers. By this time we were all laughing, and we explained what was happening so Christine could join in the joke. Christine caught on right away. She laughed and assured them there would be no police. We were all chuckling while the Brajshoris signed the papers. A good joke, I thought to myself, but I wonder where it comes from? Perhaps in Kosovo the Albanians always had to wonder when they were going to be hauled off to jail. Maybe Hajji needed reassurance that it would not happen here.

The signing ceremony complete, Christine started to say goodbye. We looked on in anticipation, knowing what was going to happen. Hajji pulled Christine towards him, shook her hand vigorously, and gave her a big, spontaneous bear hug, repeating over and over the new words that he had learned, "Thank you, thank you, thank you." Christine's look of surprise turned quickly to a smile, and she acknowledged their gratitude with grace, wishing them well in their new country. "Good luck you guys," she called out to us, as we disappeared down the hall.

The day of the picnic finally arrived, sunny, and hot as usual. The Kosovar refugees had been here in Ottawa for ten days. Today our couple and five other families would get together for an afternoon pot luck lunch at Vincent Massey Park. It was our turn again to visit the Brajshoris, and we would drive them over to the Park.

On our way to their apartment, Anne told me about the plan she had to manage the exuberant but overwhelming greetings she always received from Hajji. He was strong and he did not seem to know his own strength. Every time he hugged her he almost crushed her, and she would go home to nurse her neck and shoulders with ice packs, only to have them injured again by the next massive hug. Her plan, that she had developed in consultation with the other female sponsors, was to hold her purse in front of her with her left hand, and offer her right hand directly in front of and close to her body. This way, Hajji would have only his left arm to effect the hug, and would likely grasp her with less force, as both their right hands and her purse would be in the way.

The plan worked. Hajji greeted Anne with his usual ebullience, but the purse and hands deprived him of his leverage and resulted in a more gentle hug. We were ushered into the living room. The room looked different. The sofa cushions were wrapped neatly in a blanket, giving a slipcover effect. Prayer mats featuring Muslim holy sites in Saudi Arabia were laid carefully over the backs and seats of the two armchairs. A gold plate with an Arabic inscription had been tucked behind the top of the mirror, and several strings of prayer beads dangled nearby from a tiny nail. We commented on the new decor. "*Allah*," Hajji intoned, tracing his finger backwards over the inscription on the gold plate. "*Allah*." Then he proudly showed off his prayer rugs, before asking us to sit down.

Nazife carefully placed a glass of coke in front of each of us. Hajji wanted to sit and talk, *"tora tora"* as he called it, but Nazife knew she was going to see other Kosovars, and she fussed around impatiently, urging him to finish his drink so we could go. Seeing her eagerness, Hajji willingly relented, and soon we were all out the door, Nazife carrying a bag of kiwis, her contribution to the pot luck.

We arrived at the park, and began to look around for the large Canadian flag that was to indicate our group's location. Three times we spotted a flag, only to find it belonged to some other group. We were in a maze. There were hundreds of people and dozens of groups. The sun beat down on us, and made our coolers and folding chairs seem all the heavier. We stopped to reconsider our strategy. We thought we would recognize Nancy, the sponsor who organized the picnic. There was an even better chance of the Brajshoris recognizing some of the Kosovars. I would take Hajji to scour the grounds for our group, while Anne and Nazife sat on our chairs under the shade of some trees. Hajji and I took off, but found no one. When we came back, we saw Anne and Nazife talking excitedly to a teenage girl and her father. It was Metije and Rrahman. The Kosovars had found us!

They led us to our picnic site, a spacious private site with grass for the children to play on, lots of trees for shade, and two large wooden picnic tables that had been placed end to end so that we could lay out the pot luck lunch. Metije, who spoke a little English, introduced us to her family: her mother and father, Hava and Rrahman, her two brothers, Qemail, almost 15, and Murat, 7, and her sister, Iba, 12. They had met the Brajshoris at Camp Borden, and had become good friends.

We set up our chairs under the trees and sat for a while, eating chips and drinking lemonade, while the Brajshoris chatted with Hava and Rrahman at a hundred miles an hour, making up for lost time. Leka, the crop duster, spotted us and came over to talk. Then a tall, pleasant looking man and a smiling black-haired woman in red shorts came over to greet the Brajshoris. After a few moments he turned to Anne and me and addressed us in perfect English, "Allow me to introduce myself. My name is Eduard, and this is my wife, Juljana. We met the Brajshoris at Camp Borden. I am a doctor, an osteopath. We have three children, playing over there." He pointed in the direction of a group of children playing volleyball on the grass without a net.

We talked with Eduard and Juljana about their experiences so far in Canada. They were happy, and their sponsors had treated them well. They wanted to stay and make a new home for themselves in Canada. Eduard was hoping to be able to work as a doctor again, but his inquiries so far about how to get accredited had run into a brick wall. However, it was early days, and he had not given up hope. Of course, his future also depended on how his wife and children fared.

As the afternoon wore on we noticed a subtle change in the dynamic of the picnic. Nazife and the other women gravitated over to the picnic tables and stayed there, looking after the younger children and organizing the food. The men sat in chairs under the trees and smoked and drank coke. We asked Eduard about the coke. "That is the most popular drink in Kosovo," he laughed. "There is a coke plant in Kosovo, and it has no shortage of customers. I guess you could say it is the national drink."

We also noticed how happy Hajji and Nazife were to mingle with their friends and speak Albanian to people who could understand them. Nazife was radiant. We made a special point of thanking Nancy for including them in her picnic. Anne collected the phone numbers of all the women, so that Nazife could maintain social contact over the phone. I could hear Anne laughing as she sat with the women, trying to learn Albanian phrases. Occasionally she would come over and try out some new phrase on Hajji and the other men. They would laugh and correct her, coaching until she got it. A difficult language, I thought, looking on.

One thing really struck us as we observed the Kosovars enjoying themselves. Our couple were the only people with that "old world" look. Nazife always wore her white silk head scarf when she went out, long and loose around the back of her neck and coming down in two long points in front, where she fastened it with a decorative pin. She favoured silk or polyester blouses in bright colours, which she buttoned tightly around her neck and wrists. Invariably she wore pantaloons in a contrasting polyester pattern that billowed out like a long skirt, but which she drew in and tied at her ankles. The overall effect was as elegant as it was practical but somehow out of place in modern day Canada, and made me think of a picture I had enjoyed as a child of the little genie on a magic carpet in the story of Aladdin and the magic lamp.

Hajji had an elegance of his own, preferring long sleeved dress or sport shirts, buttoned at the neck without a tie. Over this he always wore a vest, often in light grey or tan tones, complemented by a dark business suit and black dress shoes. Tall and straight as an arrow, even at the age of 68, and with the upper body build of a heavyweight boxer, he cut a distinguished figure indeed. Everyone else was dressed just like any other Canadian on a steaming July afternoon – T-shirts, cotton pants or shorts, short sleeved shirts or blouses, and sandals. Although all the Kosovars were nominally Muslim, none except Nazife wore a head scarf and only Hajji wore a skull cap. I wondered, watching them dressed in all those clothes on a muggy July afternoon, whether they were hot. I noticed later on that Hajji had taken off his suit coat and hung it on the back of his chair, in concession to the heat.

The afternoon passed quickly, and no one noticed the clouds begin to seep in from the West. But then they suddenly rolled across the sky like a closing clamshell, and we knew it was going to rain. Within seconds tables were cleared, rubbish deposited in the bins, and goodbyes said. We found ourselves rushing across the grass in the direction of the cars. Just in time! Hardly had we closed the trunk and jumped into our seats when the rain came down in sheets, almost obscuring the road as we drove out of the park. Hajji and Nazife talked excitedly as we drove home, first about the force and abruptness of the storm, then about the friends they had met in the park. They were both wound up like tops.

The rain stopped as suddenly as it had started, just as we pulled up to the Brajshoris' apartment building. We got out to say our goodbyes. The air was cooler, and there was a freshness that always comes after a sudden storm. The Brajshoris invited us up for tea but we declined. Okay, they told us, next time then, as they gave us goodbye handshakes and hugs even warmer and more intense than usual. Then Hajji went into the street to direct traffic for us, making a big show with police-like hand signals and waving us forward when it was safe to go. We came to the stop sign at the end of the block and I looked back in the rear-view mirror. There was Hajji in the middle of the street, both hands high above his head and waving rhythmically in long arcs up and down. Anne opened her window and extended her arm so that Hajji could see her waving in return. We rounded the corner. Anne raised her window and looked over at me, her smile practically ear-to-ear. We were both thinking the same thing. How wonderful it was to see them so happy, if only briefly, as they began the long adjustment to their new home.

four

ADAPTATION

Over the next few months we visited the Brajshoris two or three times a week. Our mission was to help them adapt to their new land. We would show them the "Canadian way," and they would become more and more independent. In no time at all they would become fully adapted, and our role as sponsors would come to a close.

At least, that was our theory. We would be the teachers, and they the students. In fact, it did not work out precisely that way. True, they learned about Canada. But we also learned about Kosovo. Cultural assimilation went in both directions. Every day was an adventure, for us as much as for them.

Hajji attacked the job of his own integration into Canadian culture with enthusiasm and confidence. A week or so after the picnic, he treated us to a detailed commentary, accented by bursts of laughter and lively gestures, on his initiation to the local bus service. He had taken the bus to visit Hava and Rrahman, he told us, and had gotten hopelessly lost. It all started when Hajji had mistakenly copied down the word "Finish" instead of "Fisher" on the note he wanted to show the bus driver. The bus driver, thinking Hajji wanted to get off at the end of the line, took him right past Fisher Avenue and deposited him on the outskirts of town. Not to be defeated, Hajji got on another bus and again showed his note to the driver. Again he was driven to an unknown location at the end of the driver's route. Hajji kept trying,

72

but soon realized he was going in circles. Repeatedly, he saw the same brightly painted concrete cows – "moo moos" he called them, to ensure we understood. We knew the cows he described because they were unique in Ottawa, an advertisement for a steakhouse in the West End, far from Hava's. After a whole day of riding the bus looking for Hava's, his funds depleted and the sun sinking in the sky, he turned his attention to the more critical task of finding his way home. Jumping in a taxi, he asked to be taken to "Parliament," a central landmark that he knew. Once there, he motioned for the taxi driver to carry on straight down the street to "Loblaws," the store near his apartment. From there he knew the way home. The taxi driver, recognizing that Hajji was a refugee, refused to take any money from him.

When he arrived home, eleven hours after setting out, he told Nazife he had been at Hava's all day, so that she would not worry about his getting lost. "No you haven't," she replied. "I've been on the phone off and on all day with Hava, and you were never there." Hajji was forced to admit the truth. It was all a big joke, and he loved recounting the story, over and over again.

As we got to know Hajji better, we were struck by his ability to relate positively to people. An extrovert, he would approach people openly, with a wide grin, spouting Albanian in rapid fashion with the odd English word thrown in here and there, and gesturing in a friendly, reassuring manner. Whether or not one understood his words, there was no mistaking his benign intent. Even little children were instinctively drawn to him by his warm voice and friendly, beckoning gestures. His character, we felt, would be a powerful ally in his adjustment to his new land.

Of all the Brajshori traits we felt were indicative of Albanian culture, none was more endearing than the warmth of their greetings. They always greeted each person in turn, with the appropriate handshake or embrace. They always enquired as to our health, and the health of our loved ones. They always strove to make us as comfortable as possible, giving us the place of honour, ensuring that we had something to drink and eat, and generally fussing over us. If they had not seen us for an unusually long time, or if there was some other reason for them to feel that a special welcome was in order, they would come around to us a second time, after we had been seated. Then they would start the greetings all over again, the hugs and handshakes even warmer than before.

At one point Anne took her brothers and sisters unannounced for a quick visit to meet the Brajshoris. Family ties are treasured in Albanian culture, and meeting Anne's family was an honour. Eyes aglow, touching and hugging each brother and sister in turn, Hajji moved around the room, personally welcoming each brother and sister. Nazife followed in his tracks, offering her more reserved and demure welcoming handshake. There was a moment of concern, as Hajji realized there were too many visitors to serve tea. Since they had arrived unannounced, he had nothing prepared that he could readily offer. Realizing the importance of his giving something, Anne pointed to the bowl of sugar cubes. Relieved, and with a big smile, Hajji made the rounds again with the bowl of sugar, everyone gladly accepting his modest but heartfelt gift.

Greetings were not limited to social occasions. Business relations were equally important. When workmen came unexpectedly to the apartment to verify or repair the plumbing or electricity, they would be received warmly at the door, invited in, and offered a cigarette or a coke. Delivery men were similarly treated. While they were not always able to accept, we could see from their reactions that they were touched by this unexpected gesture of goodwill.

The Brajshoris' expressions of gratitude were equally heartfelt, and seemed to us to reflect a particular Albanian cultural twist. The Brajshoris never forgot to thank people for service rendered or a helping hand offered, and here again Hajji took the lead. Wherever possible this meant a traditional Albanian hug. We would watch with amusement as the scene unfolded, surprise and uncertainty on the part of the unsuspecting recipient usually giving way in short order to expressions of pleasure and a reciprocal hug.

One day we took the Brajshoris to Parliament Hill. Because he associated Parliament with democracy and the benevolence of all Canadians in taking in the Kosovar refugees, Hajji was naturally looking around for some official figure to thank. When we introduced him to the fully uniformed Mountie standing in front of Parliament, there was no holding Hajji back. "Thank you, thank you, Canada number one," he asserted, shaking the Mountie's hand vigorously. Then he grabbed the equally robust Mountie in a full embrace, knocking his glasses askew and tipping his broad brimmed hat to the side. A look of amazement flashed into the Mountie's eyes, but quickly gave way to one of curiosity. "They are refugees from Kosovo," Anne explained. "He is thanking you for bringing them here."

"Welcome to Canada," came the Mountie's instant response, his face breaking into a welcoming grin.

Hugs were not the only item in Hajji's repertoire. Sometimes hugs were neither appropriate or possible, as in the case of his weekly visits to the bank. Here he was separated from the tellers by a counter. By the time of his third or fourth visit, he had gotten to know all the tellers, and they him. What could be more appropriate, thought Hajji, than to offer them a small bowl of sweets in appreciation for their efforts. "Oh, thank you Mr. Brajshori," came the response, "but we are not allowed to accept gifts of any kind. Thank you anyway. A hand shake will have to do." And so he made the rounds, thanking everyone and shaking their hands. "Bring his wife in next time," one of the tellers asked me. "We would like to meet her, too."

Unfortunately, this was to prove to be impossible. Nazife never went anywhere with Hajji, when the outing was for business purposes. This included all the daily chores of living which in Canada are shared between the sexes and often left to women outright: grocery shopping, banking, and visits to the pharmacy or corner store. In fact, Nazife never left the apartment alone, either. Her sorties were limited to social outings where we, the other sponsors, or their Albanian friends would come and pick them up together to take them out in the car. This concerned us a lot at first, as we knew her spending all that time alone in her apartment meant that she was being short-changed in the long process of cultural acclimatization. As time went on we learned to accept it, however, as a cultural stricture that would not be overcome. At least she did enjoy her outings with us, and would often be waiting, fully dressed at the door and eager to go, when we arrived to pick them up.

Hajji reserved his biggest expressions of gratitude for gestures that touched him personally and intimately. He was ever so grateful to anyone who helped him maintain good health. Help in getting his false teeth was no exception.

We had been told before the Kosovars arrived that many would need extensive dental work. Years of poor or non-existent dental care had taken their toll. We were therefore not surprised to see that our elderly couple had only a few teeth left. They would need dentures.

For years Hajji had dreamed of getting dentures. In Kosovo it had just never been possible. Now he demonstrated over and over through imaginary gestures how he would pick up first the top and then the bottom dentures and click them into place. It was time for action. We set the wheels in motion.

There were many dental appointments and many dentists' offices. Hajji always entertained us and the dental staff with stories of dentistry in Kosovo. His favourite tale described how he found himself one day sitting in a crowded dental waiting room, waiting his turn. Every chair was taken. Without warning, the patient being worked on in the inside office let out piercing screams of pain and agony. It sounded like the dentist had slit his throat. For an instant the patients in the waiting room looked at each other in fear, and then all bolted for the door. All except Hajji, who kept his cool. A few minutes later the dentist emerged, and looking around the empty room, asked Hajji where everyone had gone. "They all ran away," Hajji told him. "All right then," the dentist said, looking at Hajji. "You're next. Come on in."

We were always a little suspicious that Hajji was more frightened of dentists than he let on, especially at first. He would manufacture excuses to delay trips to the dentist. We compensated by allowing extra time to get him moving. One day he gleefully showed us, in the palm of his hand, one of his own teeth that had been aching and that he had pulled out himself. Toothache and painful home remedies must have been normal experiences for many people in Kosovo, we reasoned, especially in the old days.

By the time the day for getting his dentures drew near, Hajji had developed a remarkable relationship with everyone in the dentist's office. They all loved him and took special care to look after him. "It makes our days more interesting," the receptionist said to me, "to know that a patient appreciates our services so much."

When Hajji finally got his teeth, his eyes sparkled as he tested them out, clicking them together and repeating over and over, "Very good, very, very good." He warmly thanked everyone who had had a hand in his treatment with his usual handshakes and bear hugs. Then he went to his coat hanging in the wardrobe and pulled out a bag containing a box of figs for the dentist, a necklace for the assistant, and toffees for the front office. "Thank you, thank you," he repeated as he made the rounds again, looking everyone in the eye and making sure they were convinced of his sincerity. Goodbyes said, I guided him out of the office and down into the car.

In the car on the way home he turned to me. "Thank you Davi, thank you Anna, thank you Claira, thank you Theresa, thank you Don, thank you Rose-Alina, thank you sponsors," he rhymed off, making sure to include everyone. I reminded him that we did not pay for the dentures, the government did.

"Thank you government," Hajji responded. Looking around as if to include all Canadians and gesturing broadly with his arm, he exclaimed, "Thank you everybody. Thank you Prime Minister. Thank you Canada." I glanced at Hajji again. His expression was intense. Then he explained that his parents had needed dentures, too, but had never been able to afford them. I could see tears beginning to form in his eyes. He would be eternally grateful for what people had done for him. This had been one of Hajji's most wonderful days.

As time went on, we came to realize that the core of the Brajshoris' life philosophy was their ability to live the moment. Although undoubtedly related to their particular characters, we believe that this trait was also culturally based. It revealed itself as a tendency to focus on the here and now, to give priority to the people that they happened to be with, and to dedicate attention to the task at hand, no matter how small or mundane. This had a very exhilarating effect on us. When we were with them we always felt special. It had another very practical effect on them, seeming to allow them to forget the pain and distress of their recent past.

One fine autumn day several months after their arrival we paid them an afternoon visit, only to find them a little down. Thinking it might perk them up, we took them to play miniature golf. It was obviously their first exposure to a mini-putt. They looked on with curiosity as Anne and I demonstrated, without any particular professional flair, how to play the first hole. Hajji caught on right away and in less than five minutes the roles had reversed. We followed Hajji around the course as he explained at length how to calculate the necessary angles, how to get around obstacles, and how to negotiate the particularly onerous curves and slopes. Nazife accompanied us, laughing and talking to herself as she flayed away with one hand, missing the ball more often than hitting it, and sometimes batting it right off the course. Occasionally she would get lucky, and once she narrowly missed a hole-in-one.

Halfway around the course we stopped to catch our breath and sat on a bench in the autumn sun. Suddenly their demeanour changed, and their mood became sombre. This time it was Nazife who told the story, while Hajji translated as best he could with pantomime and the occasional English word. Nazife had learned of the news yesterday, when she accidentally overheard some of her friends talking at a gathering of Kosovars. One of Nazife's sisters, her brother-in-law, and their three children, reported missing during the war, had now been confirmed dead. They had been shot, and their bodies had been found in a makeshift grave. It was all over. May Allah save their souls.

We were stunned. This explained why they had been depressed. But there was nothing we could do, save offer our comfort and sympathy.

Then the game continued. Levity returned. Hajji continued around the course ahead of us, intent on winning the game. Nazife followed, batting her ball this way and that. We caught up to Hajji at the last hole, a circular maze turned on its side, giving players the possibility of a free game if they scored a hole in one, but otherwise causing them to forfeit their ball which then rolled back to the clubhouse through an underground tunnel. Not knowing what it was, Hajji hit his ball ever so gently, and it fell immediately into the tunnel and rolled out of sight. Then I hit my ball with more force. It made a whirring sound as it went round and round in the maze, but eventually suffered the same fate as Hajji's, falling into the tunnel. Hajji felt he had been tricked, as his ball had not made any sound at all. Anne offered him her ball. He hit it with full force, and exclaimed contentedly as the ball whirled around the maze, reverberating loudly before finally dropping out of sight. His goal had been achieved.

For the rest of the afternoon, the Brajshoris concentrated their full attention on us and on the particular task at hand, whether shaking apples from a wild apple tree and picking up the good ones to take home, preparing tea for us back at the apartment, or meticulously peeling an apple into four quarters and ceremonially offering one quarter—carefully skewered on the end of the paring knife—to each of us in turn. The sad story of Nazife's sister and her family appeared to have been shelved, completely out of sight and out of mind. How wonderful, we thought, to be able to live the moment. We resolved to do more of that ourselves.

It took us several months to fully comprehend the enormity of the cultural gap that our refugee couple had to bridge. Cultural differences were partly due to geography, partly to religion, partly to our couple's age, and partly to the rural environment where they had passed the major part of their life. Hajji was about 26 when he married. Nazife was three years younger. They settled on a small farm in Sharban, a village about fourteen kilometres from Kosovo's capital, Prishtina. They had five hectares of trees, three hectares of crops, and two hectares of hay, which Hajji cut with a scythe. In fact, they had no power tools of any kind, only hand tools and oxen to plough the fields. They kept chickens, goats, cows and sheep. The farm was not productive enough to support their family, so Nazife stayed home to look after the animals and raise the children, and Hajji walked into Prishtina six days a week, where he worked in road construction. The family moved into a small apartment in Prishtina in 1983, when the daily walk from Sharban into Prishtina became too onerous. Hajji retired from his construction job at age 60 when he became eligible for a state pension It was from their Prishtina apartment that they were abruptly evicted during the war.

Given this background, it is perhaps not surprising that Hajji marvelled at his new environment. For several months after his arrival he was fascinated by the features of Canada's capital, particularly the Ottawa River, the high buildings, and the freeways. Nothing like that existed in Kosovo, not even in Prishtina, and he would let out little whistles under his breath as we passed by in the car. Nazife was equally impressed. "You can look this way, and you can look that way. No matter which way you look, it all looks nice," she commented one day, as we drove around town.

At home, they rather quickly fell into a routine. Nazife would do her housework in the morning, and soon we noticed that she would do it without fail, every day of the week. Everything had to be dusted every day, whether it needed it or not. Everything was always pristine.

When her cleaning was finished, Nazife would set about preparing lunch, which they habitually ate around two or three in the afternoon. For some time after their arrival, she seemed to prefer doing this on the floor. In particular, she seemed to prefer to prepare her dough and to roll it out on the floor, or rather on newspaper that she would spread out on the floor for this purpose. As time went on she gradually moved up, first to the coffee table and then to the kitchen counter. We bought some thick plastic to replace her newspapers, and eventually she started rolling her dough on the bare counter, as she must have seen others do.

Hajji's routine was conditioned mainly by his prayers, which he dutifully performed five times a day, every day. Then he would do the shopping or any other daily chores. He loved to shop at Loblaws, where he quickly befriended all the clerks, and joked with them and other customers as he put his purchases through the cash. Shopping was not always straightforward, however, as he could not read in English and had to go by the look of the package. One day I was shopping with him, and he asked me to show him where to find the "kripë." "Kripë, kripë," he insisted, showing me how it was something you picked up between your fingers and put on something else. Then he remembered the word "chicken," which he repeated over and over again. So "kripë" has something to do with chicken, I thought, and showed him the cranberry sauce. It was all to no avail, and we left the store without the "kripë." When we got home, he immediately went and got a bowl of something that looked like sugar. "Kripë," he explained, picking some up between two fingers. I tasted it. It was salt. Of course, they kept their salt in a bowl and sprinkled it over the chicken with their fingers. He probably did not use a salt shaker at home. Otherwise, he would have shown me a shaking motion in the store to try to illustrate his meaning.

One change they made to their apartment very early on was the installation of carpets. This was all the more intriguing to us as the entire apartment other than the kitchen, entry hall, and bathroom was beautifully finished in fine hardwood. For some years now Canadians have been tearing out their carpet to install hardwood, or even its poor relation, laminate. It seems the Brajshoris could hardly wait to do just the opposite. Indeed, someone else's thrown-away carpet became Hajji's treasure, and he looked at us with obvious pride when we arrived to find that a carpet had been laid. "Mirë, mirë?" he enquired, seeking our approval. "Yes, mirë, mirë," we responded, not wanting to let him down, even though the off-white carpet was showing its age and was marred here and there by stains and cigarette burns.

A few days later we arrived to find that an orange carpet had been neatly cut to fill in all the gaps around the white one, and completely cover all the tiles in the entry hall and kitchen. Hajji was more pleased than ever, as his carpet was now wall to wall. We had barely accustomed ourselves to the new arrangement when we arrived one day to a sea of green. It was a newer carpet, quite clean, and there was enough to cover every room, including the bedroom. It felt very soft underfoot, and we hardly had time to wonder what he had done with the other carpets when our minds registered simultaneously what had happened. He had laid the new carpet over the old one! Both Hajji and Nazife were beaming with the look of new proprietors who had finally managed to achieve the floor upgrade they had been dreaming about. We congratulated them on their achievement, and they sat us down for tea.

When we thought about it, their lifestyle was admirably suited for carpets. They both walked around barefoot. They were both comfortable, even happy, to sit or crouch on the floor. Hajji especially loved to sit cross-legged on the floor by the coffee table, from where he would direct the pouring of tea and lead the conversation of all seated around him.

Their balcony was another source of interest. It faced the rising sun, and Nusret had been quick to point out to Hajji that it was forbidden in Canada to call prayers at sunrise from the balcony. It was, of course, simply a matter of respect for the neighbours, who would not want to be disturbed at that hour. One day when we were having tea, Hajji put his index finger to his lips, urging us to be quiet, and beckoned us to come over to the balcony and look out. There, in a corner, was a mother pigeon nursing two light brown eggs. It was not many days before the eggs became chicks, and the chicks grew into fluffy little birds. Hajji was as happy as a nanny with his little family, although Nazife looked somewhat askance at the whole arrangement, probably because the balcony was becoming dirtier and dirtier. Then one day Hajji greeted us with a sadness in his eye. A white gull had swooped down from the sky and eaten the babies. The nest was empty. Nazife smiled and made a whisking motion. It would not be long before she had the whole mess all cleaned up.

However, the clean-up was not to be just yet. The next time we came we saw that Hajji had built a shelter around the nest, using chairs and boxes. No gull would find them now! Soon there were two more eggs, and before long another family. This one Hajji protected until the babies had grown up and flown away. Then Nazife prevailed and the balcony was spotless again.

We were to learn as time went on that Hajji had a love for all living things, and that pigeons, like all other animals, were important to him as part of the overall scheme of life. He would let them hop through the open balcony door, and on occasion would even feed them, laughing and saying they had come to join us for tea. We found the whole thing rather amusing in light of the normal Canadian rejection of pigeons as flatmates, and the tendency of apartment dwellers around the city to deter their visits, using everything from toy windmills to lifelike carved owls to scare them away.

As the summer turned to fall and the evenings shortened, we would often arrive after sunset to find the Brajshoris sitting in the gloom of the approaching night. It did not occur to them to turn on some lights. We reasoned that that they had lived in the country most of their lives without electricity, and, being farmers, had adopted the rhythm of the sun, getting up at sunrise and going to bed at sunset. They did not seem to mind when we would come in and turn on the lights. They just did not see any need for lights themselves.

We soon came to realize that they had been conditioned by their environment in matters of health as well. It was our job as sponsors to

sleep with no worries

see that they were introduced to the Canadian health system, given a thorough physical, and helped to deal with follow-up appointments, medications, and health emergencies. We realized almost from the start that this responsibility would require time, effort, improvisation, and good humour on our part. We were glad to have the help of the other sponsors, especially Rose-Aline, who shepherded them to umpteen medical appointments in the early days. Theresa and Don helped with the optometrist. It was a team effort.

It is not that Hajji and Nazife did not like going to the doctor's. They would willingly follow us, seeming to understand that we had their best interest at heart. In fact, one of their sons in Germany was studying to become a doctor. Perhaps he had told them that they could expect medical care to be different in Canada, and to be of a higher standard than what they had grown accustomed to in Kosovo.

In all matters related to health, the Brajshoris seemed to be guided by the principle that "if it ain't broke, don't fix it." This seemed to have been translated into a belief that you only go to the doctor when you are sick, and if he or she prescribes medication, you take it, provided you happen to think of it at all, only until you no longer feel sick. Then you stop taking the medication, no matter what the instructions. After all, why would anyone take pills if they are feeling fine? And if there are other priorities in life that oblige you to ignore doctor's orders, that is all right too. After all, there are higher authorities, like Allah, who will decide in the end what is to become of you.

We knew from the beginning that Nazife had high blood pressure. This had been diagnosed in Camp Borden, and would need attention. In Ottawa her new doctor confirmed the diagnosis and prescribed the required medication, which we carefully explained to Nazife and, for good measure, had a translator do the same.

We waited the prescribed interval and took her back to the doctor. Her pressure was not reacting to the medication, so the doctor raised the dose. We waited again and took her back, but there was still no reaction. "Do not worry," the doctor told us. "It is normal to proceed this way, raising the dosage until the pressure starts to go down." She prescribed a supplementary medication, just to be sure. Again we carefully explained the procedures to Nazife and to Hajji as well. We again had an interpreter do the same. We wanted to be sure the message was understood, and the required medication taken daily, as instructed. It was all to no avail. There was still no improvement in Nazife's pressure readings.

By this time a few months had passed and we began to feel concerned. We had also noticed that Nazife's bottles of medication always looked suspiciously full. Maybe she was not always taking her medication on a daily basis as prescribed. We purchased a pill box with seven compartments, one for each day of the week, and showed her how to fill it and use it as a guide to whether she had taken her daily dosage. Still no improvement. Then we started to actually count out all Nazife's medication every day for a week. Our worst fears were confirmed. She was not taking the required daily dosage. Obviously, we thought, she does not understand.

We enlisted help from Shano and Nusret. They would be able to explain to Nazife the importance of taking her medication every day. We were confident that our problem had been solved.

Several weeks went by and Nazife's pressure readings started to creep upwards. She was getting worse, not better. We again started counting her pills on a daily basis. She was taking some, but not all of her required doses. We knew she had to take them all to stay well. We called Shano, and she met us at the Brajshoris' apartment. There was a long discussion as Shano tried to impress upon Nazife the importance of taking all the required medication every day. Finally Shano turned to us. "It should be all right now," she said. "Nazife was confused because her basic belief about medication was contrary to the instructions she was being given. She believed that it was not right to take pills unless you are feeling sick. On many days she felt fine, so she was not taking any pills. Now she understands it does not work that way. She says she will take her pills every day, even if she is feeling well. I think your problem is solved."

After that day, Nazife always took her pills, and her pressure went down and stayed down. The sponsors were relieved. When we thought about it, there really was a certain logic to her thinking.

A few months later we had another scare. Without telling us, she stopped taking her medication. Then she asked us to take her pressure every time we visited. We noticed the pressure was gradually climbing.

We did not want to frighten her, but eventually it was up into dangerous territory and we had to tell her. Only then did she admit that she had stopped her medication, as a test, to see if she really needed it. She had been feeling off and getting headaches recently, and seemed to be able to link this to the fact that her pressure was too high. She started taking the medication again and soon felt better. We hoped that she had finally convinced herself that she needed the medication on a permanent, regular basis.

Hajji provided us with a similar logic of his own. One day we noticed he was limping, and as time went on it got worse. His knee was bothering him. Eventually he could hardly walk. We took him to the doctor.

The doctor took x-rays, checked for arthritis, and conducted mobility tests. It was going to be all right, he told us. Mr. Brajshori had tendinitis. He should take the anti-inflammatory, ibuprofen, for pain and to reduce the swelling, and stay completely off his left foot for a week to ten days. The inflammation should heal on its own.

Hajji was happy with the diagnosis and happier still that he had only a week or so to wait. We left him in his apartment with his foot up and instructions not to walk around, and not to pray, as this would only aggravate the tendinitis.

We might as well have been talking to the wall. Not praying was out of the question. He was in the midst of prayers when we arrived the next day. We called in reinforcements, and had Nusret explain over the phone what was wrong with his knee and what he had to do. There was a long exchange between Hajji and Nusret over the phone, and then Nusret spoke to us. "He refuses to stop praying," Nusret sighed. "I asked him what devout Muslims do who have only one leg and can not get up and down to pray. He replied that they pray sitting down. So I told him that he should pray sitting down, too, until his knee is healed. He said no, he could not do that. I asked why not. He said, 'Because I have two legs.' So I am afraid I was not too successful. We will just have to hope his knee gets better anyway."

Fortunately Hajji's knee did heal, but it took six weeks. We were relieved when we saw he could finally walk around again without pain.

Our experience with their glasses was a variation on the same theme. Within days of their arrival, we noticed they were having trouble seeing the numbers on the telephone. Theresa and Don took them to the optometrist for a check-up. They both came back with prescriptions for reading glasses. Hajji would use them to read the documents he had to deal with, do his banking, and read his Koran. Nazife would need them for her knitting, and eventually for learning English.

When Nazife took possession of her glasses, she looked at them with disdain and refused to put them on. When asked what was the matter she replied, "Glasses are for reading. I can't read, so why should I wear glasses?" That settled the matter. The fact that glasses could help her to see her knitting did not seem to be a relevant factor. Perhaps she did her knitting by feel.

Hajji was delighted with his glasses. But he promptly wrapped them up in a piece of cloth and placed them beside his Koran. They would be reserved for reading the Koran, he said. I wondered how he would manage with his banking and other reading that he had to do.

I did not have to wait long to find out. Within days, I had to explain some financial matters to him, and he produced from his pocket a pair of black-rimmed reading glasses that I had never seen before. "Money, money," he explained. "Not too much, one dollar." He looked through them at the hair on his arm, which was his method of testing glasses for accuracy. Apparently he had bought them somewhere in the Market or on the street. At least the price was right, and he seemed to be able to read the papers we were working on.

A few days later he produced another pair of glasses. These had women's frames, and bifocal lenses for reading. "No good," he said, pointing to the distance part of the lens. "Good," he explained, moving his finger down to the bifocal lens.

Two weeks later I was scheduled to take Hajji and Nazife to the Ontario Hospital Insurance Plan offices to renew their membership cards. We did not have much time, and I noticed only at the last minute that Hajji was not carrying his glasses. "Get your glasses, Hajji," I said. He disappeared into the bedroom, and emerged a few minutes later, carrying a plastic bag. He offered it to me and I looked inside. I could not believe my eyes. There were three more pairs of glasses inside, none of which I had ever seen before.

I never worried much after that about Hajji's glasses. He always seemed to be able to come up with a pair when he needed one. I doubt if very many of them were the proper prescription for his eyes, but that never seemed to bother him. If he could see the hairs on his arm, it was good enough.

When we took the Brajshoris out into the broader community, we were never sure what to expect. Behaviour that was normal and appropriate in their culture was often totally out of the question here.

The first time we took Hajji and Nazife out into the street for a walk, Nazife grabbed Anne's hand and Hajji grabbed mine. There we were, walking down the street, hand in hand. Without trying to make a big issue of it, I withdrew my hand. Hajji seemed offended, and gave me a confused look. I pointed to Anne and Nazife, explaining that in Canada two women holding hands was acceptable. Then I pointed to us, indicating that in Canada men did not hold hands.

Don, the other male sponsor, got the same hand-holding treatment. He had a harder time convincing Hajji this was not acceptable behaviour in Canada. He had to be convincing, but without being offensive and without seeming to reject a gesture of friendship. Finally, Hajji got the message, and the hand-holding came to an end.

Occasionally we would come across things that were so commonplace for us that we never gave them a second thought, but that proved daunting or incomprehensible for the Brajshoris. One day we took them on a tour of a chocolate factory. We were as enthralled as they were by the tour, seeing all those chocolate bars shooting out of the machines, onto conveyors, and into their wrappings. We feasted on fresh chocolate afterwards, and ended up with chocolate all over our hands. I took Hajji into the men's washroom, went instinctively to the sink and started to wash, assuming that Hajji would do the same. Then I looked over. There he was, eyeing the faucet suspiciously, tugging at it, and turning it this way and that, but to no avail. He did not have the least idea how to work it, as it needed to be pulled up, a totally different action from the faucets he was used to at home. He had a similar problem with the towel dispenser, which required a pumping action he obviously was not used to. How fortunate that we came into the washroom together, I thought, as he now knows how to work these kinds of fixtures.

Hajji, being a take-charge kind of person and an extrovert, was continually wanting to help people do their jobs. To him it just seemed natural to want to help out. One fine summer day we decided to take them on a boat tour on the Ottawa River, and were waiting on the dock for the tour boat to arrive. We stood behind a chain which separated waiting passengers from crew members who would help to dock the boat. As the boat approached, Hajji jumped over the chain, held out his hand, and called to a crew member on the boat to throw him the rope. He caught the rope and started to tether the boat as it eased against the dock. "Is he a retired sea captain?" a young crew member asked me as Hajji confidently took over her job.

"No," I replied. "As far as I know he is not a captain. He just likes to help out."

"Well then," the young lady offered, almost apologetically, "he will have to go back behind the chain, with the other passengers."

No matter where we went, Hajji would enthusiastically offer to help out. At the Experimental Farm his curiosity drew him towards a man using a handheld grass cutter with a long handle to cut the long grass around walkways and buildings. Hajji was sure he could do this, and asked the man to let him try. "I am sorry, I can't let you cut the grass," the workman explained. "If I did, I could lose my job."

I knew the seriousness of the man's predicament was lost on Hajji, who continued to ask to have a go. "Could you just let him hold it with the mower not running?" I asked. "He seems really intrigued with your machine."

It was a satisfactory compromise. Hajji got to examine and heft the machine at close range, and put it through its motions, without actually cutting grass and risking having the man lose his job.

Nazife's gentle, retiring character was just the opposite. Somewhere in her background of culture and religion she had been taught not to speak to strange men. This was particularly the case if her husband was not present. One morning Anne and I decided to treat the Brajshoris to a pedalo ride on Dow's Lake. Hajji was in the pedalo within seconds, but Nazife took one look at the bobbing pedalo and refused to get in. While Hajji and I puttered across the water at a snail's pace, pedalling furiously, Anne and Nazife enjoyed the sunshine on a lakeside bench, eating ice cream cones. Along came an older man in a wheelchair. He greeted them in a friendly, Italian accent and started to chat. But his chat turned out to be only with Anne. On seeing him approach, Nazife had turned her back to him, and stayed this way for the duration of his visit. Only when he had wheeled away did she turn around.

The same thing happened on Canada Day when Nazife and Anne sat on a bench outside our apartment, waiting for Hajji and me to return from the Mounties' Musical Ride on Parliament Hill. It must have been obvious to Nazife that the various gentlemen who happened along and stopped to chat were friends of Anne's, or at least knew her well. That seemed not to matter in the least. The minute a man would approach, Nazife would turn her back to him. It is not a wonder she never ventures out alone, we discussed later on as Anne recounted her day's adventures. It is just not in keeping with her culture.

One area where the Brajshoris excelled was their ability to make do with whatever products or materials they had at hand. They were masters of improvisation. When they needed some household tool or gadget, they would make it themselves. A few days after their arrival in Ottawa, we saw Nazife rolling out her dough with a long, straight stick about an inch in diameter. It looked handmade. Of course, Hajji told us. He had carved it himself using a kitchen knife, from a stick he had found the day before down by the river. Now Nazife could roll out her dough into large, thin rounds in the traditional way.

Knitting needles for Nazife were similarly crafted from bicycle spokes, taken from an old bicycle that Hajji had found in the trash. It amazed us to see the beauty of the work that Nazife would do, working from her head without any pattern, using nothing more than bicycle spokes and a few balls of mismatched wool purchased from a deep discount value store.

Hajji's cane, which he had brought from Kosovo and which he treasured like a loyal friend, had been hand-carved from an appropriately shaped tree branch. It was therefore with some consternation that we learned a few months later that he had lost it at the grocery store. Don replaced it with a store-bought cane, but we could see that Hajji's feelings for the new cane were not the same. We therefore should not have been surprised when Hajji took matters into his own hands.

We were taking advantage of a beautiful late summer day, the kind where you can sit outside in the woods under the shade of a tree and not worry about mosquitoes. We were at Lake Mulvihill, a tiny picture-postcard lake in the Gatineau Park just north of Ottawa. Hajji and I had lugged coolers, blankets and folding chairs to a clearing where we would have a fine view of the lake. We were waiting for the women to arrive when, without warning, Hajji took off into the woods.

Hajji had already been counselled on numerous occasions that it was illegal to cut trees in any of the city's parks. Anyway, he had no knife or axe, so I was not particularly concerned about this particular escapade off into the woods. Anne and Nazife arrived and we all sat down in the shade, speculating that perhaps Hajji had gone to pray.

You can imagine our surprise when Hajji marched triumphantly into the clearing carrying not just a stick or branch, but an entire tree about eight feet long, pulled out by its roots. "Cane, cane," he observed, turning the tree upside down and showing us the crook in the trunk just above what would have been ground level, which would make a perfect handle for a cane. We all admired the wounded tree, but inside my mind was racing. Obviously we could not replant the tree. I looked around. Fortunately we were alone. No one need to ever know we had plundered the forest of Gatineau Park. I grabbed the tree and made for the car as fast as I could. Opening the trunk, I stuffed the tree inside and closed the lid.

As we drove home later that day, the real story of Hajji's tree began to emerge. It was true that he had pulled it out of the ground, but he had had help. And it had not been taken from park land, but from a forest lot where workmen had been cutting trees in order to build a house. Hajji had stumbled on the lot, drawn there by the sound of chain saws. He had identified the perfect tree for his cane, with a right angle bend in the trunk just above ground level, and had asked the men if he could have it. They had readily agreed, and helped him pull it out. This made some sense to me. Although I knew Hajji had the strength of two normal men, I knew it would nonetheless have been a superhuman feat for a single old man to pull a healthy eight foot tree out by the roots all by himself.

Some of the most enjoyable occasions in the first months after the

Brajshoris' arrival were the get-togethers of Kosovar refugees. Hajji and Nazife could let their hair down, relax, speak only Albanian, and generally forget for a short time all the hassles of adapting to a new culture. We were the ones who had to adapt. It was interesting for us to see how the Albanians socialized. We always had a good time.

We were often invited to these gatherings. It seemed that no excuse was too small to bring a group of Kosovar refugees together. Birthday parties were a favourite. One of the first we went to was put on by Hava and Rrahman for their son, Qemail, on his fifteenth birthday. The Brajshoris always took a gift of food to these affairs, and this was no exception. Nazife had made a pan of *fli*, a dish that can be best described as several layers of unleavened pancakes, flavoured with yoghurt and olive oil. We were greeted at the door by Hava and Rrahman with warm Albanian-style handshakes and hugs. Everyone took off their shoes, and we were escorted into a noisy, smoke-filled room.

There were a few young children, but almost no teenagers. Qemail was nowhere to be seen. It was mainly adults. They virtually all jumped up when we entered and offered us their seats. Rrahman directed us to the seat of honour on the sofa. I am not sure whose places we took, but anyway everyone sat down. Glasses of orange drink appeared magically in front of us, and Ismail, one of the refugees who spoke good English, enquired how we were. We chatted with Ismail for a while, and then I noticed that Anne was the only woman in the living room. All the others had disappeared into the dining room and kitchen. The genders had separated like two repelling magnetic fields. We were a room of men.

I looked around, peering through a bluish haze. All the men were smoking. They were talking in small groups, leaning forward and listening intently. I guessed that they were sharing notes on their experiences in their new country. Occasionally there was a burst of loud laughter. I could hear Hajji sounding off from his corner seat in a huge arm chair. I could tell from his facial expressions and his hand gestures that he was telling a story. All the other men deferred to Hajji when he wanted to speak. It must be a matter of respect for elders, I thought.

A number of other sponsors arrived. The men and women were reintegrated and some of the Albanians started to practice their halting

English. They were all at English school during the day, and seemed eager to try out what they had learned. They were obviously working very hard at school but progress was slow. The Kosovars who had spoken some English before coming to Canada had to do a lot of translation so that everyone could be understood. The Kosovars told us that they liked Canada and wanted to stay. They were eager to learn English and find a job.

It was almost time for dinner. The teenagers started to arrive. Qemail came in with two male friends. Qemail's sisters, Iba and Metije, and some of their girl friends were there, too. The teenagers spoke English more readily and with more confidence than their parents. They had all recently started back to regular high school and were liking it. We could see from their level of confidence that they were integrating faster than their parents. Some of the youngest children, still in elementary school, seemed to be making the fastest progress of all.

Dinner was served. The women served the food on the plates in the kitchen and brought the plates out to the guests sitting around the living and dining rooms. Every plate had chicken that had been braised in a tomato and paprika sauce, rice, *pite* (a kind of pasta dish with spinach and yoghurt), a salad of tomatoes, cucumbers and hot peppers, and a large slice of *fli*. It was excellent, and we were given large portions of everything. It would have been difficult to go away hungry.

After dinner, Rrahman gave Qemail his birthday present, a watch. Some of the sponsors had also brought presents. Then it was Qemail's turn to cut himself a piece of birthday cake. His sister finished cutting the cake and the other teenagers brought a piece around to everyone. We finished off with Turkish coffee, and everyone sat back and chatted.

As the evening drew to a close, Hava and Rrahman escorted all their guests downstairs to the waiting cars. None of the Kosovars had cars yet, so the sponsors drove them home. When they took us down, they thanked us for bringing Hajji and Nazife to the party, and for coming ourselves. We could tell they were sincere and that they had really appreciated having the sponsors come to share their evening. Hava gave us a piece of *fli* to take home with us. Qemail said, "Everyone in Kosovo likes this *fli*."

On the way home, we could tell that Hajji and Nazife were tired but this did not stop them from brimming over with excited chatter and jokes about the evening's celebration. Hajji kept asking us if we had had a good time. He was thrilled to know that we had enjoyed ourselves. We could see that an evening with their Albanian friends had really boosted their morale. It had been fun for us, too.

It gave us comfort to see the Kosovars adapting so well to their new country, so soon after having been unceremoniously thrown out of their old one. It was good for us to see the changes in the Kosovars, especially the younger ones with children, since our first encounter with them coming off the bus. They were happy, smiling, settled into their new homes, established in school and in some cases already at work. Their English was improving, and they were entertaining a mixture of Albanians and Canadians in their homes. We were pleased to have a role in this adaptive process, and especially happy to be able to help our elder couple, who were obviously loved and respected by their compatriots and had made a large place for themselves in our hearts.

five

FAMILY REUNIFICATION

From the beginning, anyone familiar with Kosovar culture always expressed surprise when we told them we were sponsoring an elderly couple with no other family members in Canada. That is not possible, they would exclaim. Kosovars always come with their family, and usually the family is a large one. Where are their children?

We would explain that the family had been scattered by the war and the events leading up to it. Their four sons had ended up in Germany, and their daughter, Xhevrie, was left behind in Kosovo. They had no relatives at all in Canada. They were alone.

That is not to say they were not treated well by the other Kosovars, especially the ones they had met in Camp Borden. Hava and Rrahman had taken a particular liking to them in Camp Borden, and another couple they had met there, Rukije and Ismail, also seemed very close. We were happy to see these relationships carry on after they came to Ottawa, and we drove them over for visits whenever they asked. It was heart-warming to see the love and affection these two families showed towards Hajji and Nazife. In our imaginations, it seemed to us they played a kind of grandparent role. Hajji would gather the children around him and regale them with stories of his childhood in Kosovo. The children would sit wide-eyed as they took in his exaggerated facial expressions and extravagant gestures, their gazes never wavering. Stories finished, the children would go off to play. Hajji would offer a cigarette to his host, and the two men would sit back and discuss politics or other matters of great import. Nazife would disappear into the kitchen to help her hostess with the daily chores, and non-stop chatter would ensue.

Although the Brajshoris' friendships with other Kosovar families played an important role, there was no way they could replace real ties of family. The Brajshoris made it clear to us right off the bat that they wanted their youngest son, Ramadan, to join them from Germany. Several times over those first few weeks, they spoke about Ramadan in tones of urgency and concern. Hajji would adopt that rare serious look he took on only for matters of great importance. He would gesture that he wanted to write something, and then, pencil in hand, carefully craft a make-believe map showing Germany on one side and Canada on the other. With a flourish, he would pencil in an arrow starting in Germany and ending in Canada. "Dani. *Hajde* Canada. Dani English. *Shkollë. Punë, punë. Familje.*" He always repeated the words several times, making sure we got it. Ramadan, Dani for short, was to come from Germany to join them in Canada. He already spoke English. He would go to school here, and get a job. They would be a proper family.

We had no way of knowing at the time how critical this arrangement was to them. Without any of their children, and unable to speak English, the couple felt they could not cope with the stress of adjustment to Canada. They would have to return to Kosovo, and take their chances in the war-ravaged country, in hope that some of their sons would return and look after them there.

It had been carefully negotiated over the phone while they were in Camp Borden. All the sons had been asked. Which one would come to Canada to live with them and help them adjust to life in Canada? Avdi had already spent seven years in Germany learning German and studying medicine. It seemed logical he should stay in Germany and become a doctor. Ali had also been seven years in Germany, and hoped to be accepted for German citizenship, so did not want to go to Canada. Sabri had been in Germany only one year, but his wife wanted to go back to Kosovo.

Dani, their youngest son, knew nothing of Canada and envisaged his future somewhere in Europe. For a time he hesitated, too. After all, he had learned German, and had a job in a restaurant. Canada was a great unknown, and even his visit to the library turned up almost no information, save a few paragraphs on Toronto and Montreal. By early July, his parents had given up hope that any of their sons would come, and advised the sons that they would be returning to Kosovo. Then the negotiations began in earnest. Going to Kosovo is out of the question, the sons told their parents. Kosovo is in tatters. You would have no pension and no one to look after you. You must stay at least for now in Canada. One of us will come to help you there. And so it was decided. Dani would take the plunge. As a young, single man, not in school, he had fewer ties to Germany than Ali or Avdi, and fewer ties to Kosovo than Sabri. His parents needed someone. They seemed to like Canada and none of his brothers wanted to go. Dani agreed. He would go to Canada.

We had no idea how to go about bringing Dani to Canada. The war had been over since early June. Kosovars were no longer being admitted into Canada as refugees under the emergency program, because, technically at least, it was safe for them to return to Kosovo. We had heard about something in Canada called the Family Reunification Program, and we wondered if it might apply to our family. So one day, a few weeks after the Brajshoris' arrival in Ottawa, we went to check out the Program at the Regional Office of Citizenship and Immigration Canada, better known by its acronym, CIC.

The building where the CIC office was located was familiar to us. It was here we had earlier attended meetings on the sponsorship of Kosovar refugees. However, the office we were directed into this time bore no resemblance to the plush, wood-trimmed quarters in which the earlier meetings had been convened. We opened the door to find ourselves looking at a robust security guard dressed like a policeman. I instinctively looked at his belt to see if he was carrying a gun, and was relieved to see nothing more threatening than a cell phone. We explained our purpose. The guard smiled, and explained that, if we wanted an interview, we should take a number from a ticket dispenser mounted conveniently on a column beside us. Otherwise, we could peruse the pamphlets and application forms in a stand at the back of the room, and take what we needed. We thanked the guard, ignored the ticket dispenser for the time being, and made our way into the room. It had the allure of the waiting room of a bus depot, and was full of people awaiting their turns. The three people whose numbers had just been called were standing at three windows lining one side of the room that could have been wickets at a pari-mutuel betting house. I guessed that the security was probably equivalent. I could not see anyone behind the windows, but from the amount of talking and gesticulation that was going on, I assumed that someone was there. We turned our attention to the pamphlets. There were pamphlets on student and visitor visas, on the point system for independent immigrants, on applying for refugee status, and on family reunification. It was the latter that particularly interested us, but for good measure we took one of each. It was high time we learned more about the various ways and means of immigrating to Canada.

We were just about to leave the room when Edith emerged from an inner office. She was clutching some files tightly in one hand and looking harried as she dashed across the room, almost running into us. "Oh, hello!" she exclaimed, as she looked up just in time to see us and came to an abrupt halt. "How are you, and how is your elderly refugee couple?"

"They are doing very well. And now we are investigating how we can bring over their son from Germany to help them adjust." I decided to get right to the point, sensing that Edith was stressed and would not have time for pleasantries.

Edith's eyes shot from us to the files in her hand and back to us. She hesitated momentarily, as if doing a quick mental recalculation of her priorities. "Oh, all right," she assented, settling the issue in our favour. "Why don't you come in for a few minutes. We'll see what we can do."

Edith led us back across the room, punched a code number into a security pad on an unmarked door, and ushered us into the inner office. We followed her down a short hallway into a small interview room whose windows looked out into the hall. Someone had decided the view was not worthwhile, and had shut tightly the floor-to-ceiling vertical drapes. Edith sat behind a desk and motioned us to the two guest chairs across from her.

Edith got down to business immediately, enquiring about Dani's age, his address, what he did in Germany, and whether he had been a full-time student in Kosovo before fleeing to Germany as a refugee. We did not know the details, but answered the best we could.

"Your best hope is a special program that was in place up to July 11 to bring in dependent children of Kosovar refugees who were separated from their parents during the war," Edith told us. "Dani could be eligible retroactively for this program, but only if his parents applied before July 11, if Dani is 19 years old or less, and if he is dependent on his parents. We would have no record of any application here. Could you check the papers that the Brajshoris brought from Camp Borden? If they applied to bring Dani over during their stay at Camp Borden, they probably have a copy of the application."

We agreed to check the Brajshoris' papers, and also to get Dani's exact age and address in Germany. "If Dani meets the criteria, we will get in touch with our Embassy in Bonn," Edith offered, "and they will send him an application form. But they have to have his exact mailing address."

I felt encouraged by what Edith was telling us, but I wondered what we would do if Dani did not meet the criteria for the special program. I asked Edith, and she responded by outlining in rapid fire the particulars of several programs having to do with refugees and immigrants in general. I was totally lost in the maze of program terminology and said so.

"I'm sorry," Edith retorted in a somewhat condescending tone. "I can't explain Canada's immigration policy in twenty minutes."

It really was time for us to leave. After all, this was an impromptu meeting and Edith was obviously busy with other things. We promised to get back to her as soon as we had collected all the necessary details.

Edith led us back to the outer office. We said our quick goodbyes and watched her pick up from where she had left off, in headlong rush across the room. We left the building and went straight over to the Brajshoris' apartment.

After a suitable prelude of greetings, coke, and a sample of Nazife's latest batch of rice pudding, we got right down to business. Most critically, we needed to know if they had applied while in Camp Borden to bring Dani to Canada. We asked to see the file folder they had brought from Camp Borden. Nazife disappeared into the bedroom and emerged a few minutes later carrying a red manila file. I opened it and started thumbing through a thick sheaf of papers. On top were all the documents we were already familiar with: Minister's Permit to be in Canada as a refugee, Work Permit, and temporary Social Insurance Number. Next were the papers outlining the terms of the Emergency Refugee Airlift Program that had brought them to Canada, and the details of the financial assistance they were receiving from the federal government. Then there were handouts from the course given them in Borden on orientation to Canadian life and culture, in both English and Albanian. This was followed by what could essentially be described as scraps: menus, old ticket stubs, a map of Camp Borden, and some tourist brochures. I was almost at the bottom of the pile, rapidly losing hope. Then I found it – the very last document – a single page beginning with the words, "Family members you would like to help come to Canada." Underneath were written the words, "Ramadan Brajshori, son, 17 years old." The document had been signed on May 23, 1999 by both Hajji and an official at Camp Borden. It was the document we were looking for. "We're in business," I found myself saying under my breath. "This will allow Dani to come to Canada under the special program that ended on July 11."

"Now we need his address, his phone number, and his birth date," Anne reminded me.

We asked Hajji for Dani's address, and were rewarded with an extended shrug of his massive shoulders. He got up and went over to the telephone table, where he picked up a tiny booklet. He opened it and handed it to us. There were names and numbers scrawled in large letters and numerals on several of the booklet's pages. Each of his three elder sons were there, of which two were listed twice, under two slightly different numbers. Dani's name was not there. Hajji motioned for us to dial the numbers. We will, we tried to explain, but first we have to go and buy a telephone card. I came back a few minutes later with the required card, and started dialling the numbers of his sons in Germany. None of them worked. Sometimes we got a dead line, sometimes a busy signal, and sometimes a message saying we had dialled the wrong number, and to try again.

We went back to basics, examining the numbers carefully. There were some suspicious looking zeros, ones and twos at the front of most of the numbers. Maybe these were codes for dialling the numbers from within Germany, we reasoned. We tried Ali's number again, this time leaving out the introductory code, and were rewarded with a masculine voice at the other end of the line. It was Ali. We passed the phone to Hajji. A long, back and forth conversation ensued, with Hajji explaining things at great length and then listening to equally lengthy responses. Finally he hung up.

"Well, Hajji," we asked, "do you have Dani's address?" Hajji shook his finger from side to side, as if to say no, then put it to his lips, as if asking us to be quiet. Then he indicated that we should sit down, relax and have tea, and promptly went out to the kitchen to prepare it. Anne and I looked at each other with raised eyebrows. This was an unexpected deviation from the script, but there seemed nothing else that we could do, so we decided to enjoy the tea.

A few minutes later the phone rang. Nazife pounced on it. It was Dani. Hajji went on the second line. There was another long, animated conversation. Both Hajji and Nazife were obviously very excited, speaking fast, and appeared to be answering questions. Then Hajji passed his line to Anne. Nazife handed me her phone so I could listen in. Anne spoke slowly in English. She greeted Dani warmly, telling him who we were and what we were trying to do. Dani responded in slow, simple English sentences. He said how happy he was to be able to talk to us, and how eager he was to join his parents, who were old and alone and needed a family member to help them. Anne explained the steps that would be involved in bringing him to Canada, and that at some point he would be receiving an application form from the Canadian Embassy in Bonn, that he should fill out and send back to them. Then he would be called for an interview, and would have to go to Bonn. But this was all in the future. For now we needed his exact birth date, address, and telephone number. Dani gave Anne the required information. He said that he lived in the little town of Bad Sachsa, in central Germany not far from the former border between East and West Germany. I could hear him having trouble spelling out the address. The English alphabet was giving him problems. But his spoken English seemed perfectly adequate. He gave us his phone number and the fax number of a friend where he could be reached by fax. Then he gave us his birth date. He was 19, not 17, but still young enough to qualify for the program. He thanked us for helping his parents, and repeated that he could hardly wait to come to Canada. Then it was time to hang up, and we said goodbye.

We were all so happy that we had made contact that we had an extra glass of tea. When we left them a little later, Hajji and Nazife were in a positive mood, calm, and looking relaxed. Their anxiety over Dani, so evident in our recent visits, had at least momentarily been assuaged. It was beginning to dawn on me that bringing Dani over was very important to their health and well being.

Over the next two days we exchanged faxes with Dani, confirming all the information we had exchanged over the phone. We are all ready, we thought, to get back to Edith with the information she needed to send to Bonn. Fortunately we were going that very night to a meeting for sponsors at the CIC office. We would be able to give Edith the information on Dani while we were there. She would initiate the required procedures. We speculated that we would be seeing Dani in a month or two, possibly less.

I ran into Edith just before the meeting, and showed her the information. "Oh," she responded, "he'll be 20 before he arrives in Canada. In principle we should be able to manage this, as he was 19 when his parents applied. We'll have to see."

"What is the next step?" I asked.

"Well," the answer was a bit hesitant, "maybe you could send me a letter. I'll forward it on to Bonn. But it won't be for a while. I'll be out of the office next week." She disappeared into the meeting room with her colleagues, before I had a chance to grasp that we were talking almost a two-week delay. It was Thursday, so it would be at least a week and a half before she even looked at our letter. And who knows what other priorities would intervene during her first few days back in the office?

I felt dejected when I reported this back to Anne. "Don't worry," Anne consoled. "We'll talk to her again at the break. We can't let this go on hold for two weeks, now that we have all the necessary information."

When the break came, we buttonholed Edith in the lobby. She repeated the rather dismal prospect of maybe being able to send the information to Bonn when she came back from her trip. Anne enquired as to just what exactly had to be done. Edith explained that she needed to write a covering letter outlining the specifics of the Brajshoris' case, explaining their predicament here in Canada with no one to look after them, and asking Bonn to initiate proceedings to bring Dani over to Canada under the special program that the Brajshoris had applied for while in Camp Borden. Unfortunately, she did not have time to do this the next day, her last day in the office before her trip. Well, we would do it for her, Anne offered. We would write the letter that night, and bring it to her office first thing the next morning. All she would have to do would be to fax it over to the Embassy in Bonn. Edith accepted this offer at once.

The next morning we hand delivered the letter and necessary attachments to Edith at the CIC office. She came out into the waiting room to meet us, looking even more harried than usual. "Please send it over today," I appealed, "and let us know that it has gone so we can tell the Brajshoris the process is under way. It means so much to them and they could take a bit of good news just about now."

"I'll try," Edith managed, as if burdened by a thousand pounds. "But I can't guarantee anything."

We watched as Edith hurried back to the security door and disappeared into the inner office. We stood there for a few moments eyeing the closed door. "Well, we've done everything we can for the moment," I offered. "Now all we can do is keep our fingers crossed that the letter goes out."

We contacted Edith by phone a week and a half later when she came back from her trip. She sounded rested and rejuvenated, although she assured us the office was as crazy as ever. She agreed to look into the status of the Brajshori file. She phoned us back a few days later. "The Embassy in Bonn has looked over the papers," she told us. "Everything appears to be in order, provided Dani can substantiate that he is a dependent minor. The Embassy will send out an application form to Dani, for him to fill out and send back to them."

We immediately faxed Dani to tell him what was happening, and that he should expect to receive the application. The next morning at 6:00AM our telephone rang. It was Dani, all excited that the wheels were now in motion, and wanting to know if now was the time for him to go to Bonn. "No, that will come later," Anne explained. "For now just fill out the application when it comes to you, and return it to the Embassy."

We went to see the Brajshoris later that morning. As usual, they welcomed us warmly and served tea. Hajji was laughing and joking as he always did. This time the big joke was about the milk, which they had accidentally put in the freezer, and of course it would not pour. Then their questions turned to Dani, and their mood became more serious. There was anxiety in their voices. Nazife let Hajji do most of the talking, but she was clearly on edge, sighing and taking deep breaths in the background.

We tried to make the news about Dani sound positive, but we could not be definitive, as we did not know for sure that he would be accepted by the government. We could see their eyes cloud over with disappointment when we had to shrug our shoulders as to the timing of his arrival. We gestured as though we were stamping papers, and then we pretended to be doctors checking over Dani's health. Things were moving along, but there was a lot to do. We did not want to mislead them into thinking Dani's arrival was imminent, and we did not know ourselves. We thought it would be better to overestimate rather than underestimate the time required. We turned over several pages of the calendar to show that it could be several months. The Brajshoris looked dejected. After all, they had asked to be reunited with Dani at the end of May, and it was now almost the end of August.

In early September we had a pleasant surprise when Dani phoned to tell us he had received the application and was filling it in. Avdi, his brother in Essen, also spoke English and would help him on the weekend. They would send it back to the Embassy next week.

We went over to the Brajshoris to tell them this news. When we had been welcomed and had finished our tea, the talk turned again to Dani. He must have called them right after he called us, because they already knew about the application. They seem to have interpreted his call as a sure indication that he was coming. Not only that, they seemed to think that we would now know the date of his arrival! It was hard for us to see the disappointment in their faces when we told them we did not know.

We waited another month without any word of what was going on. Every time we saw Hajji and Nazife they would ask about Dani. Every time we gave them the same answer. "We think he will be coming but we do not know for sure. The government has to decide. It may still be some time." Hajji would become quiet at the news, and get a far away look in his eyes. Nazife would always protest. We never knew exactly what she was saying, but we knew she thought the delay was ridiculous. In addition, her health was starting to fail. She complained of headaches, stomach cramps, and lack of sleep. We took her to the doctor and she was given medication to treat her symptoms. There was nothing physically wrong, except the high blood pressure for which she was being treated. We thought her malaise might be due to the trauma of the war, and were convinced that the long wait for Dani to arrive was a contributing factor. We started to become anxious ourselves to have Dani arrive.

On Thanksgiving weekend in mid-October we had another pleasant surprise. Dani phoned and announced he had been accepted by the Embassy for immigration to Canada. We had a little difficulty understanding exactly what was going to happen next. Dani said something about next Tuesday, as though something important were going to happen on that date. We were not sure what it was. But the overall message was unquestionably positive. We both heaved a sigh of relief. At last something was happening, and we could relax a bit.

On Tuesday after the Thanksgiving weekend, we decided to go over to share the good news with the Brajshoris. Before going, Anne phoned the CIC office to see if they could tell us what it was that was supposed to happen today. Maybe it would be relevant to what we told the Brajshoris. I thought it would be a simple, routine telephone conversation, but I could hear Anne's voice start to rise. There was a long argument, and I could hear the frustration in Anne's voice. "Of course the Canadian Embassy in Bonn has the application from Dani," I heard her say. "He told me himself over a month ago that he had filled it out and sent it in." I heard Anne hang up and immediately dial another number.

Now my attention was focused 100% on Anne's conversation. She was explaining to someone that Mai, the new immigration officer who had replaced Edith, had just informed her that the Canadian Embassy had never received Dani's application form. According to Mai, a new application would have to be filled out and the process started all over again. This was absolutely not acceptable to Anne, as she knew for a fact that the Embassy had been sent the application over a month ago. Then she asked her interlocutor to go back and check the records and find the misplaced application. She explained that there was an elderly couple who had been waiting since May to be reunited with their son, and that another long delay would be devastating for them and injurious to their health. As I listened, I got the sense that the person on the other end of the line was listening and trying to be helpful. Anne's voice was determined but more relaxed than it had been a few minutes earlier. Finally she hung up.

"I was just speaking to Denise in CIC head office," Anne related. "She is going to check into the supposedly missing application, and get back to us. I can't believe this is happening. Dani just told us two days ago that the Embassy had accepted him, and now we are being told here in Canada there is no record of Dani's application ever arriving at the Embassy. There is something very wrong here. Someone must have forgotten to make an entry into the computer, or perhaps someone has misplaced the application. This absolutely has to be fixed! In the meantime we can say nothing to upset the Brajshoris."

I was discouraged. It seemed we had been working on the file forever, and it was almost five months since the Brajshoris had asked to be reunited with Dani. To have a government official suggest that we would have to start the application process all over again was too much to take. Our nerves were becoming a little frayed, but there was nothing we could do for the moment but wait for Denise to call back.

Fortunately, Denise called back in a couple of days with good news. The misplaced application had been found, and the appropriate computer entry made. Everything was in order. Dani had to pass a medical exam and a security check. Then arrangements would be made for his flight to Canada. He would be here within six weeks. He was scheduled for an interview in Bonn on October 29. Assuming a successful interview, and that he subsequently passed the health and security checks, he would be coming to join his parents. It was a promise.

We were relieved, but our frayed nerves of two days before had left us feeling apprehensive, and we were becoming suspicious of the governmental immigration procedures, with their rules, regulations, and delays. Normally we would be ecstatic at the news from Denise, but something was telling us to keep our emotions under control. In any event, we had to keep ourselves on an even keel so that the Brajshoris would not be subject to unnecessary emotional ups and downs. We decided not to tell them about the six week time line promised by CIC head office. It would be just too hard on them if we told them and there was another unforeseen delay.

We faxed Dani, telling him he should be receiving an invitation for his interview in Bonn on October 29. When Hajji and Nazife asked us about Dani, as they always did, we told them about the interview, that the government was still in the process of making its decision, and that we expected Dani would be coming but that we did not know when. It was a dilemma for us. We hated their long looks whenever we told them that this was still a work in process. We wanted to be positive, but had to restrain ourselves. We knew how devastating it would be if they thought he was coming for sure, and then it turned out that the government had turned him down.

On October 27 we were visiting the Brajshoris when the telephone rang. It was Avdi. He was happy to find that we were there. The Embassy had sent Dani some more forms to fill out, and Avdi was helping him. Avdi wanted to know if he could put our names in the documents as references for his parents. We told him that of course he could put our names. Then we asked him if Dani would be staying with him the night before the interview on October 29. Avdi had no idea what we were talking about. Dani had not received any invitation to an interview. We were a bit shaken to hear this. Yet another thing that was not going according to plan. We told Avdi we would look into it, and get back to him and Dani.

After we got home, we phoned Denise, our new contact at CIC headquarters. At least we were beginning to understand how the system worked. Denise knew us now, and seemed receptive to our concerns.

She agreed to find out when the interview was being scheduled, and to get back to us right away, just in case it really was on October 29. In that case we would have to get the information back to Dani right away. There would be no time to lose.

Denise called us back the next morning. For some unexplained reason, there had been a delay. Bonn was now scheduling the interview for November 5. They would be sending the invitation out to Dani today or tomorrow. There would be one last flight organized before Christmas in mid-December, and then another one in February. With the interview scheduled for November 5, Dani would be in time for the December flight.

We faxed Dani the new date right away, and asked him to let Avdi know, too.

The interview happened as expected on November 5. Our phone rang at 5:30AM Dani was talking excitedly on the other end of the line. It was 11:30AM in Bonn, and the interview had just finished. It had gone well. Now he had to be scheduled for his medical exam. The interviewers had told him they had just one outstanding question. They wanted to be absolutely sure his parents would be staying in Canada, and not taking advantage of the provision in the Kosovar refugee program to go back to Kosovo. Someone would be contacting his parents in Ottawa to ask them that question. Other than that, everything was in order. "I can't wait to come to Canada," Dani was saying. "It will not be long now before I see you in Canada."

We made a special trip to the Brajshoris' apartment that morning to give them the news of the interview. Their sons had already phoned them and their spirits were high. We were more convinced than ever of the important positive psychological role that Dani's arrival would play. It was great for us to relax a little, too. Our project of bringing Dani over had grown stressful for us as well. We were now trying to second guess everything that was going on, without having any direct line of communication with the Embassy in Bonn, and without any influence over their actions in any event. We were just the go-betweens.

Our moment of relaxation was brief. We knew that if a government official contacted the Brajshoris and asked them their intentions, they would get nowhere, as the Brajshoris did not understand English. If this were to happen, an inconclusive message, or the wrong message, might find its way back to Bonn, and Dani's arrival would be delayed again. We knew we had to act. We telephoned Denise to find out what the Brajshoris had to do to confirm that it was their intention to stay in Canada. The policy on that is very clear, she told us. The fact of applying for Landed Immigrant status will be taken as a confirmation of their intention to stay.

We were despondent. We had had an opportunity to help the Brajshoris apply for Landed Immigrant status several weeks before, but had not done it. The reason was very simple. The fee for becoming a Landed Immigrant was $975 per person. This was an expense the Brajshoris could ill afford. On the other hand, there was talk in political circles in Ottawa that the fee might soon be eliminated entirely for refugees, in recognition of the hardship it imposed. In fact the Minister of Immigration had been quoted in the Ottawa paper that she was considering doing this in the very near future. Therefore, we had held off filling out the applications, in hopes of being able to save the Brajshoris a hefty sum by our delay.

Now we were concerned that our delay might introduce another glitch in bringing Dani over. "No," Denise told us. "There won't be any problem. Just fill out and send in the applications for Landed Immigrant status, but do not attach any payment. Instead, attach a letter explaining the circumstances, indicating that you are not paying now because you believe the annulment of the fee for refugees is imminent, but you are sending in the application now because the Embassy in Bonn requires proof that the Brajshoris intend to stay in Canada."

We jumped at this proposal, as it seemed to meet all our needs, but questioned Denise further. By taking this route, were we in danger of introducing another delay into Dani's arrival? No, she told us, everything would be fine.

We started filling out the Landed Immigrant applications that very day, and by the next day had the required signatures from Hajji and Nazife. Then I hand-carried the original to the local CIC office, from where it would be actioned by sending it to the CIC office in Vegreville, Alberta. I also hand-carried a copy over to the CIC headquarters, which happened to be just two blocks down the street. What an advantage to live in Ottawa, I thought, as I walked into the office and asked to be directed to Denise. I found her in a room full of computers, with two other young women. They welcomed me with smiles and cheery hellos as I introduced myself, and Denise happily accepted the copies of the applications for her records. She asked after the Brajshoris, and seemed genuine in her concern for their well-being, and more than willing to help us expedite the arrival of their son.

When I left Denise's office, I felt satisfied that we had done everything necessary to expedite Dani's arrival. However, given the glitches, misunderstandings, and delays that had already occurred, we decided a few days later to follow up to ensure that the Embassy in Bonn now had all the information it needed to proceed with Dani's case. I called Denise, confident that she would be able to check on this for us. There was no answer, only a voice mail message saying she would call us back. I left my name and number, certain that she would call back.

Two days later we had not heard back from Denise, so I called again, only to be faced with the same voice mail message. My goodness, she must be overloaded this week, I thought, and left my name and number again. I really was not expecting her to call back call right away, however, because it was nearly the end of the week.

By this time the Brajshoris had come down from their high over the news of the interview. They were noticeably anxious at our lack of definite answers. Nazife was at her wits' end and her health problems were getting worse. She was constantly sighing. Hajji mentioned that some friends had told him to just tell Dani to get on a plane and come. He assured us this was not his intent. He wanted Dani to arrive legally even if the wait seemed eternal. Nazife seemed just to want him here by whatever means. She could not take much more of this uncertainty. She was very worried and truly doubting, we think, that he would ever arrive.

By the following week we had not heard back from Denise, and both Anne and I were getting edgy. Time was moving on. It was mid-November, and if Bonn did not have all the information they needed, the processing of Dani's case might be delayed and Dani might miss the December flight. That would mean he would have to wait for the February flight, another two-month delay. We knew this would be unbearable for Hajji and Nazife. We were fearful what this would mean for Nazife especially, as her blood pressure was still not under control and she was still complaining of headaches, stomach problems and sleepless nights. Waiting for February was not an option.

As Anne and I sat over our morning coffee, discussing our options, I happened to look at my watch. It was 10:00AM We were just in time to catch the responsible officials over in Bonn before their office closed, if we phoned right away. We could ask them directly if they had all the information they needed to proceed with the case, and make sure Dani was on the December flight to Canada.

I found the number for the immigration section of the Embassy in Bonn and dialled it straight away. An unidentified male voice answered. I asked if I had indeed reached the immigration section of the Canadian Embassy in Bonn, and the voice replied in the affirmative. "Good," I said, and I explained my reason for phoning, as quickly and as clearly as I could.

"I'm sorry," the voice responded. " I can't talk to you about that. The information is confidential."

I explained again that we were sponsors, that we were working on the Brajshori case with CIC officials from both the regional and the head office in Ottawa, and that if he checked his files, he would see that we had written and signed the original letter that had initiated the case some months ago.

"It doesn't matter." The voice had a bit of a hard edge to it. "Unless the Brajshoris signed a letter making you their agents, I can't discuss the case with you."

I protested that we were indeed their agents, but that none of the Ottawa-based CIC officials had ever mentioned any need for a written document to that effect.

"This is a matter of confidentiality and protection of personal information. There are no exceptions." The voice had a ring of finality to it, and was tinged with bureaucratic rectitude and more than a little frustration. I knew I had only one more chance.

"OK," I said. "I accept your policy. I am not asking for any confidential information. I only want to be sure you have all the information you need to process the case and get Dani on that December flight. Could you please just tell me that you do not need any more information from me?"

There was a short pause, a sigh, and the voice took on a more conciliatory tone. "All right. But I can't do it now. It's after hours here. I'll ask someone to look into it in the morning."

"Thank you so much," I responded, mustering all the goodwill at my disposal. "You can't imagine how much I appreciate this, and how grateful the Brajshoris will be to you. By the way, could you please tell me to whom I am talking?"

"I'm the Head of the Immigration Office," the voice identified itself, and took on a friendly tone. "You are very lucky that I picked up the receiver. It's after hours and officially there is no one here at this hour. I was just on the way out myself."

"Thank you for listening to my story," I finished off. "Your Office's work on this case is going to make a huge difference to the health and well-being of two elderly refugees. Please pass our thanks on tomorrow to the officer who is working on this case."

When I got off the phone, we felt good about the commitment the Head of Immigration had made, and lucky that he had picked up the phone. We were not too pleased about being blind-sided with the requirement for a signed letter making us the Brajshoris' agents, and wondered why no one at the local office of CIC or at CIC headquarters had ever asked for one. In any event, we were pleased to have finally made a direct connection with the responsible officials in Bonn.

By the next day our confidence was starting to wane. What if the Head of Immigration forgot to pass on instructions to his staff? What if the instruction became garbled as it went down the line? What if another piece of paper were misplaced? Our past experience had made us cognizant of how easily something could be forgotten or delayed at CIC. Without our initiative, the original request made by the Brajshoris in Camp Borden would not have been acted upon at all. Without our letter, Bonn would probably never have sent an application form to Dani. Without our follow-on through CIC head office in Ottawa, Dani's application might have been irretrievably lost somewhere in the paper shuffle. Now, without our initiative to make sure the applications for Landed Immigrant status were received in Bonn and properly recorded, there could be another long delay. There were too many "withouts" and too many "what ifs."

By the third day we noticed the Brajshoris' level of anxiety had risen close to the breaking point. Nazife was visibly angry, and the couple was arguing openly in front of us. Nazife wanted to bring Dani over on the next plane, regardless of the consequences. Fortunately, Hajji was still resisting this, and trying to stay calm. We told him he was doing the right thing, and tried to convince Nazife that it would be pointless for Dani to come illegally, as the government would probably not let him stay.

We knew we had to act again. We got straight at it the next morning, without even waiting to have breakfast. We tried to phone Denise, but only got her voice mail. We decided to phone Denise's director general. This was the level of authority we thought would be best placed to get fast action on an operational matter. The director general's secretary answered the phone. Her boss was out and would not be able to return calls before tomorrow at the earliest. Denise was off on sick leave, and had been for some time now. Leave your number, the secretary advised, and she would have someone call us back.

I felt a tug of anxiety at my stomach, and my breathing accelerated. I had visions of another round of message passing and telephone tag consuming several more precious days. It was already November 18. We knew the Embassy in Bonn had been waiting since the interview on November 5 to have proof that the Brajshoris would stay in Canada. We had sent the proof ten days ago. Now we needed verification that the proof had arrived, and that Bonn could now move to get Dani on that December plane.

"I absolutely have to speak to someone right away," I said. "Could you please pass me on right now to someone who is in a position to verify that the file is complete, and that the information Bonn has requested has reached them. This is critically important to two elderly refugees whose health and well-being are dependent on Bonn taking immediate action to get their son on that December flight to Canada."

"I'll pass you on to a senior officer familiar with the Kosovo program," came the reply. "I'm sure he will be able to help you."

I felt my breathing return to normal. A man's voice answered the phone. I explained what we needed to know.

"I'm leaving the office at four this afternoon for an international trip," the officer explained. "I'll pass this request immediately to an officer who can look into it, and I'll call you back before I leave this afternoon, to advise you of the status of this file."

There was a confidence and level of certainty in the man's voice that put me immediately at ease. I knew he was going to do exactly what he had said.

Sure enough, at 3:30 the telephone rang. "We contacted Vegreville," it was the same confident-sounding voice. "The information on the Brajshoris' applications for Landed Immigrant status was put into the computer today. Bonn has been advised. They have all the information they need respecting the Brajshoris' intent to stay in Canada, and will be able to proceed with the case."

I felt a little lump rise in my throat as I listened to this calm citation of the day's events. Visions of the Brajshoris hugging their long lost son in the Ottawa airport flashed before my eyes. Overcome with relief, I had to swallow to compose myself. "Thank you so much," I offered back, as soon as I could find my voice. "This will mean so much to Mr. and Mrs. Brajshori. I am so grateful for your help. You'll never know how much I appreciate what you did for us today."

"You're very welcome," the man spoke in a matter-of-fact tone. "I am glad we could help. We are just doing our job. Good luck with your sponsorship." The phone call came to an end. We both heaved a sigh of relief. Our project was back on the rails. We immediately went over to the Brajshoris' apartment to reassure them that everything was now in order and that we were expecting to see Dani in mid-December. Our news had a calming effect, although Nazife was still looking a little sceptical.

November 18 was a bit of a turning point for Anne and me. We knew there was nothing more that we could do. We were now totally dependent on what happened over in Bonn. We were confident that we would see Dani in mid-December. While we made no promises to the Brajshoris over the weeks that followed, they must have sensed our confidence. They seemed more relaxed as well. They stopped talking about putting Dani on the next plane.

After a couple of weeks we started to wonder how things were going at the Embassy in Bonn. I decided to call John, one of my favourite contacts over at the CIC local office. He had been introduced to us
at the first meeting of sponsors, and had always bent over backwards
to be helpful in providing information, even though he had no formal
responsibility for our case. Maybe he could shed some light on where
things stood.

John seemed happy to hear from me, even though I called him at
6:30AM In fact, whenever I wanted to talk to John, I always called at
6:30AM, as this was the only time of day I could expect him to be in
his office, able to answer his phone. At one point he confided that he
started work at 6:30 every day because the "slow" time between 6:30
and 8:00AM was the only time of day quiet enough to get any work
done that required concentrated thinking. After that his day was so
hectic that all he could do was react to the crisis at hand.

As usual, John had just the information we needed. "There is a
flight from Germany scheduled on December 14," John told me.
"We'll get the list of passengers on December 8. I'll be able to let you
know then if Dani is on the plane." Then John thanked us for all the
work we had done to help the Brajshoris. We had always been sure to
thank all the CIC officials for the work they had done to help us and
the Brajshoris, but this was the first time any official had thanked us.
I knew he meant it. I was very touched.

We waited eagerly for December 8. On December 7, our telephone
woke us at 5:30. It was Dani. "The Embassy told me my flight is next
week," he said eagerly. "I'll call again as soon as I know the date and
flight number."

This was the moment we had been waiting for. We both wanted to
jump in our car and head over to share the good news with Hajji and
Nazife, but we knew Rose-Aline was already there, as it was her turn
to visit. We settled for second best, and picked up the phone. We gave
the good news to Rose-Aline and she told the Brajshoris. We could
hear Hajji's deep-throated exclamation of joy, followed by loud chatter and commotion. After a slight delay, Rose-Aline came back on the
line. "Hajji's and Nazife's eyes lighted right up when I told them," she
said. "Now Hajji is dancing around the apartment like a schoolboy.

They are in their seventh heaven."

On December 8 at 9:00AM we had a phone call from Sally, who worked for the Refugee Assistance Program in Toronto. Sally had helped the Brajshoris in Camp Borden, and had helped us with the financial details of Hajji's and Nazife's government allowance under the two year federal program. Now she was calling to let us know that Dani would be arriving in Ottawa on December 14, at 8:00PM "Say hello to Mr. and Mrs. Brajshori for me," she asked. "They are such a fine couple. Isn't it wonderful their son can come to join them?"

This time we did jump into our car and headed over to the Brajshoris' apartment to give them the news. They were ecstatic. Nazife was walking with a spring in her step. Hajji looked like a thousand pound weight had been lifted from his shoulders.

The next day Dani called to give us the same information. Then John called from the CIC local office with his confirmation of the date and time.

On the 10th, Denise called. She was back in the office, and spoke with bubbly enthusiasm. "I just noticed Dani's name on the passenger list for December 14," she said. "I know you have been waiting a long time for this. I wanted to be sure you knew as soon as possible."

Anne thanked Denise for thinking of us, and taking the time to call. She did not have the heart to tell Denise that we already knew all the details of Dani's arrival.

When Anne got off the phone I noticed a slight smirk on her face. We both sat down and burst out laughing. We were being inundated with telephone calls from every direction. Getting the CIC moving had been a gargantuan effort, like pushing a cement mixer up a hill. Now that the CIC machine was in motion it was unstoppable. "Maybe the Head of Immigration in Bonn will call us next," we joked with each other. "They are probably all saying, 'Thank goodness Dani is on the next flight; at least now those two sponsors will be out of our hair,'" Anne laughed. It was great fun, and as we sat there laughing, we felt the stress of the whole ordeal gradually fall away.

It was December 13 before we heard again from Dani. He was calling from Avdi's place, in Essen, and he sounded apprehensive. "They are telling me the airport in Frankfurt is very big," Dani explained. "I am afraid I will get lost and not find my plane." He also sounded sad. "I want to come to Canada, but I am sad to leave my brothers. And I do not have time to go to Oberhausen to see Ali before I leave for Frankfurt tomorrow. I do not know when I will see him again."

We tried to cheer him up by telling him how keen his parents were to finally see him again. We also told him not to worry about the airport. We knew he spoke good German and would be able to ask directions if he got lost. We assured him everything would be fine, and that we would definitely be waiting at the Ottawa airport with his parents to meet him when he got off his plane.

The next morning we were awakened by the telephone at 5:00AM It was Dani, calling from the airport. His voice sounded relaxed and upbeat. "I found my plane," he said. "It leaves in half an hour. But I can't talk for long. I don't have very much money."

We thanked Dani for calling. Throughout our long wait to bring him over, he was always so good at calling us to let us know what was happening. He had been our lifeline, for without his calls there was no doubt in our minds that the whole immigration process would have careened off the road into the ditch long ago. This one last call was just what we needed to assure us that we would indeed witness the family's reunion that night.

Our day started early and went by ever so slowly. The sun shone in the morning, but as the afternoon wore on dark clouds rolled in. The weather station announced freezing rain, starting in Ottawa late in the evening, but much earlier in Toronto, around 5:00PM We were wondering if this might mess up Dani's flights, but since there was nothing we could do, tried to put the thought out of our mind.

We went over to the Brajshoris' apartment early, arriving around 6:00PM We wanted to have plenty of time for a social visit before leaving for the airport. Nezir and Nazife answered the door together. Both were dressed to the nines. Nazife had on her new blouse and vest, pantaloons in matching colours, and matching jewellery. Hajji was dressed in a gorgeous green shirt with matching bandana around his white Muslim skull cap. He wore a dark three piece suit. They looked wonderful.

The atmosphere in the apartment was heavy, and the two Brajshoris seemed nervous, as though they did not really believe Dani was about to arrive. Hajji was trying to be nonchalant, acting as though nothing special was happening, but his acting made him stiff and unnatural and quieter than usual. Nazife was obviously tense, walking from room to room for no apparent reason, and doing little make-work projects like dusting the furniture and straightening the shoes in the entrance. We had our tea, and then Nazife was ready to go, but Hajji was stalling. It was the same kind of practised delay and hesitation that Hajji used whenever we would come over to pick him up for a doctor or dentist's appointment. He would sit at the coffee table, peel another apple, cut it meticulously into quarters, spike a quarter on the tip of his paring knife, and offer it ceremoniously to each of his guests in turn. Then he would settle back and start into a story of his early life in Kosovo, or describe at length a parable from the Old Testament. Tonight, as we were eating our apple, I noticed that Nazife had disappeared. Curious, I went to check, and saw her in the bedroom, crouching and smoking a cigarette. Her nerves had gotten the better of her. We knew that she smoked, but she never smoked in front of guests, and when she saw me standing there she looked up guiltily and then started to chuckle. Her cover had been blown, but she did not care. She really needed her nicotine fix that night!

At 7:00 o'clock we had to put an end to Hajji's stalling. We got up and started putting on our coats and boots. Nazife eagerly joined in. Hajji saw that the jig was up, and joined in, too. We were off, with a lot of deep breaths and nervous sighing. The trip to the airport was quiet, without the usual chatter.

We arrived at the airport at 7:30, in plenty of time for the 8:00 o'clock plane. I dropped them off at the door, and went to park the car. Hajji motioned that he was going to have a cigarette before going in. Anne took Nazife inside. Theresa, Don, and Rose-Aline were already there. Theresa spotted Anne and went immediately to her side. "Dani's flight was cancelled – not delayed, cancelled," Theresa breathed in a low tone, as nonchalantly as possible under the circumstances. Anne felt her stomach squeeze, like she had just been punched in the gut. Her mind raced as the adrenaline kicked in. Above all else she had to remain calm. "You look after Nazife," Anne said to Theresa, with all the composure she could muster. "Hajji is outside having a cigarette.

I'm going to the Air Canada counter to find out what is happening."

At the Air Canada counter Anne was received by a smiling, efficient ticket agent. The agent did a few quick checks on her computer. "Don't worry," she counselled. "The flight from Germany landed in Toronto this afternoon at 1:30PM, and Mr. Brajshori was on it. It is only his connecting flight from Toronto to Ottawa that was cancelled, because of the freezing rain. I'll check to see whether he is booked on another flight."

The agent busied herself on the computer screen for what seemed like an eternity. Finally she looked up. "I could not locate him anywhere," she explained. "He is probably on standby, waiting in the airport. Another plane is due here at 9:00PM, but it is full. There is another tentative arrival about 10:30, then another after midnight. He could be on either of those flights."

Anne was devastated. She explained her dilemma, that she had two elderly refugees with her who had been waiting seven months for their son to join them in Canada, and that this was supposed to be the day. She did not know how to explain to them that their son might not arrive, or that if he did arrive it might be after midnight. Was there anything else the agent could do?

The agent asked Anne to wait a moment, picked up the phone and made a call. After a short conversation she hung up and turned happily back to Anne. "Good news! Mr. Brajshori is on a plane full of passengers on the tarmac in Toronto, ready to leave as soon as it has been de-iced and it is safe to go."

Anne thanked the agent profusely. She was thrilled to at least be able to tell Hajji and Nazife that Dani was on his way and would likely be there in an hour or so. What a relief!

By the time Anne got back to Nazife and the other sponsors. Hajji had joined them and I was back from the parking lot. With help from Nusret, whom we got on the phone, we explained to Hajji and Nazife the reason for the delay. We were so grateful for Nusret's help at this critical moment.

We had some time to kill, probably an hour or so. We trooped into the cafeteria, put two tables together, and bought coffee, tea, and cookies. Every once in a while, someone would get up to check the flight monitor or to go for a quick turn around the terminal to calm his nerves. After a while the table was half empty. Hajji noticed the number of people around the table had diminished, and made a joke out of it. Here we were, waiting to greet Dani, and half of us had already gotten lost.

The flight monitor was projecting Dani's arrival for 9:00PM, so about 10 minutes before 9:00 we all headed down to the arrival gate. All, that is, except Hajji. By this time he had disappeared, and was nowhere to be found.

Finally, just before the passengers started coming through the door, we found Hajji outside having a cigarette, and brought him back. Hajji and Nazife stood there motionless, looking serious. This was a big moment for them, perhaps one of the biggest in their lives.

There was a moment of comic relief as the first passengers started coming through the door. Every one of them had a cell phone to his ear, talking as he came through the door. It was hilarious, as though this was some necessary part of disembarking from a plane.

"Ramadan!" Hajji suddenly exclaimed, pointing to a dark-haired, good looking young man in a yellow jacket who had just come through the door. Dani spotted his parents, who by this time were rushing toward him. It was a flurry of smiles, hugs, and excited talking and introductions, as the Brajshori parents greeted their son, introduced the sponsors, and posed for snapshots to capture the happy moment. It was a very special moment for Nezir and Nazife, finally reunited with their son after an absence of over two years. It was also very special for Anne and me, as we had made the Brajshoris' quest our own, and were able to share vicariously in their happiness at being together at last.

Dani had no luggage other than his carry-on bag, so we headed for the exit. On the way over, a man rushed up to us and introduced himself as an officer from CIC. He asked if this was the Brajshori family, and if we would be driving Dani home with his parents. He had come out to the airport to meet Dani, just in case his family or the sponsors had not been able to come. We told him yes, we were the sponsors and we would take all the Brajshoris home. We thanked him for his thoughtfulness. It was a nice gesture for CIC to look after their clients this way.

There was confusion as the other sponsors started to say goodbye to the Brajshoris. We had agreed with them beforehand that they would all go directly home from the airport, and that we would take the Brajshoris back to their apartment and drop them off, without staying. Our reasoning was that the family would want some private time together to celebrate Dani's arrival, and that Dani would be tired anyway, since for him it was already 3:00 in the morning. When Hajji finally understood what was happening, he ran and brought the other sponsors back. All the sponsors are invited to his apartment, he was gesturing. We will celebrate Dani's arrival together.

Hajji, Nazife, and Dani drove back with us. The car was full of happy chatter, so different from the tense silence on the way to the airport. Ottawa looked beautiful with all the Christmas lights aglow. We purposely passed in front of the Parliament building because we knew the Brajshoris loved the lights in front of it and Hajji was proud of the democratic values that it symbolized. Hajji pointed it out to Dani as we passed. "Parliament, *mirë, mirë*!" When we arrived at the Brajshoris' apartment, Dani and Nazife went up, and Hajji stayed at the front door of the building to make sure that all the sponsors arrived and were brought safely inside.

After a short wait, Hajji escorted the final sponsors to arrive into the living room. Dani sat in the place of honour on the sofa, and we spread out in a big circle around him, some beside him, some on kitchen chairs and some on the floor. Nazife went into her hostess mode. First she brought everyone a coke. Then she started warming up a huge meal of chicken, rice, salad and *fli*, all her specialities. All the sponsors were trying to tell her to forget about serving a meal, and to come instead to sit beside Dani and chat with him. Finally she relented, but only if we would agree to have tea and dessert. So we all sat around and had tea and rice pudding, with Hajji leading the conversation in an animated mix of Albanian, gesticulation, demonstration and the odd English word. Everyone was laughing and joining in the fun, even if it was not always clear who was saying what, to whom. Dani described his last few days in Germany, his recent visits with his brothers, and his trip on the plane, which had included a stop in Toronto where he had been met by CIC officials and processed through immigration as a Landed

Immigrant. He had to say everything at least twice, once in Albanian and once in English. He seemed remarkably fresh and awake, given that it was about 5:00AM Germany time.

By 11:30, dessert had long since been finished, and it was time for the sponsors to go. Dani had to sleep, and everyone else was tired, too. Anne and I made our way out into the street. The air was still warm and the freezing rain had not started yet. We stopped for a moment and took a few deep breaths of the fresh air before getting into the car. It had been an exhilarating evening. We felt fulfilled. Having Dani finally there after months of waiting made the many ups and downs along the way all worthwhile.

six

DANI

The next few days were a whirlwind of activity. The day after Dani's arrival we went over to Reception House to pick up sheets, towels and a pillow. Dani was also allocated a bed and dresser, but since there was no room for them in the Brajshoris' apartment, these would have to wait. When we arrived at the Brajshoris' apartment with the linens, the family was in celebration mode. Nazife had prepared a full Albanian meal, and insisted that we stay. Dani seemed rested and ready to begin his new life in Canada. "Tomorrow we will register you at Reception house," we told him. "You will be added to your father's file and he will receive an allowance to pay for the extra costs of a third family member."

Then we explained to Dani all the other things he would need to do. He would have to register for Ontario medical insurance, OHIP, and for the permanent Social Insurance Number he would need when he started to work. Then he would have to be tested to determine his competence in English, at the Language Assessment Centre. This would lead to placement in a language school to upgrade his English to the level needed for college or university. At the same time we would help him investigate admission requirements for university and college, so that he could begin his studies as soon as possible.

Dani seemed particularly keen to get back to university. He had completed his first year of studies in arts at the University of Prishtina, and thought that now he would like to study computers.

On December 16 we began all the necessary registrations, and on December 17 Rose-Aline called us to say that a great job opportunity had come up. Would Dani like to work as dishwasher in a restaurant where Anne M.'s son, Ryan, was chef? The job would be part time, in the evenings, and could be co-ordinated with Dani's English training.

We raised the possibility with Dani. In our opinion, we told Dani, it was a bit too soon to start a job. We suggested his priority over the next few months should be English, especially if he wanted to go to university or college in the fall. Later on he could take a part time job to earn a little money to help pay his way through college. Lots of Canadian students held part time jobs.

"I think I would like to take the job," Dani told us. "I could go to school and work at the same time. But I will have to ask my father."

We saw Dani the next day, and asked him what he had decided. "I am going to take the job," Dani replied with a grin. "My father preferred that I just concentrate on school for now, but Nusret was there. He said that if the sponsors suggest I take a job, then I should do it. So my father agreed. I will start tomorrow."

To say that we had suggested that he take the job would have been an exaggeration. However, we could see that Dani was keen. "Good for you," we told him. "Go for it. But be sure to give priority to your English. If you see that you need to cut back on your working hours, or drop the job altogether, that is all right, too."

Within a week of arriving in Canada, Dani had a job. He worked from 5:00PM to 11:00PM, five or six days a week. It was almost full time. His boss liked him from the start, and told us that he was a hard worker, and very thorough. "None of the pots get sent back to be washed a second time," he pointed out.

By January 5 Dani was also putting in a full day at the English school. When his classes were finished, he would come home for lunch, and then head straight off to his job. We were often over at the Brajshoris' apartment when he came home for lunch. "I am halfway through level three of five levels of English instruction," Dani told us soon after he had started. "It is going well and I am liking it."

Nazife was immediately comfortable with this new arrangement. She would run around the apartment like a mother hen, making sure everything was clean, orderly and ready for her son to return. The apartment was filled with the smells of Albanian cooking – mouth-watering aromas of chicken, onions, paprika, tomatoes and beans. She would lovingly show us the thick soups, stews, and traditional Albanian pasta that she prepared almost every day. Every time she showed us something new, Hajji would observe jokingly that Nazife no longer cooked for him, only for Dani.

The apartment was crowded, but that did not seem to be a problem. They organized themselves in a way that seemed to meet everybody's needs. Dani slept in the bedroom, Nazife on the couch, and Hajji on a makeshift bedroll between his easy chair and the wall, concocted out of foam salvaged from a neighbour's cast-offs. We were happy to see them getting along so well in such tight quarters, but we made a mental note that eventually, when the lease ran out, we would have to help them find something more appropriate for three.

By mid-January we noticed that the communication dynamic between us and the Brajshoris had been completely transformed. We were thrilled and somewhat relieved to be able to speak English with Dani, and in any event we had a good deal of business to conduct directly with him over matters related to job and school. In addition, we found it highly convenient to use Dani as a shortcut to communicating with Hajji and Nazife. When we needed to be absolutely sure that we were understood, we would simply tell Dani in English and he would translate into Albanian for his parents. After a time, we found ourselves spending a great deal of time speaking English with Dani, and less and less time labouring over the gestures, charades, pictograms, and broken mixture of English and Albanian that had become our staples of communication with the elderly couple.

We also began to notice a change in Hajji. First it appeared in his body language, his drooping shoulders and sad eyes. Then finally he said it outright. "You don't need me anymore," he observed, with a graphic thrust of his arm to indicate that he was throwing himself away. "*Tora, tora, tora*, Dani English." And with that he got up and removed himself to the far side of the room, where he slumped lotus style onto his bedroll and became silent.

At that moment we finally woke up to what was happening. From then on we made a conscious effort to include Hajji in our conversations, and to address him directly in our habitual mishmash of signs, gestures, written scribbles and mixture of languages. When we did need an exact translation, we would address our English comments to Hajji, not to Dani, and Hajji would reply to us. Dani took on the role of a pure translator. The conversation itself was between us and Hajji. With these few simple changes, our relationship with Hajji was back on track.

We still found enough time to speak directly to Dani in English. Sometimes he would come to visit us, and we would take advantage of these occasions to grill him on his past in Kosovo and Germany. Gradually, his story emerged.

Dani moved from the farm to Prishtina with his family when he was about four. By the time he was in high school, Kosovo had lost its autonomous status, and the government began to clamp down on the Albanian language. In March 1991 the government halted funding of Albanian schools, fired many Albanian-speaking teachers, and imposed the Serb curriculum in language, history, and music. Dani found himself in the parallel school system set up by the Kosovars to get around the Serb restrictions. The parallel system was funded by a 3% "voluntary" tax on Kosovars living in Kosovo, as well as on the many Kosovar expatriates who by this time found themselves in Germany, Switzerland and Scandinavia.

"Our classrooms were moved into private houses," Dani told us. "We sat on wooden planks resting on cement blocks. At first we had nowhere to put our books and papers. We had to write with our paper on our knees. Later they put up a second plank for us to write on.

"It was very cold. We had to wear our coats in school, and learn to write with our gloves on. I remember feeling cold almost all the time.

"There were very few books. Only the teacher had a textbook. The teacher would write the text on the blackboard, and we would copy it down. We spent a lot of time copying like that from the board."

At about the same time a parallel health system also emerged. It had its origins in a public health scare in the spring of 1990, when Albanian school children mysteriously began to suffer from nausea and stomach pain. The rumour spread that Serbs were introducing toxic gas into the school ventilating systems. Whether true or not, it made Albanians hesitant to go to Serb doctors and health facilities for treatment. An alternative health system was set up, with clinics in private houses and voluntary staff. The system was run by a humanitarian organization named after Mother Theresa, who was an ethnic Albanian born in Macedonia.

For Albanian Kosovars, life became more and more difficult. There were fewer and fewer jobs, as Albanians were dismissed to make way for Serbs. Everyday life continued much as before, but Albanians were routinely harassed by police, arbitrarily arrested or beaten. There was an ever-growing sense of frustration.

By the summer of 1997, frustration had reached the boiling point, and it was among the students that the pot was first to boil over. Dani had finished his first year of university in the parallel system, and became an organizer for peaceful student marches. The marches were banned, and when they went on anyway, were brutally repressed by the police. Dani was not in the front lines, but saw his friends being beaten. Later, a meeting of the student organizers was surrounded by the police within five minutes of starting, but again, Dani escaped unhurt.

"My father told me that I would not always be so lucky," Dani explained. "He told me to leave the country, to go to join my brothers Avdi and Ali who were already in Germany. I went by bus to Germany, and stayed with my brother Ali in Oberhausen for a little while.

"After a few weeks I went to register as a refugee. They sent me to Hanover at first, and then to Bad Sachsa, a pleasant little town in the hills of Saxony, south of Hanover. I was allowed to work, and I got a job in a restaurant. I liked Germany. I already spoke some German when I arrived and my German improved fast. But I never felt really welcomed by the Germans. I guess I stood out as a foreigner because of my dark hair. And Germany did not seem to want immigrants. I was not allowed to go to school."

Dani had been in Germany about two years when his parents were evicted from Kosovo and ended up in Canada. Soon he was on the move again, this time to join his parents in Canada, which was to him a great unknown. "I was hesitant to come at first," Dani admitted. "But when you were nice to me on the phone, I thought other Canadians would probably be nice, too. Anyway, my parents needed me, and I wanted to go to university again."

Hearing Dani talk about his aspirations for a university education made us realize that we had better start looking into university registration. We had heard that the deadline for September entry for some of the courses was the end of March, and we would be away in France from mid-February until the beginning of April. If we were going to help Dani with registration for the fall term, it had to be right away.

We went to the University of Ottawa, Carleton University, and Algonquin College and brought back the calendars for study in computer-related fields. There were excellent courses of study at all three institutions. We gave all the material to Dani and asked him to have a look.

A week went by and we asked Dani what he thought of the various courses. "I have not had time to read it," he told us. "I have been too busy with my school and my job."

If we had stopped to think about it, or been more perceptive, we would have realized that we were going too fast. Dani had only been in Canada for a month and had his hands full adjusting to a new culture, to his school and to his job. There were only so many hours in a day, and his days were already full to overflowing. He had many months of English training in front of him before he would be at a level adequate for university or college. Dani's eagerness, his ambition to go to university, and his seemingly inexhaustible supply of energy had lured us into a false appreciation of how much he could take on and accomplish over the short term.

It took us a long time to wake up to the fact that we were putting too much pressure on Dani. It would have taken us even longer, had it not been for Linda.

We first heard about Linda from Hajji and Nazife. They started talking about Linda even before Dani's arrival, casually at first, and then with more and more insistence. It was "Linda this – ," and "Linda that – ," Soon they were talking about bringing Linda to Canada. "Who is Linda?" we asked.

From their description, we understood that Linda was Dani's girlfriend in Kosovo. We also understood that Hajji and Nazife thought the world of her, and wanted to bring her to Canada to be with Dani. It sounded like they expected Dani and Linda to marry.

We raised the question with Dani. "Yes," he told us. "She was my girlfriend in Kosovo. She is a very nice girl. She kept in touch with me by phone when I was in Germany, and now she is phoning me here."

"Is it serious?" we enquired.

"I don't know what to say," Dani responded hesitantly. " I am in Canada now, but I do not want to punish her life. My parents would like me to marry her. Her parents are pushing her to get married, too. They say being a single girl in Kosovo is too dangerous right now. There are too many girls being stolen by the Mafia and taken away to be prostitutes. A woman needs a man to protect her."

Dani lapsed into silence for a moment. His eyes flickered with uncertainty. He leaned forward. "She calls me late at night, when I should be sleeping. I think she wants me to go and live in Kosovo, but I cannot. My parents need me here. I tell her that it is 3:00AM in Canada, and that I must go to sleep because I have school in the morning. But she keeps on talking, and then she cries."

Dani hesitated. He picked up the glass of coke in front of him, but put it down without drinking. He leaned back and rested his head on the sofa cushions. His brow furrowed slightly and his mouth showed the hint of a grimace. "It is very stressful. I do not know what to do. I do not want to punish her life."

We sat and talked with Dani that day for a long time. He seemed to want to talk, to share his feelings and concerns. It would be good for him to get this off his chest, I reasoned. It was good for us, too, to understand better all that was going on. There were so many pressures: adjusting to a new country, going to school every morning to learn a new language, putting in what amounted to a full day of hard physical work almost every evening, dealing with an unfinished relationship, trying to please parents who were marching to the beat of a different cultural drum, and trying to meet the expectations of the sponsors. Each of these pressures in itself was manageable, but together they were pushing Dani hard. Maybe not to his limit, but beyond the threshold of reasonable expectation.

One day when we offered Dani something to eat, he refused, casually mentioning that his stomach was hurting and that he was not sleeping well. We knew we had to ease off. At least he did not have to feel pressure from his sponsors. We started by dropping any talk of registering for the September session of university or college. But how could we help him with Linda? We thought about this long and hard.

Finally Anne came up with the answer. "I've got it," she pronounced. "We don't know how close Dani is to Linda, or what he will decide to do. What we can do is help to open the door to whatever decision he eventually makes. Before we leave for France we should help him to fill out an application for a travel document to go to Kosovo. I'll give him the money to buy a return ticket. If he goes to Kosovo, he can resolve his relationship with Linda one way or the other. If he decides to break it off, he can say a proper goodbye and put closure on the relationship once and for all. On the other hand, if he wants her to be his lifetime partner, he can marry her in Kosovo and then come back and work on the immigration papers from here. That would be the fastest way to get them together on a permanent basis here in Canada."

I thought it was brilliant, and when Anne made the proposition to Dani, I could see that he was grateful. "You are doing so much for me," Dani said to Anne, after she had laid out the details of our plan. "I will never be able to repay you."

"Don't worry," Anne joked. "Just promise that you will phone us in France if you become a married man. Maybe you could join us with Linda for your honeymoon. That would be fun. We promise to give you a few short moments of privacy form time to time."

Dani laughed and said, "I promise."

The paperwork for Dani's travel document was finished the day before we left for our holiday in France. After our plane took off from the airport in Dorval, we wondered aloud to ourselves what would happen while we were away. The decision had to be his. Here was a young man who had been through a lot, leaving university abruptly, being separated from his family and his girlfriend by the threat of war, and adapting to two new countries before the age of 21. Now that he was in Canada with his parents, his life would stabilize again. He had the opportunity to work, to pursue higher education, and to choose the career of his choice. We sat back in our seats with our drinks as the plane cruised high over the Atlantic, and smiled at the potential.

Dani did phone us at the end of our stay in France. He sounded happy and well. Anne asked from where he was calling. Was he married? He replied he was in Canada, was not married, and in fact had not even been to Kosovo. He said that he and Linda had decided that, given their changed circumstances, new responsibilities and all the uncertainties of re-establishing themselves, perhaps it would be wise to be just friends for the time being. They would keep in touch from time to time, but would live their lives freely, dating others and seeing where fate would lead them.

"That sounds like a wise decision," Anne told him, validating his position. "I am sure everything will work out for the best."

Then Anne asked him the truly Canadian question. "Is the snow all gone yet?"

"Not quite," Dani replied, laughing. "But I will arrange for it to be gone for your arrival. And if the grass is not green, I will paint it green."

The conversation left us longing to see them all again and happy knowing they were all well.

When we returned to Canada, we realized just how modern and westernized Dani was in comparison to his parents. He walked around with his cell phone glued to his ear, dressed in the up-to-date styles of his generation, surfed the Internet, and blended right in to the Canadian mosaic. His English was improving fast, and he was starting to learn French. He took up roller-blading, carried a student's backpack, and was generally enjoying life.

In other ways he was becoming more like his parents. When he first arrived in Canada we had welcomed a handsome young man with a slim, athletic build. Now he had joined a gym and was putting on upper body muscle, making him look more and more like his Dad. He had a personable, outgoing manner like his father as well, and an irrepressible sense of humour that he probably picked up from both his parents. Maybe looking at the lighter side of life ran in the family. He also had the sensitive, thoughtful side that we had seen in both his parents, and which, over time, would grow into wisdom.

"I am liking Canada more and more," Dani told us one day. "I feel welcome here. I am so glad I came."

"We are so happy to hear that," we replied. "You know, there is lots of opportunity in Canada to pursue the work and lifestyle of your choosing. Have you given any more thought to what you would like to pursue as a career?"

"I am still thinking of studying computers," Dani responded, flashing us that irrepressible grin, "perhaps with an emphasis on the use of computers in business. I really like being with people, and I think I could do well in that line of work."

"That sounds good to us," we said. We encouraged him to think big, to choose a field that interested him, and to get all the education he could. We knew he had the abilities to succeed. And we knew his parents would support him in whatever career he chose. For them, seeing Dani taking advantages of the opportunities Canada had to offer would be ample reward for the hardships they had suffered in getting here themselves.

We wished Dani all the best that life had to offer. We, too, were happy that he had come to Canada.

DANI

Left: Hajji and Nazife with the Mountie who welcomed them to Canada on Parliament Hill.

Below: Nazife, in her first Ottawa apartment, on the line with family members in Germany that she has not seen for several years.

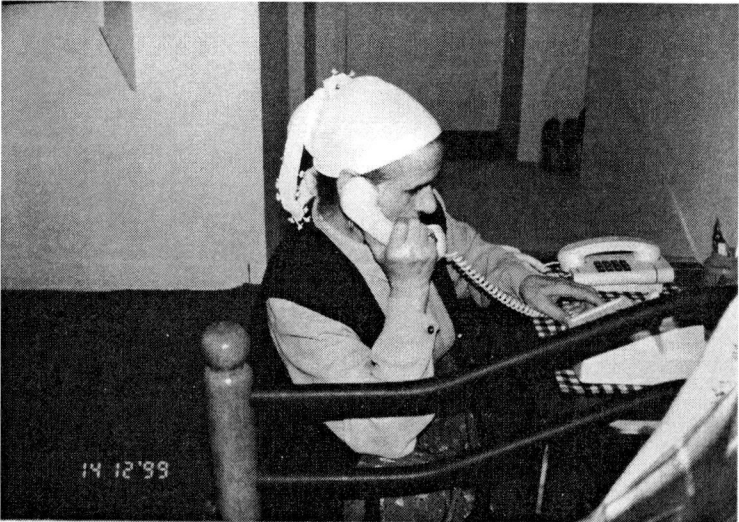

132

Above: Anne and Nazife, during a playful moment at the Canadian Museum of Science and Technology.

Left: Nazife demonstrates her golfing skills at a mini-putt, while Hajji looks on.

Above: Seven months after their arrival in Canada, Hajji and Nazife are united with their youngest son, Dani, at the Ottawa International Airport in December, 1999. Back row from left: Anne, Nazife, Dani, Hajji. Front row from left: Dave, Theresa.

Left: Hajji and Nazife's daughter-in-law, Maria, visiting from Germany in December, 2000.

Hajji, Dani, and Nazife with duffle bags in their Ottawa apartment, on the day of Dani and Nazife's departure for a return visit to Kosovo in 2001.

Nazife and Hajji competing in a game of alphabet bingo, during an English lesson. From left: Nazife, Anne, Hajji.

Left: Nazife, with her freshly-made pite, a typical Albanian dish. She made a point of never letting any guest leave her apartment hungry.

Below: The Brajshori family, with the ever-present setting for tea. Hajji always made the tea. From left: Hajji, Nazife, Dani.

*Hajji thanks Prime Minister Jean Chrétien (at right, back to camera)
for all he had done to help the Kosovar refugees.*

*The Brajshoris' cherished photo with the Prime Minister of Canada,
which Hajji hung in the place of honour over their dining room table.
From left: Hajji, Anne, Nazife, Prime Minister Chtétien, Dani, Dave.*

Hajji greets Dr. Ibrahim Rugova, future President of Kosovo (centre left),
during Dr. Rugova's goodwill visit to Canada.

The Brajshoris with all their sponsors.
Back row: Anne M., Anne, Dani, Rose-Aline, Theresa (partly hidden), Don, Claire.
Front row from left: Hajji, Dave, Nazife.

*Following the citizenship ceremony in March, 2004,
Dani tells the citizenship judge how proud he is to be a Canadian.
From left: Hajji, Nazife, Dani, Judge Suzanne Pinel (back to camera).*

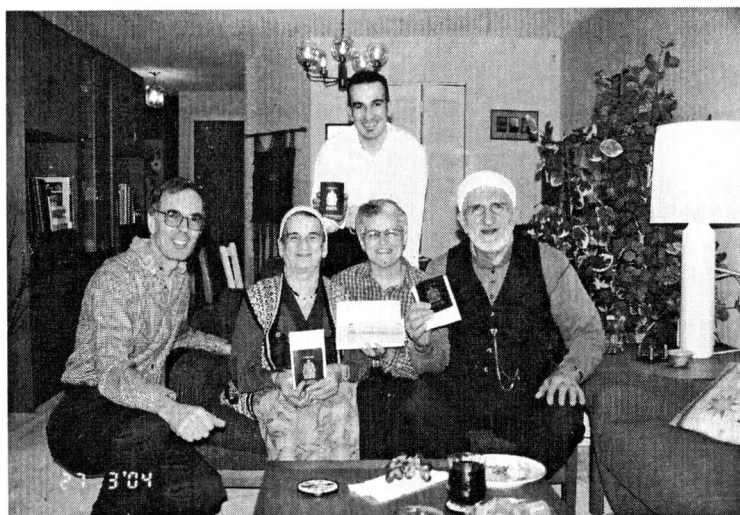

*The Brajshoris show off their treasured new Canadian passports.
From left: Dave, Nazife, Dani (standing), Anne, Hajji.*

Dani and his girlfriend, Valerie, visiting Dave and Anne
at their new home on Georgian Bay in the summer of 2005.

Nazife and Hajji stroll on a Georgian Bay beach,
during a winter, 2004 visit with Anne and Dave.

seven

COMMUNICATION

We have often wondered how an elderly couple must feel when they are dropped unexpectedly into a foreign language environment and told to make a go of it. Perhaps it would be like landing suddenly in Beijing, without knowing a word of Chinese, and being told it was your new home.

When we were told we would be sponsors of a couple who spoke no English, we reacted with more than our usual confidence. After all, there were seven sponsors, and five of them were teachers. Three, including Anne, had been second language teachers. Anne also had experience teaching reading and writing to illiterate adults. So there was, if anything, a surfeit of competence. Personally, I did not think too much about it. I would leave it to the experts. In no time at all, our refugee couple would be speaking English.

Our complement of teachers was quite excited about it. Everything was planned at one of our preparatory meetings. We would, of course, have an interpreter there on the first day. On day two, we would introduce our picture dictionary, The Wordless Travel Book. Designed for travellers, this little pocket book was chock full of pictures of every possible service or product a traveller could imagine. Want to go to church? Fine. Just point to the picture of a church. Need to buy your groceries? No problem. Point to the bag of groceries, and then point to the little building with a question mark on it, so as to say, "Where do I find groceries?"

We bought enough picture dictionaries for the Brajshoris and each of the sponsors. We would carry it in our pocket or purse, where it would always be handy.

On our very first visit, we eagerly pulled out our dictionary to illustrate our planned trip to the bank. Hajji examined the book carefully, his eyes revealing curiosity, but not understanding. "Bank. Money," we repeated each word several times, pulled out wallets and displayed the contents. "Oh, mirë, mirë." Hajji finally caught on, but it was the twenty dollar bills, not the picture of the money and the bank in the dictionary that got the message across.

We discussed our experience with the other sponsors. They had noticed the same reaction, or rather, lack of reaction, to the picture dictionary.

The next time we went to the Brajshoris' apartment, their copy of the dictionary was nowhere to be seen. We concluded that, finding it useless, Nazife had tidied it away, as she seemed to do with any loose object that was not immediately required.

Never mind, we thought, we still have our copy. "Hajji, would you like to go to the mosque?" I asked, pointing to the picture of a mosque. We knew that Hajji was devout, and that this was somewhere he would surely like to go. He peered at the picture, puzzling over it, but not reacting. Hajji motioned that he wanted to borrow my glasses. "Oh, oh, xhami, xhami!" he exclaimed, looking through the lens and finally catching on.

Our little mystery was resolved. They were not reacting, because they could not see the tiny pictures! We put the picture dictionaries away, at least until they got their glasses. Our first idea had been a total bust.

We hoped to have the help of Albanian-speaking interpreters as well, at least for those initial few weeks when there were so many administrative things to do and it was so important that they understood clearly. The problem was that there were very few Albanian-speaking people living in Ottawa, and fewer still who had put their names on the list of voluntary interpreters to whom the sponsors could turn for help. Of those on the list, most were working, so available, if at all, only during their leisure hours. Anne spent one whole day trying to line up interpreters who would be in a position to help us, and ended up with no one.

We were lucky to have met Shano and Nusret on the first day, in the parking lot, as we were picking up our couple on their arrival in Ottawa. They became good friends to the Brajshoris and to us, and we could always depend on them to translate when we had to look after an important business matter or medical question. It was even more amazing that they were always there for us when we needed them, as we knew they performed a similar interpretive function for many, many other Kosovars.

Arjeta, a hair styling assistant from Kosovo whom we had met at the initial Kosovar picnic, was similarly helpful with interpretation. Arjeta had come to Canada as a refugee a year earlier with her husband and two young children. She was often at home, looking after her children, and already knew enough English to help us get our messages across to the Brajshoris, or tell us what the Brajshoris were trying to say.

It was a bit disconcerting at first that some of our messages would be garbled in the translation process. This was, however, often to our advantage, as it enabled the translator to bridge a cultural gap that we had ignored. Once we asked Nusret to explain to Hajji the importance of always leaving enough money in the bank to cover the rent, which was paid on a monthly basis by automatic bank check. "If you do not leave enough," we told Hajji, "your check will bounce." Nusret took this useful but culture-specific jargon and translated it by saying, "If you do not leave enough money to pay your rent, the landlord will evict you and you will be out on the street."

"That is the only way we can be sure that Hajji understands your message," Nusret assured us in an aside.

Usually, over those first few months, there was no one around to interpret. We were on our own. We had to devise our own means of communicating.

It is the custom in Albanian families for the husband to take the lead, acting as spokesperson for his wife and other family members. Hajji seemed eager to fulfil this role, one which came to him naturally,

given his extrovert tendencies. Nazife would sit back quietly and observe, or go and busy herself in the kitchen. She seemed quite content
to let Hajji do the talking. It was only later that we learned Nazife was
herself an inveterate talker. Initially, our main efforts to communicate
were directed at Hajji.

There were no rules. Anything that could help get the message
across was allowed. Any technique that worked, however ridiculous or
childlike it might seem to an observer's eyes, was the right technique.

A combination of gestures and charades became the order of
the day. Hajji was a master of these techniques. In Kosovo he was a
story teller, we were told one day by Shano's son. A large part of the
Albanian tradition is passed on orally. These gestures were natural for
him. They were a communication tool he learned as a child and had
used all his life.

Many of his gestures were automatic, and we caught on right away.
The backward flick of his hand indicated "go away," the determined
thrust of his finger said "no," the finger held to the nose and moved suddenly down showed "nothing," and the beckoning motion of his whole
hand clearly defined "come here." To these gestures were added facial
expressions that would do credit to a seasoned Hollywood actor: the
raised brow for uncertainty, the hardness in his eyes for anger, the open
mouth and rounded eyes for surprise. All the while Hajji would be talking, and watching us carefully for signs of comprehension. Seeing them,
he would move on, but in their absence he would repeat, repeat and repeat. Ever patient, he would not give up, and never showed frustration.
Finally, if all else failed, he would draw a picture, or perform a charade.

It did not seem to matter where we were when he felt a charade
coming on. One day we took them to the Museum of Nature, and
they were particularly intrigued by the displays of stuffed wild animals. When we passed the wolf display, Hajji thought of a story he
wanted to tell. Without the least hesitation, he lay down on the floor
in front of the display, a few feet underneath a hovering, stalking wolf.
To convey the story of what had happened to him in Kosovo, he made
the motions and noises for sleeping, and then suddenly woke up, only
to see the wolf looking him right in the eye. From his gestures, it was
hard to say who was the more surprised, Hajji or the wolf. Both took

off in opposite directions. It was a close call.

There were a lot of wolves in Kosovo, and his job as a shepherd when he was a boy was to protect the cattle, sheep and goats from the wolves. He did this with the help of dogs, and a stout stick with a piece of iron through the end, to use as a weapon against the wolf if all else failed.

All of this was conveyed to us right there in the museum, with appropriate gestures, facial expressions, and animal noises necessary to make the point. There was no doubt at all about his story, which he managed to get across without a word of English. "Wolf, wolf," we said at the end of his story, pointing to the wolf in the display.

"*Albanski, ujk, ujk*," Hajji informed us. "*Ujk.*"

This was just one of many "wolf" stories we were to hear. To listen to Hajji, one would think that wolves were rampant in those early days in Kosovo. They certainly seemed to be the farmers' public enemy number one.

We became quite adept at charades ourselves. Browsing through the grocery store one day, Hajji found a large plastic bag of frozen goat bones, and asked us what it was. "Goat bones," we said, "Goat, goat." Seeing his blank look led us directly into action. First outlining little beards, we then braced our index fingers at the sides of our heads, pawed the ground a little, and bleated like a goat. Hajji understood immediately. "*Dhi, dhi!*" he exclaimed, giving us the Albanian word for goat, and acting out the goat charade himself.

Meanwhile all had become quiet around us. We looked around. Eight pairs of curious eyes were fixed on the spectacle of three grown adults pretending they were goats. "It's OK," we said. "He doesn't speak English. This is a bag of goat bones. We have to act it out."

We became quite adept at pictograms as well. This was particularly handy when we were in the Brajshoris' apartment where paper was available. It was a little like playing "Pictionary," the parlour game, but without the rules. Anything went, provided it contributed to getting the message across. Sometimes it went badly wrong, like my hurried sketch of a rooster that actually looked more like a dog. "Rooster, rooster," I repeated, and followed with an uninspired "Cockadoodle doo." Hajji looked sceptical and unconvinced. Peering at the picture, which I had drawn large enough for him to see, he started to laugh.

"No rooster," he chortled. "*Qen, qen*," he corrected, giving us the Albanian word for dog.

I often found myself the butt of jokes, and my hurried scribbles and complete lack of artistic talent made me an ample target. One breezy day, finding it particularly hard to draw a picture of the wind, I persisted in puffing and blowing and pointing to the outdoors until Hajji caught on. "*Mërmërima*," Hajji guessed, giving me the Albanian word for breeze. I jotted it down in haste on the notepad. Hajji perused the scribbles, and laughed heartily. You are not writing at all he gestured, you are just scribbling. What you have written is neither English nor Albanian. It is just a child's scribbles. "Baby, baby," he laughed, making the exaggerated hand motions of a child writing.

I looked down at my pad. Sure enough, the word "mërmërima" had come out as so many vertical pencil thrusts that it looked like nothing more than a repetitive scribble. "Very good English," I protested, but it was too late. Everyone else was laughing, too. I had to admit I could not write!

One of the Brajshoris' favourite excursions was a drive in the countryside around Ottawa. There are many pleasant drives past woods, rivers and farmers' fields. We would delight in trying to teach the Brajshoris the English names for the animals and crops that they knew so well from their farming days in Kosovo. For added effect, we would make the noise of the animal mooing or braying, and then give them the English name. They would do the same in Albanian. Unfortunately, little of the English stuck with them, and little of the Albanian with us, but the animal noises were easy for everyone. We were a moving barnyard, hurtling down the highway, mooing, neighing, braying, cackling, honking and barking with great glee as we spotted this animal and that along the way.

After a while we learned to combine our gestures, charades and pictograms with any convenient combination of English and Albanian that seemed to do the trick. If a few words of French were thrown in, that was all right, too. If the Albanian word for "bus" sounded like the French "*autobus*," then that is the word we would use.

A typical scenario of us telling the Brajshoris we would come tomorrow at a certain time to take them to the doctor's would go something like this. We would say the words, "tomorrow" and "Wednesday," while simultaneously pointing to the day on the calendar. We would add the Albanian word for Wednesday, "*mërkurë*," just to be sure they understood. We would say the word, "morning," and the Albanian word for morning prayers, "*saba*," and point to the hour of nine on the clock. Then we would point to ourselves, saying our names, and pretend we were driving a car, saying the word, "car," and making car-like noises and steering gestures. Pointing to each of them in turn, we would say "doctor" and "*doctorë*", and then "check-up" and "*kontroll*," and follow up with a mock doctor's examination, pretending to listen to someone's chest through a stethoscope. After this bit of role playing, and perhaps a few repetitions, the Brajshoris would nod knowingly. They had caught on.

Our mixture of communication techniques soon became second nature. We actually began to feel we were talking to the Brajshoris, although we were in fact doing nothing of the sort. But it definitely was communication. It worked for all but the more complicated subjects.

There was still something missing. We should learn Albanian, we thought to ourselves. It would obviously be a few months before the Brajshoris would be sufficiently relaxed to attempt English school, and many months after that before they become conversant in English. In the mean time, we could at least learn enough Albanian for simple communication on everyday routine matters.

We started by buying a bilingual dictionary, or at least trying to buy one. There were so many Kosovar refugees in Ottawa the stores were all sold out. We had to wait while more were ordered. Finally it arrived. I carried it with me everywhere, as though it contained the key to better living. It was my ticket to the mastery of Albanian vocabulary.

Hajji was initially mildly curious about the dictionary. I told him it was the solution to our communication problems. Whenever I heard a word I did not know, particularly if he repeated it several times, I would try to look it up. Take the word for "wind". "*Mërmërima, mërmërima*," Hajji would repeat, as I fumbled with my dictionary. But I did not know how to spell it, and I was taking too long. I was interfering with the flow of the conversation. By the time I found it, if at all, the conversation would have moved on to some other topic, and I would be hopelessly out of phase.

Often, I never found the word. Albanian phonetics differ substantially from the English, and I could not get the hang of it. Sometimes, I could not find the word because the word was not there! I asked some English-speaking Albanians about this. "That's probably because of the dialect," they told me. "Besides, the Brajshoris have a very thick accent, and use words from the countryside that we don't know. Half the time, we don't understand them either."

This was small comfort to me. We wanted to talk to the Brajshoris! But at least it made us feel better about being so slow in picking up Albanian.

It was not long before we found out that Hajji was making words up to help us. He taught us the expression "*tora, tora*" for the word "talk." We remembered it instantly, and started to use it regularly. One day we used it with some other Kosovars. "What are you saying?" they asked.

"Why, '*tora, tora*,' of course," we responded, "the Albanian word for 'talk.'"

"That's not Albanian," they laughed. "Hajji must have made that up."

We were constantly making mistakes. One day Hajji was telling us about his childhood days on the farm, where his brother, Qerkin, was initiating him into the techniques and responsibilities of being a shepherd. I thought he had said "Chicken," as the phonetic sound of "q" in Albanian is the same as our "ch." I was repeatedly calling his brother "Chicken" as I probed to get more of the story. "No chicken!" Hajji guffawed. "Qerkin!" This was all the funnier as "chicken" was one of the first English words Hajji had learned, it being the meat of preference in their daily dietary regime. Whenever the subject of Qerkin came up after that, someone would call him "Chicken" and the laughter would start all over again.

Very early on, Nazife displayed a keen interest in Canadian techniques of heating and cooling houses. Anne learned how to say "hot air," "cold air," and "ceiling vents" in Albanian, and used her newfound knowledge to explain once again to Nazife that the air was coming out of the vents in the ceiling. All the Kosovars broke up laughing. "You just said that our friend Zena lives in the ceiling," one of them explained, hardly able to stem his mirth. "Nazife has no idea you are talking about the heating system."

The other sponsors were no better. Theresa had noticed that Hajji said "*Chera, chera*" whenever he wanted to draw someone's attention. "*Chera*" means "look here" in Albanian. Theresa started going around calling out "*Chura, chura*" to Hajji when she wanted to speak to him. Hajji tried to be polite, but could not contain himself. "You are calling me a turkey," he explained to Theresa, using his usual combination of charades and pictograms. "*Chura* is the Albanian word for turkey."

We wanted to take introductory Albanian language lessons, but could not find any. We guessed there was just not enough demand in Ottawa to support that kind of thing. Maybe in the future, we thought, now that there were more Albanian-speaking people in Ottawa, someone will offer classes. For the time being, we were left to our own devices.

By the end of their first summer, we thought the time was right to enrol Hajji and Nazife in the free English classes offered to all new immigrants to Canada. Theresa, Don and Rose-Aline took on the job of introducing them to school. There were the normal preliminaries: placement tests, interviews, and discussion of the options. The best option was a class for beginning adults at the York Street Public School, less than five minutes' walk from their apartment.

By the time they were enrolled, the fall term had already begun. They were welcome to come anyway, the consultant told Theresa. They would be quickly integrated.

Theresa and Rose-Aline made up little school bags for both of them, complete with pencils, pens, erasers, paper, and exercise books. Hajji and Nazife laughed as they prepared to leave for school on their first morning. "We are your two babies," Hajji gestured, as he made a big display at being a student going off for his first day at school. "Nazife is your baby," he gestured to Theresa, "and I am Rose-Aline's baby. You are the two mamas taking us off to school." And with that, the unlikely cavalcade crossed the road to the school.

We could only imagine the commotion made by their entry to the English class. Hajji introduced himself, and went about the business of school in his normal, effervescent way. The first word he learned was "sit," and we think we know why. Nazife, on the other hand, was very ill at ease. This was quite understandable, given that she had never been to school in Kosovo and was illiterate in her own language. After that first day, she never went back. School was not for her.

Well, thought Theresa, with the creativity and guile of an experienced teacher, I'll just have to teach her English myself. Having forewarned Nazife of the plan, she arrived one morning at the Brajshoris' apartment for Nazife's first English lesson. Hajji was, of course, away at school, so Theresa had Nazife all to herself. She had carefully prepared the first lesson, keeping it simple, very personal, and in keeping with Nazife's interests. The first lesson was to be on the family, with large pictures of mother, father, and baby, identified clearly with printing in large letters. The notebook was clearly labelled "Nazife" in large letters, and if the lesson went well, Nazife would begin to learn to write her own name.

The material was spread out on the coffee table, and the lesson began. Nazife looked the other way, and began to chatter in Albanian. Theresa's lesson was falling on deaf ears. Maybe if I can just get her to pick up the pencil, Theresa reasoned, she will relax a little and start to feel more comfortable. But there was no way; she would not even hold the pencil. Within two minutes, Nazife began to clear the lesson off the table, and within five minutes there was no trace of it. Everything was folded up and put away. Nazife had more important things on her mind. She led Theresa into the kitchen, and turning the tables on her completely, began to show her how to cook, Kosovar style. Oh well, Theresa thought, at least someone will learn something this morning.

We all left Nazife alone after that. Learning English would be for later.

Hajji, on the other hand, was all ambition. He trotted off to school every morning with his schoolbag, and came home at noon. At first he talked to us excitedly about his experiences, practising his new words: "hello," "goodbye," "how are you," "very good," "come, come," and "umbrella." We wondered about the latter, until we found out that the Albanian translation was "*ombrellë*," with pronunciation being virtually identical to the English. He loved to display his new-found knowledge, and delighted in introducing himself to neighbours in the hallway or to the checkout clerks at Loblaws with an energetic "hello, goodbye, how are you." No one seemed to mind that he said "hello" and "goodbye" in the same breath. As always, it was the body language that conveyed ninety percent of the message, and Hajji's intent was always clear.

As the months went by, Hajji's enthusiasm began to wane. He did not seem to be learning very many new words, and was not so eager to show off his work. We knew that something was not right, but were not sure what it might be. We asked to see his notebook. His last lesson was all there, copied in carefully printed letters on two facing pages. It covered everything he needed to know about days of the week, months and seasons of the year. The work was immaculate. Hajji gestured that he had copied it all from the blackboard, but he was unable to read it to us, or tell us what it was about. It was a complete mystery to him. We knew immediately the source of the problem. The work was too advanced and was going over his head. No wonder his motivation was flagging.

When the month of Ramadan arrived, Hajji stopped going to school. He was not allowed to eat or drink anything from sunrise to sunset, and decided to stay at home to conserve his energy. This seemed perfectly reasonable to us. We were still visiting and encouraging him to maintain the English he had already learned. School could wait until the New Year.

In any event, Dani was about to arrive. There was too much excitement in the air to think about English school. Besides, as far as Hajji was concerned, he could already communicate with us. By this time, our technique of gestures, charades, pictograms and jumbled Albanian and English had been honed to perfection.

When Dani did arrive, one of his first suggestions was for his father to learn English, so he could talk to us sponsors. "I already talk to my sponsors," Hajji shot back to Dani in Albanian. "We communicate just fine."

We hoped that Hajji's motivation to learn English would eventually come back, and that he would return to school. We could see many motivating factors. Hajji could see for himself the advantages Dani had in communicating with us in English, and we knew he did not like being left behind. Also, the other Kosovars who had come to

Ottawa at the same time were becoming ever more fluent in English. At social gatherings where both Kosovars and other Canadians were in attendance, more and more of the conversation was being conducted in English. Kosovars who spoke only Albanian were being left out of the conversation. We could see that Hajji, used to being at the centre of the action and participating fully, did not like this kind of isolation. Finally, we could see that he really wanted to have a full, independent life in Canada, and this meant communicating with people in English. Eventually, we thought, he will be asking to go back to English school.

However, the weeks went by, and turned into months. Something was always happening to push school to a lower order of priority. Then months became a year, and one year turned into two. All the other Kosovars were by now able to converse in English. We could see that Hajji was uneasy. He spoke a few more English words, but was still mostly limited to his trusty tool kit of gestures and charades. We approached him with a proposition. Are you ready to go back to school? He agreed to try again.

This time it was my turn to guide Hajji through the administrative preliminaries. I took him to a placement test, where he had to read simple sentences and tell a story based on the pictures he was shown. He was obviously very proud of the English he knew, and rightly so. Nonetheless, his level was very elementary. He would be, for all intents and purposes, starting from the beginning. So much the better, I thought, at least this time he will get a good grounding in the basics, and should be able to follow the class.

Test results in hand, we walked through the pouring rain to the Albert Street Administrative Centre where he would be registered in a class. Sitting there like two drowned rats, we were offered the options. Daytime or evening classes, full-time or part-time. We opted for part-time evening classes, two times a week. It seemed ideal. Enough to provide some structure and discipline to the learning process, but not so much as to make school seem a burden or interfere with the many other aspects of his day-to-day life. He would have a five minute walk to get to his classes. Hajji was very pleased.

The following Tuesday evening, I took Hajji over to the school to show him how to get to his classes, and to introduce him to the teacher. It was a small seminar room, and eight or ten other students were already in the room, waiting for the class to start. The teacher welcomed Hajji warmly, and he took his place with the other students. This is good, I thought. A small class, and a sympathetic teacher. Maybe this time the conditions will be right for Hajji's learning to really take off.

Unfortunately, it was not to be. Hajji attended his classes diligently but without enthusiasm for about three months. Then he stopped for the fasting month of Ramadan. He never went back.

We were not sure what the problem was. Hajji was still professing an interest in learning English. In addition, Nazife was now eager to learn. All of her Kosovar friends now spoke English, and she was feeling left out. She had grown used to life in Canada and was liking her new home. It was time for her to speak English, too.

We mulled over the situation, wondering what to do. Then Anne had an inspiration. "We'll teach them ourselves," she told me one day. "We could introduce them to the sounds of the English language with the help of pictures. We could also include the written word, and they could use these aids to remember, review or refer back to forgotten words. I'll develop the curriculum myself, but I'll need your help. We will visit them three times a week, and give them a lesson every time we go. We will be able to give them one-on-one attention, which will be important since they are at two different levels of ability. We will make it really fun, for them and for us. I am sure they will like the idea."

She was right. Hajji and Nazife both jumped on the idea. They both wanted badly to learn English, and, like us, had probably been looking around for the right means to do so.

Anne put a lot of thought into the preparation. English phonetics would be the central principle for organizing the curriculum, and the Brajshoris' own life experience and activities would form the content of the course.

Her first teaching aid would be a book of pictures, organized by letters of the alphabet, of things and people for which Hajji already knew the English word. This would give Hajji a chance to review his vocabulary while learning English phonetics. He would also have the satisfaction of experiencing an immediate sense of success. Hopefully,

Nazife would eventually get over her inhibitions, and begin to learn some vocabulary from these same pictures.

Anne also bought large blank workbooks for each of them, reserved a page for each letter of the alphabet, and then customized the workbooks to meet her students' individual needs. Nazife's workbook would have blank spaces for Nazife to copy the letter of that page, in both capital and lower case forms. Then there would be a column of pictures of objects or people from her everyday life, and across from it another column of the written words identifying the pictures, but in random order. Nazife's assignment would be to repeat the sound of the letter, say out loud the name of the object or person in each picture, and then join the words with the pictures, using a pencil.

Each page of Hajji's workbook would have the same letter as Nazife's, and the same spaces for him to copy the letter. Instead of pictures, since he already knew how to read in Albanian and Arabic, it would have simple sentences in English, using the sound of the day. Underneath would be a short story drawn from his day-to-day life in Ottawa, or from the stories he had told us about his early life in Kosovo. His assignment would be to read the sentences and stories to us.

Anne rummaged through the teaching aids in the local teachers' stores, and came up with two additional tools: a card deck containing all the letters of the alphabet in upper and lower case letters, and an alphabet bingo game that we all could play. She wanted the course to be fun, as well as practical.

Finally the material was ready. The big day had arrived. It was our first day of school. We arrived at the Brajshoris' apartment ready to dive in to our new curriculum.

Not so fast, Hajji motioned, when he saw us trying to pull out the teaching material. We must have tea first. School can come later.

Our faces must have dropped, but we quickly composed ourselves. Of course the Brajshoris would want to observe the first rule of Kosovar hospitality, serving their guests something to eat and drink before even thinking of conducting any "business." School to them was the equivalent of business. Drinking, laughing and chatting took precedence.

After close to an hour of preliminaries, it was finally time to get down to work. Anne opened the book of pictures. It was an immediate hit with Hajji, who sang out most of the English words without prompting, and got more and more excited as he realized he could actually do the work. He rushed along at breakneck speed, urging Anne to turn the pages faster and faster. "Whoa, whoa," Anne tried to calm him down. "We will do just five sounds today. It is important that you associate a particular sound with each separate letter. It's not just a matter of spitting out the English words as fast as you can."

Anne slowed down, and turned to Nazife, who had been left in Hajji's dust. Pointing to the first word, Anne enunciated slowly and clearly, and waited for Nazife to respond. There was a long hesitation. Nazife looked embarrassed. I looked away and pretended to occupy myself with something else. Anne repeated the word. There was another long pause, and then I heard "apple" in the tiniest whisper, almost inaudible. Anne pointed to a picture of her son, Avdi. "Avdi," she said. "Avdi," came back the tiny whisper. The ice had been broken. Nazife was learning English. I breathed an inaudible sigh of relief. Anne's plan was working.

Building on that first successful day, we quickly established a routine. Every lesson started with an extended tea break. We had learned not to mess with this formula, so critical to the Kosovar concept of hospitality. Besides, it put us all in a relaxed mood, and ready to tackle the work to follow. "Laughing" and "*tora, tora*," as Hajji put it, were essential preludes to "*shkollë.*"

Hajji remembered some of the patterns and accessories of his own far-off schooldays, one of these being a rather rigorous practice of discipline. In his school, all the boys had to recite the Koran by heart, and any failings or inattention led to retribution of the crudest sort. The offending student would be told to lie on his back. He would have his ankles tied together. Then he would be beaten on the soles of his feet with a stick. We winced. No wonder all these old-timers seem to know their Koran by heart!

Hajji was keen to embellish our own school with the appropriate level of make-believe discipline. For this purpose, one day he produced a two-foot metal wand that looked something like a teacher's pointer, and was probably in reality a draw-stick for draperies. He presented it to Anne with a flourish, advising her to use it in the unlikely event that he needed correcting. "Good," he said, "no paff, paff. No good; paff, paff." Anne played the game to perfection, always threatening, but never actually delivering, the "paff, paff."

We finished the workbook of phonetics with their associated pictures in less than a month. We had covered the entire alphabet. It was time to move on to their individual workbooks of customized exercises. We soon found that Nazife loved the writing exercises. Hajji, on the other hand, preferred the oral work. We therefore separated them even more.

Hajji attacked his workbook with the relish of a dog going after a bone. I was assigned to work with Hajji because, Hajji gestured, I would be less likely to discipline him for mistakes. In fact, I took Hajji by default, as Nazife refused to work with anyone but Anne. She was proving to be still somewhat shy.

My session with Hajji always started the same. "Get your glasses, Hajji," I would plead, knowing that without his glasses my coaching would be in vain. Hajji would look around the room, hoping to spot his glasses resting conveniently on a shelf somewhere nearby. Usually, they were nowhere to be seen. He would give a shrug, and then lumber around the apartment looking. Sometimes he would find them in a pocket of a jacket he had recently worn. Sometimes they would be wrapped up and tucked away in a drawer. Sometimes they were nowhere to be found, and Nazife would join in the search. Eventually a pair of glasses would appear, but not always the same pair. It did not matter, provided he could see.

Glasses found, Hajji would lay siege to his printing as though his life depended on it, with one eye craftily monitoring Nazife's progress. Above all, he wanted to finish his printing ahead of her. "Anna, Anna, finished!" he would cry out, wanting to have some attention from the head teacher, whose praise he craved. "Very good work," Anne would respond encouragingly, after looking it over.

Then he had to read his sentences and accompanying story. He did this more slowly, with determination and a good deal of concentration. There was no race with Nazife, as she did not have this kind of work. As the stories described his recent experiences in Ottawa and his earlier life in Kosovo – "history" as he called it – he was keen. I would ask him to do the appropriate gesture or charade, to ensure he understood the meaning of what he had just read. Reading was often difficult for him, as the phonetics were different from what he was used to. Sometimes his brow would furrow, and his breathing quicken. When I saw that the stress was too much, I would suggest a break, and he would happily concur. We would sit back, hands behind our heads, relaxing. Hajji would try to catch Anne and Nazife's attention, showing them how smart we were to have finished our work so fast. We never got much sympathy, and were usually jokingly told to get back to work.

Nazife, if anything, was more enthusiastic than Hajji. She could not wait to finish our tea and get on with the day's lesson. If the tea drinking dragged on too long for her liking, she would harangue Hajji to hurry up, and even start to clear the table. Then her lesson would start, under Anne's watchful eye. Nazife loved to print, and, once the letter learned, would form her practice letters with attentive care and precision. She even did homework, which for some unknown reason Hajji refused to do.

When it came to reading words and joining them to the appropriate pictures, exercises Anne had prepared to assure Nazife's understanding of the word read, the work would always bog down. "I can't understand it," Anne would tell me later. "She knows the words, and repeats them when I point to the pictures, but for some reason does not want to join the word to the picture. I can't get her to draw the line, unless I take her hand in mine and draw it for her. What can be the problem?"

One day when Dani was home, Anne asked him to enquire of his mother why she would not join the words and pictures. "Why should I?" Nazife replied. "I know which word goes with each picture, so why should I join them?"

We could only laugh. Yet, when we thought about it, there was a certain logic, and Nazife was revealing the stubborn side of her character that we had not seen before. Anne asked Dani to explain to Nazife that, even though she knew the answers, the exercises would not be finished until the lines were drawn. By drawing the lines, Nazife would be showing Anne that she could read and understand what she had read without Anne's help. That is the way it was done in school. After that, Nazife was more co-operative in doing the exercises, though she still remained sceptical of the utility of drawing all those lines.

Over the next few weeks we worked our way through the entire range of English sounds, and in the process had covered the alphabet a second time. It was time to introduce Hajji and Nazife to "alphabet bingo."

Anne spread out the caller's sheet of letters, and allocated everyone a card and enough chits to cover the card. "I will show you letters one by one, and call them out," Anne explained, "and if you have one on your card, cover it with a chit. The first person to fill his card is the winner." Then she began to call out letters. At first both Hajji and Nazife were hesitant. They probably have not played bingo before, we surmised. At the end of the first game, Anne held out an opaque plastic bag to the winner, Nazife. "Put your hand in the bag and pull out a prize," Anne instructed. Nazife reached in and pulled out a chocolate bar. She grinned. Hajji immediately saw the point. The competition was on.

We had never seen such competitive spirit. We were especially surprised at Nazife, whom we had seen up until now as easy going, compliant, and yielding. She looked forward to every game of bingo, and she played to win. Hajji was equally determined. "*Hajde, hajde,*" he would urge Anne to speed up, "*hajde, hajde.*" He would try to see beyond the letter she was holding up, to get a jump on everyone with the next letter in line. Then when he was successful in filling his card, he would let out a whoop. "Bingo!" he would cry, and then stand up, holding out his hand so that everyone could congratulate him. "Bravo, Hajji," we would share in his content. "Bravo!"

By the time summer had arrived, both of our students had made notable progress. Hajji could read stories in simple English. He knew a lot of words and several useful expressions, and was on the verge of making simple sentences. Nazife had overcome her fear of school, had learned the alphabet, could print, and knew many simple English words that she could use around the apartment. For both, their comprehension had improved in leaps and bounds. We were convinced that they understood a lot of what we said, even though they could not repeat it themselves.

Hajji told us that when he was in Kosovo he did not want to learn

Serbo-Croatian, but it "just went in." Now he really wanted to learn English, but it "wouldn't stay in." He was gradually learning more, anyway, and refused to give up. Nazife explained that she was the only member of her family who had not gone to school. She was visibly thrilled to be able to write her name and the letters of the alphabet. She also loved using her newly learned English words. Whenever she greeted us with her "How are you?", she always got a satisfied and almost surprised expression on her face, as if to say, "I can't believe I can do this."

Their confidence had improved, and they seemed proud of their accomplishments. What more could we ask at this stage of the integration process? We were fulfilled as well, knowing that we had contributed in a small way to their well-being in their new country. But it was summer now, and school was out!

We wondered if our trips in the country would henceforth contain more English words and fewer animal sounds. Time would tell!

eight

HAJJI

Hajji and I were sitting together in the doctor's office, awaiting feedback on some routine medical tests. The doctor, a pleasant young woman who had been thorough, understanding and kindly to the Brajshoris, entered the room.

Hajji's eyes lighted up. Rising, he extended his hand, clasping hers tightly as he welcomed her in English and Albanian and then slid effortlessly into a traditional Albanian greeting, lightly touching his temples to hers. He then let go a barrage of questions, asking about her health, about her six month old baby, and whether she had a picture to show him. Grinning, the doctor produced her latest baby picture, over which Hajji made a tremendous fuss, saying how beautiful the baby looked and that she was the spitting image of her mother. The doctor welcomed and acknowledged all this unexpected attention. Then she turned to me. "What energy!" she said.

No words could have more accurately summed up Hajji's character. He was a human dynamo.

Hajji focussed all that energy on the people he was with. He used it to offer friendship, engage his interlocutors, and leave them feeling that they had participated in something interesting, rewarding, and worthwhile.

One evening Anne and I had taken Hajji and Nazife picking raspberries at a self-pick berry farm. There are many such farms around

Ottawa where, for a fee, customers can go into the fields and pick their own fruit or vegetables. On this particular occasion the farmer and his wife were exhausted and quiet at the end of a long day, waiting for the last of the stragglers like us to emerge from the rows and rows of raspberry canes. Setting his basket of berries down for weighing, Hajji immediately engaged the tired couple through an explosion of commentary, half English and half Albanian, on the beauty of the evening, the bountiful harvest of raspberries, the merits and demerits of raspberry picking as a pastime, and the particular advantage of being able to eat a few while on the job. It did not really matter that the details of this eclectic mix of English, Albanian, and charades mostly blew right by the couple like leaves in a sudden swirl of autumn wind. The love of raspberry picking and the offer of friendship were absolutely clear. The two were drawn in by Hajji's energy, and began to participate in the exchange in spite of their fatigue. It was a magic moment of human contact, though it lasted no more than four or five minutes. As we said our goodbyes the farmer was the last to speak. Eyes sparkling, voice energetic and carrying an upbeat lilt, he turned to Hajji and said, "I really enjoyed meeting you. Have a nice evening, and come again."

As we got to know Hajji better, the depth of character behind that unstoppable energy slowly began to emerge. Every incident we experienced with him, and every story he told us of his past, added to our belief that here was an extraordinary man.

Hajji's approach to life in Ottawa was imbued with youthful qualities. One thing that became very clear is that he loved to have fun, and he loved to laugh. When there were no obvious diversions, he would create his own by teasing.

He loved to tease Anne, perhaps because he always got a willing reaction. One thing that always seemed to intrigue him was that Anne often drove the car. Maybe in Kosovo it was unusual to see a woman driving. We would often drive somewhere with Anne and Nazife in the front, and Hajji and me in the back. When we reached our destination, he and I would sprint ahead to the point of interest, and Anne and Nazife would follow along more slowly. He soon developed the habit of joking that he and I would have to watch out that Anne and Nazife did not jump back in the car when we were not looking, and take off, leaving the two of us to make our way home walking, or on the bus.

Anne played along, and soon got into the habit of responding to his ribbing by saying that, yes, she and Nazife could very well take off in the car and go somewhere together, leaving Hajji and me to fend for ourselves. After this kind of good-natured banter had been going on for some weeks, Anne took me to the side. "Look," she said, "one day I am actually going to do it. The joke will be on him. When you and Hajji are off somewhere together, Nazife and I will get back into the car and leave. But don't worry. We won't go far. We'll just be around a corner somewhere, where you will easily find us. I just want to play his game, and make him think he has to walk home. It should be good for a laugh."

It happened when I was least expecting it. Anne and Nazife had dropped Hajji and me off at the supermarket. We would pick up some tea and milk, and they would wait in the car.

When we were in the store, Hajji could not resist the thought of buying some candy, to give to Anne and Nazife as a treat. He carefully picked out two bags of mints, one white and one pink. He would turn this routine stop into a special occasion.

When we returned to the parking lot, the car had disappeared. Hajji's face dropped, and he looked at me for confirmation that it was really true. I played along. I pretended to look for the car, thinking that I might see it in the distance somewhere. Actually, it was nowhere in sight. It really looked as if they had deserted us. "They've gone," I lamented. "They have left us on our own, just like they said they would. We'll have to go home on the bus."

It looked like Hajji had been duped. He was repeating, "Anne, Nazife no here. *Hoop. Autobus.*" He started to look for the bus stop.

I had not spotted the car anywhere, so now I really started to look. We rounded the side of the plaza. There it was, in plain view, but with no one in it. Where could they be, I wondered? Hajji spotted it, too. He grabbed my arm. "OK," he whispered in a conspiratorial tone. "Anne Nazife *hoop*, no *bonbon*." Then he put his finger to his lips, grinned and shook his head, to make sure I knew it was part of the joke.

We approached the car. Anne and Nazife were crouched down, one in front and one in back, where they could not be seen from a distance. They must have been awfully cramped, waiting like that all this time.

We opened the doors to let them out. Hajji feigned anger. "Anne Nazife *hoop*. No *bonbon!*" He looked at me for support.

"No candy for Anne and Nazife," I said in my sternest voice. I wondered how long Hajji would keep up the pretence of anger, but he was already smiling.

"OK *bonbon*." He threw each of them a bag of mints, laughing.

He kept laughing all the way back to the apartment. It was pretty funny, and the joke had been on him.

Of all Hajji's physical characteristics, perhaps the most remarkable, and the most astounding for those who did not know him, was his unusual strength. It was obviously a trait that had helped him cope with a physically demanding life, and it continued to serve him well after his arrival in Ottawa. It was not that he flaunted his strength. On the contrary, he sometimes seemed blissfully unaware of it, as we had earlier discovered as recipients of his crushing bear hugs. Regardless, his strength certainly came in handy during moments of need.

Knowing that Nazife and Hajji liked animals, Theresa and Rose-Aline had the idea of taking them to Omega Park, a little over an hour's drive from Ottawa, near Montebello. Omega Park is a big, natural zoo, and includes an extensive open area where many of the large Canadian mammals like deer, elk, and moose are allowed to roam free in their native habitat. Patrons are allowed to drive their cars through the Park to observe the animals in the wild.

Patrons are encouraged to buy a bag of carrots, to feed some of the animals along the way through their open car windows. There is one important proviso: you are not allowed to get out of your car.

Rose-Aline was driving, with Hajji beside her in the front seat. She had made the rules very clear: no getting out of the car. Within seconds of entering the park, a coyote appeared, casually observing the car from the brush about 100 feet away. Rose-Aline stopped the car for a better look. Before they knew what was happening, Hajji was outside, calling to the coyote, trying to get him to come closer. Rose-Aline and Theresa both hollered at the top of their lungs for him to get back in the car. Hajji complied, but reluctantly, pointing out there was no danger. This was not a wolf, only a coyote. There was no problem. It was a very small animal.

The rules were spelled out again and the safari carried on. They entered the deer area. Hajji was in charge of the bag of carrots. When the deer spotted him brandishing the carrots, they all congregated around his open window. Hajji carefully doled out the carrots, one to each of the deer. He was obviously enjoying this close contact with animals. Soon the carrots were almost all gone.

Rose-Aline drove on. They rounded a bend and came face to face with two huge animals waiting in the middle of the road. She did not know what they were, perhaps moose, or maybe elk. Anyway they were not deer. She stopped, and when the animals saw Hajji holding a carrot out the window, they shuffled around to the side of the car.

Hajji had only one carrot left. Seeing there were two animals, he broke the carrot in two, and offered half to the first animal to approach. The animal grabbed the carrot, downed it in a flash, and asked for more. Hajji was saving the second half for the other animal, so withdrew his hand from the window. The animal bent down and, still eying the last half carrot, was about to stick his head into the car. Hajji raised his right elbow to block the way. KACHOMP! The animal, infuriated at Hajji's resistance, snapped his jaw shut around Hajji's upper arm. Rose-Aline, Theresa, and Nazife all screamed in unison. Hajji reacted instantly. Twisting and jerking, he wrenched his powerful arm out of the marauder's mouth, and threw the last half carrot out the window. Distracted, the animal turned away. Rose-Aline closed the window. There was an instant of silence in the car, and then Hajji started to laugh. It was a good thing, he told them, that the animal had no upper teeth. Otherwise, it would have been a lot harder to get away. As it was, escaping had been no problem for him. Nazife, on the other hand, would have lost her arm.

The rest of the trip through the park went well. Rose-Aline did not stop again.

As we were drawn more and more into the orbit of this fun-loving, energetic, and attentive man, we also noticed the courteous regard and respect offered to him by his fellow Kosovars. This was due partly, we thought, to his age, as age commands respect in traditional Albanian

sleep with no worries

culture. We were soon to see that it was more than age. Hajji had superior judgement, tuned to the needs of his compatriots. They actively sought him out to bring this judgement to bear.

One day as we were having tea, he told us of the events of the previous day. Ismail had come to pick Hajji up in haste, and driven to the home of a mutual friend. The friend had arranged the marriage of his daughter, and the arrangement was in difficulty. Hajji was being called upon to help resolve the dispute.

We knew that arranged marriages were commonplace in traditional Albanian culture. Hajji and Nazife were themselves the product of such an arrangement. Parents traditionally determined who would marry their sons and daughters, and fiancés would often meet for the first time on their wedding day. Although this tradition was rarely followed now, it was far from dead, as the case in question clearly illustrated.

The mutual friend had promised his daughter to a young Kosovar man from Toronto. The young man had made two trips to Ottawa, to finalize the arrangement and meet his bride-to-be. Expectations had been raised, commitments made. But the young lady was protesting, saying she did not want to marry. She wanted to finish her schooling, to prepare for a career. She was not ready to settle down as a housewife and raise a family. And so she was refusing her consent.

Hajji spent the afternoon and evening with the family, talking, discussing, hearing out the arguments on both sides. It was a long and detailed mediation. We can only imagine the considerations that were brought to bear. Eventually an agreement was reached. The daughter would not be required to marry. She would continue her studies, in accordance with her own wishes. The prospective groom would give up his claim, but would be compensated for expenses incurred during the arrangement process. Everyone left the meeting satisfied, or at least in acquiescence. Hajji did not vaunt his role, but clearly he had been instrumental. It had been a duty he had willingly accepted.

It was a curiosity to us how this man, used to being in authority in his family and a leader in his community, would so willingly do our every bidding in relation to the sponsorship, and follow us around town wherever we would lead, even if he did not know exactly where we were going, or for what purpose. Usually we were able to convey the

165

general idea of what was going to happen, but we were not always one hundred per cent successful. There was a lot of scope for confusion.

It was on our very first excursion for "self-pick" fruit and vegetables that the tremendous scope for confusion on a single, insignificant detail became so graphically obvious. Our destination was a popular fruit and vegetable farm just east of the city. We would be picking strawberries.

We were greeted at the barn by a young saleslady, who handed us our empty baskets. Hajji addressed the saleslady. "Eat, eat, *dresnë*?"

"He wants to know if he can eat strawberries out in the field," Anne interpreted.

"Yes, yes, he can eat a few," the saleslady replied.

Hajji seemed satisfied. We joined a bunch of other pickers who were sitting on a large, flat wagon hooked to a tractor, waiting to be driven out to the strawberry patch that was being picked that morning. We waited while a few more pickers climbed up on the wagon. Then a young man emerged from the barn and jumped on the tractor. We chugged and bumped our way down a lane, across fields of young peas, corn and raspberries, past rows and rows of strawberries, and eventually came to a halt beside a smiling young lady in a broad-brimmed hat. "This is Emily," the man on the tractor told us. "She will show you where to pick your berries."

Emily took the pickers in little groups to areas where there were gaps between the people already in the field, and placed them one to a row. Eventually it was our turn. She assigned us four rows, and I could see right away that there were lots of ripe berries. We would not have any trouble filling our baskets.

Hajji touched Emily's sleeve to catch her attention. "Eat. Eat *dresnë*?" he enquired. Anne translated again.

"Sure," Emily responded. "Everybody eats a few as they pick."

We all started picking. I could see that Nazife was going after the berries like her life depended on it. This was not the first time she had picked strawberries. The bottom of her basket was almost covered, and I had not even started.

My gaze shifted over to Hajji. He was picking, too. Not as fast as Nazife, but quite deliberate. I watched a little longer, wondering if he was going to eat some. "It's OK, Hajji. You can eat the strawberries," I called out to him, and then, as if to demonstrate, I took one and popped it in my mouth. He just stared at me, and continued picking. I better get going, I thought, or I will be the last to finish.

I looked over several times to see if Hajji was eating any berries. I never saw him eat one. That's strange, I thought, after all that questioning about whether he could eat berries.

We all finished at about the same time. Nazife's basket was so full I wondered how she would carry it back without losing half her berries. She stuffed one last berry under the basket's handle, eliminating any hope of actually carrying the basket. I could see her looking around to find another spot where she could put one more, without having it immediately fall off.

Hajji was in the process of sitting down cross-legged in between the rows. He had filled his basket, and now he was picking and eating berries one after the other.

I glanced up. The tractor driver had already made another round trip to the barn for more pickers, and now he was sitting there while pickers with full baskets clambered up on the wagon. It looked like he had almost a full load and I guessed he would be leaving soon. I drew Anne's attention to the waiting tractor. If we hurried, we would probably get to it before it left.

"Come on, Hajji," I called out. "It's time to go. The tractor is waiting."

Hajji heard me and looked up, but did not budge. He just kept eating. "Let's go," Anne said. "We'll start off, and he can catch up."

I scooped up Nazife's basket under one arm, taking care to hold it level, and the three of us started off. Every once in a while someone would call back to Hajji, but he pretended not to hear.

The three of us reached the tractor. I carefully placed the baskets on the wagon floor, and helped Nazife up. The tractor driver noticed our dilemma. "You've lost one member of your party," he observed. "We can wait for him, if you want to go and get him."

"I'll get him," Anne offered. She ran back towards Hajji, calling as she went. "Hajji, the tractor is waiting. Come, come. Hurry, hurry."

Hajji stopped eating as Anne approached, but now he was filling a paper cup with strawberries, as fast as he could. As Anne approached, he finally relented, got up, and followed her to the tractor, his basket in one hand and paper cup in the other.

We bounced our way back to the barn. I was surprised to see that we had lost only one or two of Nazife's berries. Hajji and Nazife went to have a cigarette in the shade of a tree. Hajji was still carrying his paper cup half full of berries. Anne and I went with the baskets into the barn to pay for what we had picked.

When we came out of the barn a few minutes later with four baskets of berries, Hajji's eyes opened as wide as saucers. What were we doing with the berries that we had just picked for the farmer? Surely we were not going to keep all those berries? Suddenly we realized why he had been so stubborn about coming back to the barn. He thought we had been picking berries for the farmer, and in return we were being allowed to eat some ourselves while we were out in the field. That explained the paper cup, too. We had rushed him out of the berry patch before he had had time to eat his berries.

Now he understood, and it was all a big joke. We had paid money for the berries, and now they were ours. "Come, come, Hajji," he kept repeating Anne's words in jest. "Hurry, hurry." We laughed and joked about it all the way back to town. We thought he was just being stubborn, and he could not understand why we were not staying to eat a few berries, which after all, was a small enough recompense for doing the farmer's work. It was a good lesson in communication, and had been a really fun afternoon. The two baskets of strawberries the Brajshoris carried up to their apartment turned out to be a bonus that they had not been expecting.

There was something almost spiritual in the way Hajji seemed able to live the moment, and accept it for whatever it brought. As we got to know him better, it became evident that his ability to be accepting and to live the moment was related to his deep faith in God.

It was Hajji's belief in God, more than anything else, that conditioned his existence. As Allah had commanded, he would carry out. We both noticed that Hajji was thoughtful and caring wherever he went. A little girl slipped and fell off her bicycle, and he picked her up. An old man needed help to negotiate his way up an icy ramp, and he rushed to offer support. An overburdened shopper needed help packing groceries in a bag, and he lent a hand. A street person begged on the sidewalk, and he gave a little change. Individually these were all small things. Together, they made a pattern that defined the man. He saw me looking on one day as he dropped twenty-five cents into a beggar's hat. Saying nothing, he pursed his lips, raised his eyebrows slightly, and discreetly pointed an index finger to the sky. It was Allah's command.

Prayer was a major element in Hajji's day. Five times a day he would perform the Muslim washing ceremony to prepare himself for prayer. Soap and towels were needless extras. The procedure, prescribed in detail by tradition, required about five minutes. Hands were washed carefully, three times, taking care to rub between the fingers. The mouth was rinsed with water, the teeth cleaned, and the nose rinsed. Then it was time for the arms, followed by the face, scalp, eyes, ears and back of neck. Lastly came the feet and ankles. Washing finished, everything would be air dried. Only then was the person ready for prayer.

Hajji had been praying five times a day, he told me, since the age of 15. He had never missed his Friday prayers, the most important prayers of the week. It did not matter where he was when it was time to pray. It was not necessary to be in a mosque, or even indoors. Anywhere was fine with God. Though timing was prescribed, there was some flexibility, to allow for the convenience of others or the social necessities of life in a world where not everyone was Muslim.

We came to learn, after a while, that if Hajji had suddenly disappeared from view, he had probably slipped off to pray. He would find some corner, *cul-de-sac*, or wooded hollow where he would be unlikely to disturb or be disturbed, and he would pray. He had some favourite spots. Beside a tree was one, facing East, the tree trunk directly in front of him, a jacket or head scarf laid out on the ground. On top of rocks was another. Sometimes he found his way to the top of rocks so huge that I wondered how he got up. Once I found him praying on a rock in the Rideau River, water coursing by on both sides.

I was curious to know for whom he prayed in these ongoing sessions, and one day I asked. He gave me a solemn look, and started pointing to the people around us: me, Anne, Nazife, and the strangers just beyond. "Everybody," he responded. "Everybody. I pray for everybody. *Crete.* All the people."

His answer did not surprise me. He never spoke ill of anyone. Nor did he criticize other religions or try to convert us to Islam. In his world, everyone was equal, all descendants of Adam and Eve, and everyone deserved love and forgiveness.

One thing that struck us was Hajji's respect for all living things. All animals had a right to live. Of course he had grown up with animals all around him. He was a farmer. Animals provided his livelihood. But his respect went beyond the normal relationship of a farmer to his stock. It was a spiritual thing. We were given firm evidence of this when pigeons inhabited the Brajshoris' balcony for the second time. They had not been invited. They just arrived. The nest had been built and the eggs were laid and hatched. When Hajji showed us the nest with its precious contents, we pretended to scold him for allowing the pigeons to take over his balcony again. We knew that Nazife did not particularly appreciate the mess. Nor would the landlord be sympathetic if he found out. We kidded Hajji and made sweeping motions. Perhaps the nest should be swept away.

No, he replied. He would not do it. The nest must stay. The birds are God's creatures, too, and have a right to raise their young. If the landlord finds out about them, he can sweep them away if he must. But Hajji would have nothing to do with such an action. It was forbidden by God. He would take over the cleaning of the balcony while the pigeons were there, to save Nazife the necessity of all that extra work. But the birds would not be moved.

One of the most important events in the Muslim calendar is the fasting month of Ramadan. For the Brajshoris' first year in Canada, this month coincided with our Christmas season. It was a very special month for the Brajshoris due to two important events. First, Dani had arrived in Canada. Second, in anticipation of *Biram*, the celebration marking the end of Ramadan, the sons who had remained in Germany invited their parents to come and visit. We asked Nazife if she wanted to go with her husband to Germany. She shook her head. She would stay in Ottawa. Dani had just arrived, and she wanted to look after him. Hajji would go alone.

A trip to Germany would be a wonderful opportunity for Hajji to see his sons, two of whom he had not seen for seven years. It was also very timely, as the German authorities had just announced that all Kosovar refugees were to be sent back to Kosovo. That news had been greeted with some consternation in Ottawa. The parents knew that Ali did not want to go, and while Lujlia, Sabri's wife, was keen on being reunited with her family, everyone agreed that conditions in Kosovo were not yet ripe for a return. Destruction was everywhere. There was nowhere to live, the water and power were off more often than on, food was scarce, and there were no jobs. Besides, the countryside had been extensively mined, so it was not safe to walk or play outside.

Notwithstanding everyone's concerns, both the parents and their children seemed resigned to the inevitable. They were all aware of the efficiency of German administrative procedures, which, once decided, would move forward expeditiously with clockwork precision. It seemed likely that Ali and Sabri would be back in Kosovo in a matter of months. Avdi, as a student, would be allowed to stay in Germany.

We began immediately to prepare Hajji for his trip. There was a lot to do, not the least of which was getting him a travel document. A travel document, we learned, is a kind of special passport for residents in Canada who do not yet have Canadian citizenship. Like a passport, it involves a detailed application procedure. We picked up an application form, and went to visit the Brajshoris to get their help in filling it out. When we arrived, Dani met us at the door to let us in. We were pleased to see him, as his busy schedule usually found him away. Besides, he would be able to translate what his father told us.

We were served a coke and then quickly progressed to tea. Hajji knew the real purpose of our visit was to fill out the application for his travel document, and he was as keen as we to get to it. Soon we spread out all the papers on the coffee table. We breezed through the preliminaries concerning Hajji's own name, address and phone number, but Hajji had to pause and think when it came to his father's date of birth. His brow furrowed as he tried to recall. "My father's name was Ram," he said finally. "He died at the age of 104, and that was in 1956." We counted backwards. Ram had been born in 1852. It seemed an extraordinarily long time ago. That made Ram a citizen of the Ottoman Turkish Empire. I recalled that Turkey had ruled Kosovo until the

Turks had been expelled by the Serbs in 1912.

"Kosovo," Hajji continued. "He was born in Kosovo. He owned my farm before me. But when he was young, he spent six years in the Turkish army."

"Did he fight any battles?" I enquired, getting curious.

"No. There was no conflict. It was a time of peace."

I paused, marvelling at the huge span of time accounted for by this sixty-nine-year-old man sitting in front of me together with his one-hundred-and-four-year-old father. Together, their lives had spanned almost a century and a half. What a wealth of history and experience! I wondered what sort of man this Ram had been.

Hajji grinned, as though he were reading my mind, and launched into a story. It was a story about his childhood on the farm, when he was about 13.

"There was a marauding wolf," Hajji began. "A big *ujk*, that was systematically plundering the countryside for miles around. I heard a lot of stories about it, even before it came to our farm. And then finally it struck, killing one of our cows in the pasture on the other side of the ravine. My father seemed unsure about what to do to protect our animals. My older brothers were away, and my father was getting too old to track down the wolf himself.

"I knew exactly what to do," Hajji went on. "I waited that night until everyone had gone to sleep." Hajji tilted his head to the side, closed his eyes, and imitated his father's snoring. "I tiptoed over to the wall brackets where my father kept his gun. I took it down off the brackets, grabbed some ammunition, and sneaked out the door, taking care to close it quietly." Hajji glanced furtively from side to side and pursed his lips, as though seeking to ensure that no one saw him, and then made little walking motions with his hands, joined thumb and forefingers suggesting a light-footed creeping out the door.

"I went immediately to the scene of the crime. The carcass of the dead cow was still there, where the wolf had killed and partly de-voured it. I made a few quick calculations, and climbed a tree to lie in wait. I knew that the *ujk* would come back to finish his meal, and I would be waiting for him."

Hajji got up and demonstrated his stealth, showing us how he climbed a tree and braced himself between the trunk and a large branch, where he could survey the whole area around the dead cow and easily spot the approaching wolf. He raised the imaginary gun to his shoulder and took fictitious aim, clearly telegraphing his intentions.

By this time he had entered body and soul into his story. I knew he had completely forgotten the more mundane purpose of our visit. The application form could wait. We were all transported back in time. Our would-be hero was braced for action in his tree, knowing that there was a job to do and that he was the one to do it.

"I stayed in the tree a long time. At last, just a little before dawn, I spotted the wolf. He approached the cow tentatively, keeping to the trees. I waited until just the right moment to shoot. POW! I hit him in the rump."

Hajji slapped himself in the rump to make the point, and emitted shrill yelping noises while using his hand to illustrate how the animal had run off in circles on three legs, limping badly.

"No *ujk*," he admitted. "*Qen*! I shot a dog!" He burst out laughing. "I couldn't see well in the half light. It looked to me like a wolf. It was a very wolf-like dog. How was I to know?"

Hajji put an imaginary wolf in his left hand, and an imaginary dog in his right, and pretended to balance them out. They were about the same. It was not his fault.

Now our young sharpshooter's biggest worry was what would happen to him. He had shot the neighbour's dog by mistake. He was in big trouble.

Hajji continued his story. "I sneaked back into the house, put the gun away, and went to bed. The next morning, I acted as if nothing had happened.

"For two days everything seemed normal. Then my father's neighbour came to call. Someone had shot and killed his beloved sheep dog, and he was searching for the culprit. Whoever had done it would be brought to justice. They would have to pay for their evil deed, the neighbour assured, quoting an exorbitant price. It was far more than any dog was worth.

"My father invited the neighbour in for tea. I was secretly listening to their conversation from the bedroom. My father consoled the neighbour, agreeing that it was a dastardly act, but at the same time denying any knowledge of who could have been so stupid or so cruel to have done such a thing. He was very convincing. After about two hours the neighbour went home, I am sure not harbouring the least suspicion in my regard.

"After that I really began to wonder if my father knew all along that I had done it, and was just protecting me. It is very possible. That is the kind of man he was. He was very strict with us kids, but he supported us through thick and thin."

Hajji paused wistfully, thinking of his father. "Well," I interjected, taking advantage of the pause to pose a question, "did you ever tell him that you did it?"

"No," he replied. "I never did."

"Did your father ever punish you for anything?" I asked.

Hajji thought for a moment, and then launched into another anecdote. He was about the same age as in the first story, or maybe a little older. In their village they had a well, where everyone went to draw water. Sometimes the villagers left their pails beside the well.

"There was this old woman that none of us kids liked," Hajji recalled. "She used to yell at us for almost anything. One day she left her pail by the well. One of the boys took a nail and punched holes in it. When she came back and saw it, she immediately blamed me. She went straight to my father, and told him I had done it. I told him I was innocent, but he believed her, not me. He said what I had done was inexcusable, and that I must be punished.

"My father was an old man by that time, and walked with two canes." Hajji got up to demonstrate, walking across the living room with two imaginary canes. Then he motioned for Anne to get up, too. He wanted to demonstrate the punishment. He threw one of his imaginary canes to the ground, and grabbed Anne by the arm.

"He had to drop one of his canes in order to hold me. Then he started to whack me across the rump with his other cane. He was old but still strong, and it hurt. Without thinking, I pulled away from his grasp, and ran away." Now Hajji was pretending to be himself as a boy. He jerked his arm violently, as though trying to break from someone's grasp, and then feigned running away with his fingers while emitting a series of fast little whistles to go with the running motion.

Hajji's eyes twinkled with mischievous joviality. He was one of those amazing types who could be imagined almost perfectly as a young boy. "Hajji, I am sure you were a handful. Was that the only time your father hit you?" Anne asked.

"Yes, it was the only time. Anyway, I was getting too big to punish. And I was much stronger than average. By the time I was 16, I could throw a man down with one hand. I got so strong I surprised myself with my own strength. Sometimes I felt so much strength in my hands I really believed I could crush rocks in my fist."

"What about your mother?" I asked, suddenly noticing all the paper spread out on the coffee table and remembering we had a job to do. "Where was she from, and when was she born?"

"Her name was Fazile," Hajji replied. "She was from the village of Majanc. She was my father's second wife. My father had one son, Qerkin, with his first wife. That is why my half brother, Qerkin, was so much older than me. He was 26 when I was born."

"What was your mother like, Hajji?" Anne asked.

"She was a big, strong woman." Hajji brought his two fists up in front of his chest and flexed his muscles. He raised his hand over his head. "She was taller than me, with broad shoulders. She ran the farm and milked the cows until she was 87 years old.

"I guess you could say that she spoiled me. I was the youngest in the family. Her first son, also named Nezir, died as a baby. Then there was Shaban, my brother, who was about eight years older than me. Finally I came along, and they named me Nezir after my brother who had died.

"My mother always told me I was a little trouble maker. She was always looking forward to the day I would be old enough to do my military service. Then when I was 18 and joined the army, she cried."

Talking about his parents had put Hajji in a reflective mood and kindled memories of life on the farm. He loved to tell stories of his early life in Sharban, and he was a gifted storyteller. He liked to make people laugh. Melancholy rarely appeared in any of his tales. It was fun for us to sit and listen. I put down my pen. Filling out the application for his travel document could be finished later.

"When I was a little boy I used to follow my brother Shaban everywhere. One day I stopped to eat some raspberries. I looked up and found myself face-to-face with a rabbit. I don't know who jumped the highest, me or the rabbit. We both turned and ran. I ran all the way back to my house. This is one of my first memories of life on the farm.

"The boys were trained at an early age to look after the sheep and the goats. My older cousin supervised. He was a good teacher, but a very strict disciplinarian. It was like being in the army. One day he got tired of the lackadaisical way my younger cousin and I did the sheep-watching and goat-watching. He had decided that enough was enough. I knew we were in for a severe upbraiding. He was very tough. I was shaking, and my mouth was quivering. I couldn't form my words. When he had finished raking us over the coals, he asked me if I had understood. I wanted to be polite and say, 'Yes, Mr. Smitte, I understand,' but it came out as, 'Yes, Mr. Shit.'"

Hajji looked at us to make sure we had understood, and then made a little motion with his hand to demonstrate discreetly the meaning of what he had said to his cousin. We all burst out laughing, and did not stop for a long time. Even Nazife was laughing, in spite of herself.

"I took off running and never looked back," Hajji sputtered, in between bouts of laughter. "I didn't stop until I reached the next village. I desperately wanted somewhere to hide until my cousin's anger wore off.

"Actually, I later realized that my older cousin was right. My younger cousin and I had a pretty relaxed approach to goat-watching. Sometimes the whole family paid for that. Once our carelessness resulted in several goats being killed by the wolves. My young cousin and I were sent out to survey the damage and count the goats that were left. We counted three times in a kind of haphazard way and got three different numbers. Even with the lowest number, we had one more goat than we started out with before the wolves came along. My cousin broke down laughing. When I could get him to talk, he said, 'These are fine wolves. They bring goats to us, instead of taking them away!'

"A little later we actually did find some dead goats. It was pretty gruesome, but of course by then the wolves were long gone. I went to examine one of the dead goats, and bent over to inspect it closely. Just as I went to turn it over, the goat stood up. I screamed in surprise and jumped about six feet backwards. The goat took off like a shot. He had only been sleeping.

"I finally got tired of taking orders from my older cousin. This was when I was a little older. One day we had a disagreement, and when I turned to run away he reached out with his shepherd's cane and caught me by the ankle. I came down hard, because I was already in full flight when he tripped me. When I got up, I went back, grabbed his cane right out of his hand, and heaved it as far as I could down the slope into the bush. He saw that I had grown too strong to push around. He never tried to give me orders after that."

Hajji bounced up off the couch again to provide another demonstration, first showing how his cousin had extended the cane to trip him up, then showing his reaction, picking up the imaginary cane and hurling it down the hill.

We were captivated by Hajji's stories, and we could tell he loved telling us about his early life in Kosovo. His face came alive when he spoke and his voice pulsated with energy, hands and arms dancing in accompaniment. Even without Dani's translation, there would have been little ambiguity. We were taken with his clear, vivid memory, and his playful demonstrations that transported us back to those eventful moments in another world.

But now Hajji had paused. Talking about his cousins had reminded him of something. His face clouded over somewhat and his mood appeared to change. When he resumed speaking he had a more serious tone.

"When the Second World War started I was about nine or ten years old. The Germans had come and occupied the area. We got used to them, and they never did anything to us. One day my cousin and I were out with the goats, a little distance from the village, when a bunch of planes suddenly appeared. They flew right over the village and started dropping bombs and shooting at a German camp nearby. My cousin and I ran for the nearest ravine and jumped in. We figured we would be safe in there from any stray bullets. After a while the commotion died down, and my cousin said he was going back to the village to see if everything was all right. I said, 'No. Wait here. It's too soon to go out.' But my cousin was already gone, running across the field. He was halfway to the village when the planes suddenly reappeared, out of nowhere. This time the shooting and bombing seemed even worse than before. My cousin was hit. I was sorry I had let him go."

"Did your cousin die?" Anne asked.

"Yes, he died," came the response, simple and unadorned.

"What country did the planes belong to, Hajji?" I asked.

"I don't know. Maybe they were British."

I was surprised by his answer, but then I recalled reading somewhere that in the early years of the war the British had established bases in Albania, from where they supported the remnants of the Serbian army before it was finally destroyed. Maybe they were British planes.

Hajji was recalling other aspects of the war. He started up again. "When I was 12, Shaban decided to join the German army. The Germans were being harassed by Tito's partisans, who were conducting a guerilla campaign. The Germans decided to deal with the guerillas by sending Albanians out after them. Shaban was keen to go, and for some reason, Qerkin sent me with him. We had to walk for a whole day to get to the training camp, but when the German doctor examined me he told me I was too young and sent me away. I went back to Sharban, to help my father on the farm. He was pretty old, and needed my help.

"After the fighting ended a few years later, Shaban came home. My father told him right away to go and join Tito's partisans. 'Now that the Germans are not here,' my father told us, 'the partisans will be coming around to seek revenge.' So Shaban did join the partisans, and my father and I stayed to work the farm. Pretty soon the partisans showed up. They took my father and me out beside the barn and told us to start digging. We were digging our own graves. Fortunately for us, a man from our village who was trusted by the partisans happened to come along. 'What are you doing?' he asked the soldiers. 'They are digging their own graves,' the soldiers replied. 'We are going to shoot them.' 'Why would you want to do that?' the villager asked. 'They are just an old man and a boy. They have done nothing. And this man's other son is a partisan. He is on your side.' After a long discussion, the partisans let us go, and then they went away."

Hajji stopped speaking. His story was over. He had just told us about his own near-death experience in casual, unemotional tones, as though he was describing a trip to the market. What an amazing man, I thought, and what foresight on the part of his father, to send Shaban to join the partisans. If Hajji was a survivor, his old father was his teacher.

We could have sat and listened for hours. Nevertheless we did have work to do and it was urgent. We had only two weeks before he was expected in Germany, and we wanted to be sure we had his travel document before we reserved the flight and paid for his ticket. Hajji found paperwork boring, but when we insisted he co-operated willingly. He knew it was crucial for his trip. We soon had the rest of the application completed, and I finished the required second copy later at home.

The next day I took Hajji to get his passport photos taken. Then we went down the street to the bank, where his friend, Patrick, signed the applications as guarantor. Patrick was in his usual good humour. Hajji took the opportunity to try out a few new English words, and thanked Patrick profusely, gathering him up in a huge bear hug.

I took Hajji home, and rushed over to the Passport Office across the River in Gatineau. I got there just before closing, and luckily there were no lines. The lady at the desk, Bernice, looked through the material I had brought, checking off the required items one by one. When she saw that his father had been born in 1852 as a citizen of the Turkish Empire, she looked up. "This is really unusual," she commented. "I can't remember ever seeing anyone going this far back."

"Yes, I know," I replied. "His father was already 15 years old when Canada became a country. It is so interesting to listen to Mr. Brajshori's stories of life in Kosovo in the early years of the twentieth century. They transport us back to a time and place that is reminiscent of Canada's own Upper Canada Village. All the farm work was done by hand, with ploughs drawn by oxen and hay cut with a scythe. It is hard to believe we have someone in our midst who actually cut hay with a scythe."

I explained how important it was that Hajji go soon to Germany, as his sons could be deported back to Kosovo with little notice. I hoped that Bernice would be able to give Hajji's application priority, under the circumstances.

"Everything seems to be in order," Bernice told me. "And Mr. Brajshori has a good case to be given priority. It will take me about three business days. I will call you when the document is ready."

I thanked Bernice and drove home. Things were falling smoothly into place. It seemed too good to be true.

We took advantage of the next few days to help Hajji and Nazife with some of the more personal aspects of their trip planning. They had told us they wanted Hajji to take gifts to the grandchildren, and they wanted the gifts to be watches. We knew they considered watches to be a very special gift. We decided to scout out the stores to find one where there would be a good selection of moderately priced children's watches. Then we could take Hajji and Nazife shopping, and they would be able to select what they liked best. There were three grandchildren old enough to wear a watch: Muhamet, Fitore, and Safet, Ali's three children.

We spent an afternoon checking out stores in the downtown region. We settled on the Hudson's Bay Company, which had a large selection of watches, including some youthful looking watches that we thought would be particularly suitable.

The next day we went to pick up the Brajshoris to go shopping. We were invited up first, as usual, for a visit. We could see immediately that Hajji was again in an expansive storytelling mood, and we encouraged him. I had been wanting for some time to find out more about his stint in the Yugoslav army, and this was my chance, particularly since Dani was home and could translate for us again.

"I was 18 when I joined the army," Hajji began. "It seemed all right at first. They trained me to be a sniper. Maybe they noticed that I was always on the lookout, always thinking ahead."

Hajji started to laugh. We asked him what was so funny.

"I had to be on the lookout to stay ahead of our officers. They would often try to trick us. It was their method of discipline. One day we were at lunch, but they told us not to start eating until they gave the word. We were all sitting there, just eying our food. I thought something was fishy, that it was a trick, so I cut up my food and got it all ready to eat. When they gave the signal to eat, I ate as fast as I could. After about a minute, they made us stop eating, and sent us back to work. Most of the men had barely started eating, but I was almost finished."

Hajji paused for a moment, but as usual one story had made him think of another. We did not deter him.

"In the army there was a very strong man. He was a sort of champion, who would challenge all comers to wrestle with him, and had never lost a fight. He was bigger and older than I was. I did not know if I could beat him, but anyway I did not like fighting much, so I kept quiet. My philosophy was to mind my own business to avoid attracting attention. That way I was less likely to be disciplined by the officers."

We were trying to picture the scene. Hajji was a big man, six feet tall. For a man of 69 he was in remarkable shape, perhaps weighing just over 200 pounds. Most of his weight was in his upper body – his back, arms and shoulders. His neck looked like it was fastened to his shoulders with steel reinforcing rods. The gentleness of his eyes and the smile lines emanating from their corners was the only thing that gave him away. To us, he was a gentle giant. We wondered how big the other man must have been.

Hajji continued his story. "Without telling me, a friend of mine went boasting to the officers that he had found a man who could beat the champion. The officers said, 'Bring him to us.' When my friend took me to see the officers they just laughed, saying, 'He is just a kid. He will not stand a chance.'

"The next day all the officers and men formed a big circle around the champion and me. I grabbed the champion and threw him down so fast the officers said it must be a mistake, that I must have started too soon before the champion was ready. They said we had to fight again. The second time the champion managed to grab me from behind and spin me around and around, trying to make me dizzy. Then he threw me down, but I was lucky, I landed on my feet. I grabbed the champion and threw him down, and landed myself face-down on his chest. He was so mad at being beaten twice in a row that he bit me as hard as he could in the chest. I still have the scar to prove it."

Hajji paused just long enough to pull up his shirt to show us the scar. Sure enough, there it was, a large mouth-shaped scar just above his left nipple. Hajji's lips parted in a grin, and he started to chuckle from deep inside, a rolling infectious chuckle that soon had us going as well. Everything was a big joke to Hajji.

"Nobody ever challenged me after that," Hajji concluded in an understated manner. "My life was easier. It also attracted the attention of the officers, but in a good way. They decided to send me to Vienna, to officer school."

"When I got to Vienna, I was happy at first. I had an opportunity to get an education and have a lifelong career in the military. Then I started to think about my parents back in Sharban. They were too old to farm alone and needed my help. What could I do? I wanted to do the right thing, and in Albanian culture respecting and helping one's parents is very important.

"After classes I would go into the park to think things through. The first day I was there a Canadian diplomat came along and started to talk with me. We talked about all kinds of things: politics, family life, travel, and the military. Canada sounded like a good country, a lot like Kosovo with forests and mountains, but in some ways even better than Kosovo. He told me that Canada was a democracy, where people were free to live the way they wanted and to vote for whomever they wanted. In Kosovo, Tito had come into power after the war, and communism was being forced on us. My father hated the communists, and so did I. In fact, all the farmers hated the communists because they wanted to take away the farmers' land, to make us live on communal farms.

"I went to the park several times that first week, and my new Canadian friend was almost always there, too. I think he went there every day after his office closed. He asked me if I wanted to go to Canada as an immigrant, and offered to help. The idea of going to a democratic country like Canada appealed to me, but I told him I could not because my parents needed me in Kosovo. My friend only said, 'That's OK. Maybe someday you will change your mind. In the meantime, take this charm as a symbol of our friendship.' I took the charm. It was a little gold clasp. I took it and hid it in my prayer beads. To me it was a symbol not only of friendship, but of democracy. I have treasured that charm and had it with me now for almost fifty years."

With that, Hajji got up and went over to where his prayer beads were hanging on the wall. He brought them over to where we were sitting and pointed to the silk tassel hanging from the centre of the string of beads. Turning the tassel upside down and carefully parting the mass of pink threads, he exposed a tiny gold charm. He took a pen knife from his pocket and cut the threads that bound the charm in place. Then he handed the charm to me.

"This is for you, to keep," Hajji said. "It represents my dream of living in a democratic country. Now that I am in Canada, I don't need it any more. I want you to have it as a symbol of our friendship. This way, the charm has come full circle, from one Canadian to another.

"My only regret is that I did not come to Canada as a young man. There are so many opportunities here. I could have made a good life for Nazife and my children, and had a good career. But it is too late for that now. At least Dani has that opportunity."

I could not believe that Hajji was giving me his treasured possession of fifty years, but I could see in his eyes that he meant it. I took the charm. "Thank you, Hajji. *Falleminderit*," I said. "I will treasure this always, just as you have done." I got up and shook his hand, and gave him an Albanian-style hug. I felt at a loss for words. It meant such a lot to me to have this special gift from this very special man.

As I retreated momentarily into silence, Anne took over the conversation. "So what did you do next, Hajji?" She asked.

"Well, I left Vienna at the end of that first week. I told them my mother and father were sick and needed me. I had decided to stay in Kosovo and settle down on the farm to help my parents.

"When I got back to Kosovo I did see my parents, but then I had to go back to the army for another year, to finish the mandatory two-year term. As soon as the two years were up, I went back to the farm for good, and moved back in with my parents.

"A few years later my parents arranged with Nazife's mother for us to be married. Nazife came to live with us. It was a beautiful place to live and raise a family. Our house was in the family compound, on top of a flat hill. We could see hills and valleys for miles around. Nature was all around us."

"What day were you married?" Anne asked, eager to get a few more details.

Hajji thought for a moment, and then entered into a long exchange in Albanian with Nazife. Finally he turned back to us. "We can't remember the date," he said. "Anyway, that was important then, but it is not important now."

Here was another example of Hajji and Nazife living the moment. It would be unusual for a Canadian couple to forget their wedding anniversary date. For Hajji and Nazife it seemed quite normal. The important thing was that they were married now.

Nazife had taken this slight hiatus in the conversation to slip into the kitchen. Her shuffling of dishes and pots and pans made us suddenly aware that she was about to prepare more food. We looked at our watches and were shocked to see that over an hour had passed since our arrival. We immediately rushed into the kitchen to urge Nazife not to prepare anything. We were supposed to take them shopping for their grandchildren's gifts!

Dani left for work at the restaurant, while the rest of us bundled ourselves off to the Hudson's Bay Company on the edge of the Market. The watch department was large, but we knew exactly where to find the watches suitable for children and teenagers. We led Hajji and Nazife to the appropriate counter.

Hajji looked no more than ten seconds at the watches and turned away, mumbling, "*No mirë, no mirë.*" Then he walked straight over to the adult watches with gold coloured cases and bracelets. "*Mirë, mirë!*" he exclaimed.

Of course, we thought to ourselves, we had forgotten. The Kosovars seemed to have a particular penchant for gold. It is important that the watches be gold.

Hajji and Nazife soon picked out three moderately priced gold watches, but the bracelets were designed for adult arms and were far too large for children. The salesclerk assured us that the bracelets had removable links, so could be adjusted to fit the children's wrists. The watches would still have an adult look, but that did not seem to be of concern to the two grandparents. Hajji went over to pay, and was just about to do so when Nazife approached him with a questioning look. The two entered into an animated exchange. Then Hajji spoke to us. Two more watches were required, one for each of their daughters-in-law.

The clerk soon helped them pick out two beautiful women's watches, quite reasonably priced for quality instruments. It was another demonstration to us of the importance of gift-giving in Albanian culture.

Hajji and Nazife were visibly pleased with all their purchases. We deposited them safely back at their apartment and then drove home ourselves. As we drove we listed off the steps we still had to complete to get Hajji airborne. First, we had to take possession of the travel document. Then we would arrange his flight, flight insurance, and medical insurance. We would ask for Muslim meals on the plane. We would help him change some money into German marks. He would have to communicate his itinerary to his sons in Germany, and we would have to ensure someone would be at the airport to pick him up. He would have to pack. Then we would see him off. It seemed a straightforward plan. We felt good about helping this elderly gentleman with his mini family reunion, and we were getting to know him better. He was becoming a good friend.

Over the next ten days the plan went exactly as we had anticipated. The day before the flight, everything was in order. We would pick up the Brajshoris early the following day, to be sure to arrive at the airport on time.

We were relaxed—a little too relaxed—when we arrived at the Brajshoris' apartment on the day of the flight. When we entered their apartment it was mayhem. Hajji was rushing around trying to get dressed. A huge duffle bag lay in the middle of the living room floor, with articles of clothing, shoes, and sundry articles strewn all around. I picked up the bag, which was already full. It weighed a ton. "What has he got in here?" I asked Dani.

"Oh, he has everything," Dani replied, "but I think it is his prayer mats that make the bag heavy. He has two or three prayer mats in there."

"We must be sure he at least has all the essentials," I proposed, while mentally calculating the activities that had to be squeezed into the remaining time before the plane took off. "Where are his ticket, his travel document, and his money?"

Dani produced a leather satchel with no top closure. It was so full its sides bulged out like a pregnant dog, and bits and pieces were spilling out the top. "His ticket and his travel document are somewhere in here, and his money is in his wallet."

We located the ticket and travel document stuffed inside the satchel. Hajji came over and produced his wallet for us to see, with the German marks tucked inside. "Good," I said. Now we have to finish packing your duffel bag."

"You're not going to fly dressed like that!" Dani broke in. He had been surveying his father's clothing, and finally could not hold back. "Go and put on something dressier."

Hajji was wearing old clothes that were frayed. It was clothing I might have worn myself on a plane, to be comfortable, so I had said nothing. But Dani was right. It would be better if Hajji wore something that made him look like the distinguished gentleman he really was. It might make things easier for him on the plane and in airports when he changed planes. After all, he could not speak English or German.

Hajji obligingly went off to change. "Look," I said, "we'll just have to stuff the rest of his things inside the bag ourselves. We don't have much time. Dani, are the gifts packed yet?"

"I don't know," Dani replied. "I'll have to go and look."

Dani went off to check into the status of the gifts, while Anne and I pushed and shoved and finally secured all Hajji's things inside the duffle bag. I tried to lift it, but it would barely budge.

Dani came back juggling four or five boxes of watches and other assorted containers, which he put down in order to test the weight of the bag. "This won't be any problem for my father," he confirmed.

I thought momentarily of the check-in ladies at the airport, trying to place Hajji's bag on the conveyor belt. We did not have time to split the contents into two bags. Nor did we have any way of checking to see whether our one huge bag came in under the weight limit, which I recalled was 30 kg. We would just have to cross our fingers and hope.

"What about all these watches and other gifts?" Dani was saying. "My Dad forgot to pack the gifts."

Out of the corner of my eye I could see everyone with rather blank expressions, staring at the bulging bags. I suspected I looked about the same. There were no obvious options. Maybe we could just stuff them in the duffle bag, someone offered. We all thought about it, and then rejected the idea. They might get broken, or worse still, stolen.

"I know," Anne lit up. "We'll stop at our place on the way to the airport. We'll pick up a larger carry-on bag with a zippered closure, and put the gifts in there. This open topped satchel is too risky in any case. Something is sure to slip out."

"Good," I said. "Let's get moving. Whatever we do, we can't miss the plane."

Hajji appeared from the bedroom just in time to join us. He was wearing a stunning combination of clothing, including a navy blue vest with a gold watch chain hanging from the watch pocket. His suit coat was the top of a tuxedo someone had given him, and it fit him perfectly.

We whisked him out the door, down the hall, and into the elevator. Dani had already carried the duffle bag to the car. In no time at all the five of us were all inside the car and I started off, confident that we could still make it to the airport, but knowing we had no time to spare.

We had gone no more than two blocks when the sound of worried debate in Albanian began to fill the car. "What is it?" I asked Dani.

"It's my father's glasses. He forgot his glasses. He won't be able to read the Koran. He is very upset."

I made a hurried U-turn and drove back to the apartment. Dani rushed upstairs and down again, carrying the treasured glasses. Hajji was visibly relieved. We started out again, and in almost the exact same spot the debate started off anew.

"This time it's his cane," Dani informed us. "He wants to go back for his cane."

I looked at my watch. "I'm sorry we can't go back for the cane, Hajji," I apologized. "It will make us late. You can buy another cane in Germany if you need to. In the mean time you will just have to walk carefully."

I really was sorry about the cane. Hajji's knee had been bothering him, and, while he could still walk without it, it would have been a help.

We were fortunate in getting through downtown Ottawa without getting caught in the traffic. When we stopped at our apartment, I raced upstairs to get the carry-on bag, and Dani and Hajji transferred the material from the satchel to the new bag on the way to the airport.

At the airport I dropped everyone off at the door to the departure area. By the time I had parked the car, they were all standing just outside the security check. We had just enough time to say a proper goodbye. Hajji gave his usual Albanian bear hug to everyone except Nazife. He shook Nazife's hand. It seemed a rather formal goodbye for someone who had been married forty-three years. Perhaps it has something to do with the religious rules governing marriage, I thought to myself.

The guards allowed me to accompany Hajji through security, so that I could escort him to the flight ramp. Though he had emptied his pockets and taken off his watch, he still set off the alarm. For a moment we were all baffled. Then the security guard noticed Hajji's gold watch chain. It had set off the instruments. The guard checked the chain manually, and let us through.

I asked the ladies at the flight ramp to look after Mr. Brajshori carefully. "He is travelling by himself to Germany and he speaks neither English nor German. He has to change planes in Toronto, and he will need help there. Someone will be meeting him at the airport in Frankfurt, but he may need help finding his bag and going through customs. There is a note in English in his wallet explaining who he is, where he is going, and who is meeting him in Frankfurt. It also says who to contact in Canada if need be."

"Don't worry about anything. We'll see that he gets to his destination. I'll have someone come and escort him to the plane," one of the ladies confirmed.

I said goodbye to Hajji, and then watched as he followed his escort down the ramp. I had a good feeling about this trip. Something was telling me it would be a real success.

While Hajji was away in Germany, the sponsors made a special point of visiting Nazife. They took her out for walks, to museums, and to visit her Albanian friends. On one visit to the Museum of Science and Technology, Anne posed with Nazife in a little two-seater antique roadster, with Nazife at the steering wheel. We blew the photo up on the computer and framed it. Nazife would tell Hajji on his return that she had taken driving lessons, and was now able to drive a car.

When Hajji finally did return, he looked calm and happy. We

asked him whether he liked Germany, and he said, "Germany *mirë* but Canada *shum mirë*. Canada number one." His visits had gone very well. He spent a little time with each of the three sons, which was easy since their three cities – Essen, Oberhausen, and Mulheim – were fairly close together. Hajji was happy to report back to Nazife that all their children and grandchildren were doing well in Germany. They had comfortable, well furnished places to stay and enough food to eat. The children were well dressed, happy and healthy. This was great news and a big worry off their shoulders. Hajji and Nazife were visibly content, and, for a short time at least, the worried talk about deportations to Kosovo was put on hold.

By the time he had returned from Germany, we had known Hajji for almost a year. Our relationship had blossomed beyond mere sponsorship. We thought of how fortunate we were that we had been matched to this unique individual. He was a true mixture of the old and the new. Through him we learned so much about the Balkans, a part of the world we must confess was pretty vague and blurred in our minds. We also gained insight into the Muslim religion, which while superficially different from Christianity, was not different in its fundamental beliefs about loving God and loving your neighbour.

We had seen firsthand how Hajji overcame adversity and accepted present realities, while still remaining positive. He was a survivor who stuck to his principles and was fair in his treatment of all men and all living creatures. He enjoyed life to the maximum, lived the moment and loved a good laugh. He was a robust man who could be as gentle as he was strong. He had the knack of making everyone feel welcome and special, no matter what the circumstances. He had a take-charge personality, and tackled life with all the energy and enthusiasm he could muster. He was a man who turned to religion to guide his actions and explain the mysteries of life. We have met many interesting people over the years, but Hajji, we have to admit, was unequalled. As one of the neighbours in his apartment building said to us once, "This man is special. Everybody likes this guy."

nine

MEETING THE PRIME MINISTER

It was a measure of Hajji's uniqueness that within two and a half years of being forcibly expelled by war from his old country and finding himself plunked down in a new one, he had personally met with the leaders of both.

All the reasoning in the world will tell you that this can not happen. In Kosovo, Hajji had been a farmer and construction worker, hardworking and respected by his peers, but well removed from the social and political elite. In Canada Hajji was a refugee, struggling to adapt to his new country, and speaking little English or French. How does a man in this position find himself chatting over coffee with the President of Kosovo, or being welcomed by the Prime Minister of Canada on Parliament Hill?

Shortly after arriving in Ottawa, Hajji told us the story of his first encounter with Canada's Prime Minister. The Brajshoris, along with other Kosovar refugees, were living temporarily at the Canadian Forces Base, Camp Borden. There they were being oriented to life in their new country and awaiting their assignment to sponsors in various Canadian cities. As a gesture of welcome and goodwill, Canada's Prime Minister, Jean Chrétien, came one day to visit them. Seeing some of the Kosovars engaged in a game of basketball, the Prime Minister decided to join them and was soon out on the court, passing, dribbling, and shooting baskets. All was well, until without warning the Prime

Minister tripped and fell.

Within seconds, Hajji rushed out onto the court, helped the Prime Minister up, and dusted him off. The Prime Minister thanked him, and carried on with his game.

Later, the Prime Minister asked for a private meeting with Hajji, who willingly obliged. They hit it off very well together – so well, in fact, that before the meeting ended, the Prime Minister had invited Hajji to come and visit him in Ottawa.

Hajji liked the Prime Minister, and wanted to take him up on his invitation. So when the time came to choose where to live in Canada, Hajji chose Ottawa.

When he had finished telling his story, Hajji turned to us. Would we help him arrange to visit the Prime Minister? We thought about his request for a moment, and then took the easy way out. It was summer and the Prime Minister was on vacation. A visit to the Prime Minister would have to wait.

We liked the idea of a return visit between Hajji and the Prime Minister, but we were glad the question was put off for the time being. We had no pipeline into the Prime Minister's Office and no notion of how to go about making the arrangements. "Oh, no problem," Anne commented wryly. "I'll just call Jean up and make an appointment." In any event, there were a million and one other priorities that had to be addressed in order to get the Brajshoris settled in to their new country. We put the whole question of a visit with the Prime Minister to the side.

Hajji accepted the decision with good grace, but it was obvious the Prime Minister's invitation to visit was never very far from the top of his mind. He questioned us about where Mr. Chrétien lived and worked, and was keenly interested when we passed his stately residence on Sussex Drive and his offices on Parliament Hill. The first time we passed by the Centre Block of Parliament, with its majestic Peace Tower and stunning gothic revival architecture, he let out a little whistle and shook his head slowly from side to side. "Parliament, parliament," he repeated. "Mirë, mirë."

It was a ritual we were to become used to over coming months. Every time we passed in front of the Parliament, we would hear his little whistle. After a while we became curious. What was so remarkable, we asked him? It's not just the building, he told us, but what it stands for. The Parliament stands for democracy. It is the visual confirmation that Canada is a democratic country.

As the months went by we heard many stories underlining Hajji's lifelong belief in democracy. His distaste for the communist system he had lived under in Yugoslavia was obvious. He had always refused to sign that he was a communist, and had therefore been denied the right to vote. When Tito died and the communist system gradually started to unravel, ethnic rivalries intensified. In Kosovo, the Serbs and the Albanians saw their relationship deteriorate from uneasy coexistence to revengeful persecution. Albanians were in the majority, but had little in the way of civil and human rights. A group of Albanian intellectuals, led by Ibrahim Rugova, a Professor of Literature, established the League for a Democratic Kosovo, the LDK. The LDK espoused democratic principles, and its ultimate objective was independence for Kosovo.

"I became a member of the LDK," Hajji explained to us one day, with Dani translating. "My membership card was in the form of a little booklet, with my photo and an official party seal. I treasured that booklet because it was my way of saying I wanted a more democratic Kosovo. When we were thrown out of Prishtina, I had to leave the booklet behind. If I had been caught with that on me, I would have been jailed or maybe killed. I hid it inside the wall of our apartment. It is probably still there, and maybe some day I will get it back.

"Ibrahim Rugova was the party leader. He told us we could get our rights through non-violent action and help from the international community, and I believed him. We hoped for better conditions for many years, but things just kept getting worse. After a while, we could not even mention the LDK, because it would risk reprisals. Nazife embroidered the initials, LDK, on my headband, but I had to wear it inside out so the initials did not show."

Hajji went into the bedroom and we could hear him rummaging through a drawer. When he came out he was holding a white scarf with "LDK" in large embroidered letters on one end. He showed us how he folded the scarf so the letters would not show, and wrapped the scarf in a band tightly around his Muslim cap.

"This is how I would dress when I went out," Hajji continued.

"Nazife had to be careful when she did the laundry not to hang this scarf outside. We would have had a visit from the police, if they had seen it.

"When the students started to organize their peaceful demonstrations, I knew it was time to act. It was our best hope to improve our conditions and to reclaim our rights to hold good jobs and to speak Albanian with pride. The students accepted me in their marches, even though I was much older. I always went to the front of the march. In one of the early marches we were blocked by a police barricade, so some of the students just stood there holding up the Albanian flag, and the ones in front sat down.

"The next day my photo was in the paper, and there were shots of us on TV. I was sitting there, in front of the flag, with my chin resting on my thumb and my index finger on my cheek. I guess I looked defiant, and, because of the finger on my cheek, I looked thoughtful, too. If they had put a caption under the photo it might have read, 'There has to be a better way.' Anyway the photo became a bit of a rallying call for the Albanians. The students even published it in their yearbook.

"After that the harassment got worse. One of the marches was broken up violently, and many students were arrested. I ran down a side street to escape, but I knew the police had circled the area and would soon find me. Then I thought to myself: I am older than the students, so I will pretend I am just an old man out buying bread. I went into a bakery and bought two loaves and stuck them under my arm. Then I walked right through the police lines as though nothing had happened. They did not even stop me.

"Unfortunately by this time I had developed a reputation, and the police now had my photo from the marches. One day I was sleeping in our bedroom, with the door closed. There was loud knocking at the apartment door and Nazife knew immediately it was the police. Before opening the door, she picked up my cap off the sofa and stuffed it inside her blouse. She opened the door and there were two militiamen standing there, fully armed. It looked like they meant business, and they were looking for me. When they asked where I was, Nazife told them I had gone to pray at the local mosque. She was very calm and they believed her. We heard later that the mosque had been blown up that same day. They probably thought they got me. I was at home all the time, sleeping."

Hajji's stories of civil disobedience and his narrow escapes from the law always amazed us. Now we were seeing that, under pressure, Nazife was just as cool as Hajji. They were willing to risk their lives for democracy and civil rights, but it was a calculated risk. Their fast thinking and sly behaviour had served them well, and helped them extricate themselves from a number of tight spots.

Throughout the early months of the Brajshoris' new life in Canada, Hajji kept asking about the Prime Minister, and whether it was now the appropriate time for his visit. He wanted to tell Mr. Chrétien that Canada was "number one," that Canadians treated them well, and that they liked their new country. It was evident he was not about to forget Mr. Chrétien's invitation. Of course we were unable to make any commitment, but we could see how much it meant to Hajji, and we puzzled over what to do.

Then Anne had an idea. "I'm going to contact the public relations people in the Prime Minister's Office," she said. "We need to see whether they will honour the Prime Minister's invitation. The timing is good, because it is almost one year since the Kosovars came to Canada. Hajji is obviously happy to be in Canada and keen to thank the Prime Minister for helping the refugees. For Mr. Chrétien to meet with Hajji on the anniversary of his arrival would be good public relations. I'll tell them how Hajji always sticks out in a crowd and has an impressive stature. I've got nothing to lose. I'll see what response I get."

Anne called the Prime Minister's Office, explained the purpose of her call, and was put in touch with Bill in Public Relations. Anne went over her story, taking care to point out that it was the Prime Minister who had issued the invitation. "It sounds like a good idea," Bill concluded. "I'll run it up the pole and see what reaction I get. The Prime Minister will be going to Japan soon for the G8 Summit. I may have a chance to raise it with him during the trip."

After the Summit, Bill called back. "The visit is on," he reported. "The Prime Minister has agreed. We won't make a public relations event out of it. The Prime Minister would prefer a private meeting of maybe twenty minutes or so. How many people will be there?"

"There are Mr. and Mrs. Brajshori and their son, Dani. He will be there to translate."

"What about you? Won't you and your husband be coming?"

"Sure, that would be great! And I wanted to ask you, would it be possible to have a picture taken? Mr. Brajshori had one from the earlier meeting in Camp Borden, but it was lost, and I know he would really like to have one."

"I am sure that can be arranged. It will take a couple of weeks to set up the meeting. It will probably be in the Prime Minister's office in the Centre Block. I'll get back to you."

Anne thanked Bill and hung up. After the call she reported excitedly back to me. We shared the good news with the Brajshoris, and then sat back to wait.

Bill never called. Anne waited a month, and then called back, only to find that Bill had changed jobs. Yvonne was her new contact. But by then the Prime Minister's Office was absorbed in new priorities. A fall election was called. We reasoned that the Prime Minister would not have time to meet Hajji during the election campaign. The Liberals were re-elected on November 27, 2000, but the timing did not seem right to pursue an early visit. The Brajshoris' daughter-in-law visited them from Germany, and then we helped them move into a larger, two bedroom apartment, close to the downtown core. Other governmental priorities came up, including the Summit Meeting of heads of state to discuss the Free Trade Area of the Americas in Quebec City in April, 2001. After the Summit, Anne began to communicate more resolutely with Yvonne, but she was absorbed in other things. In fact, she seemed to have forgotten about Mr. Chrétien's invitation to Hajji and the promised visit. Then summer came, and everyone went on vacation. The visit would have to wait until the fall.

In September, while Anne and I were away on a camping trip, Ibrahim Rugova, President of the Democratic League of Kosovo and soon-to-be-elected President of Kosovo, paid a goodwill visit to Canada. In Ottawa he met with the Minister of Foreign Affairs and senior officials of the Department of Foreign Affairs and International Trade and the Canadian International Development Agency. He also met socially with Kosovars at the Chateau Laurier, and Hajji and

Nazife were invited.

As two of the senior members of the Kosovar community in Ottawa, Hajji and Nazife were invited to join Dr. Rugova at his table for coffee. For Hajji, who had worked for democracy all his life, and who had been a member of the LDK since its creation in 1989, it was a great honour. It was wonderful that these two men, who had both worked tirelessly in their own way for democracy in Kosovo, could at last meet for the first time here in Canada.

Dr. Rugova told the Kosovars how grateful he was for Canada's help since 1999 in humanitarian relief, police training, education, health, and mine clearance. He hoped for a continued strong relationship and close ties between Canada and Kosovo in the future.

After the meeting, Hajji and Nazife posed for a photo with Dr. Rugova and the others at their table. The meeting was to become one of their most treasured memories.

If Hajji and Nazife had met with the President of Kosovo, they were still waiting for Hajji's promised return visit to the Prime Minister of Canada. Over a year had gone by since Mr. Chrétien had reconfirmed his invitation to Hajji, via his office staff, and we believed it was time for action. Anne got on the phone again, and was passed to a new contact in the Prime Minister's Office, Danielle. Finally a date was set. It was to be on October 30, 2001, at 3 o'clock. We wondered about going to question period which was from 2:00 to 3:00. We thought the Brajshoris would really enjoy seeing the Prime Minister in action before the visit. Danielle said that would be fine. Our Member of Parliament would also come to meet us and join us for the visit with the Prime Minister. The visit would be in the Prime Minister's office on the third floor of the Centre Block. When we had gone through security we should go to the commissionaire's desk. He would ring the Prime Minister's office and someone would come to meet us.

Hajji was elated when we went over to their apartment to tell them that the visit was on. He had been preparing a long time for this moment, and it meant a lot to him. He began to make up a speech, and he recited it over and over to us in the best English he could muster, punctuated with his usual energetic gestures: "Hello Mr. Chrétien. How are you? Canada is number one. People are good. Food good.

Home good. Everything, *crete*, very, very good. Thank you." After his speech, he would present a personal gift to Mr. Chrétien, in the form of a tiny heart-shaped gold charm.

A few days later, Anne received another call from Danielle in the Prime Minister's Office. Something had come up and our Member of Parliament could not make it on the designated day. She had, however, rescheduled the visit for November 20. Anne noted that this was far from ideal, as the fasting month of Ramadan would begin on November 16. It was decided that we would talk to the Brajshoris about the timing, and that Anne would then get back to Danielle.

The Brajshoris were disappointed the visit was now scheduled to take place on a fasting day, but they decided we should proceed anyway. It was close to the beginning of Ramadan, and they felt they would still be strong enough to handle it.

Anne phoned Danielle to relay their decision. While she had Danielle on the phone, she asked if it would be all right for Hajji to give the Prime Minister his little gift. He really wanted to give something and it would not be big, just a token of thanks. Danielle replied that it was not at all necessary, but if he felt that way she was sure the Prime Minister would accept the gift with pleasure.

When we arrived at the Brajshoris' apartment on November 20 to take them to see the Prime Minister, the air crackled with excitement. People were running around putting the finishing touches on their wardrobes, and chatting back and forth as they moved from room to room. Valerie, Dani's new Canadian girlfriend, had come over to be with Dani for this very special event. She asked if she could come to the meeting with the Prime Minister, but unfortunately we had to tell her no; the arrangements with the Prime Minister's Office were for five people only. She would accompany us as far as Parliament. Hajji recited his speech one last time. Then he asked if they looked good. "*Mirë, shum mirë,*" we replied.

In fact everyone had taken special care to look their best. Hajji wore a dark blue vest and suit over a blue chequered sports shirt. Nazife had on a classic sand coloured sports jacket and blue-grey pantaloons, set off by a light blue polka-dotted headscarf with a longer white silk scarf around her neck to keep out the autumn chills. Dani wore a smart light blue pullover and dark wool slacks.

We walked the short distance to Parliament Hill, the cold autumn wind biting at our faces and driving the occasional snowflake straight at us. It was cold, but not cold enough to chill our spirits. We passed between the ornate stone gateposts and through the black cast iron gate, and entered the parliamentary grounds. The eternal flame, at the entrance to the broad concourse leading to the Centre Block, was burning warmly and as brightly as ever. We made our way towards the Peace Tower, standing sentinel in gothic majesty. The gigantic Canadian flag at its summit stood at attention as we skirted the tower's base and made our way to the visitors' entrance at the ground level. We passed the spot where Hajji had thanked the Mountie more than two years earlier. I wondered if Hajji recalled that event. Now he was about to meet the Prime Minister.

The security clearance for visitors resembled the clearance at an airport, with the agents carefully scrutinizing all the key chains and other objects in our pockets before giving us the go-ahead. We emerged into a lobby, and were directed by the commissionaires to an elevator that would take us up two floors, to the level of the Prime Minster's office. When you get off, they told us, turn right, and carry on until you reach the security barrier.

The security barrier on the third floor looked as though it had been recently improvised, perhaps in response to the recent terrorist attacks in New York. We passed through another metal detector, and were asked to leave our coats. Then we were directed to another security barrier, this one blocking access to the Prime Minister's suite of offices.

The commissionaires quickly verified our identity, and then called ahead, announcing our arrival to Danielle, Anne's contact. Within seconds Danielle appeared, offering a welcoming smile and handshake. Then her expression turned serious. "I'm sorry to say we will not be able to use the Prime Minister's office. He will be giving an interview that will be televised nationally after he sees you, and his office is full of television cameras and floodlights. Unfortunately the boardroom is also in use. There are people waiting to see him in there as well. So I will be putting you in one of our auxiliary offices, just over here beside his office."

With that, she turned and led us to a smallish room whose main item of furniture, apart from a standard office desk and chair, was a seat from the old Montreal Forum, with a dedication on it to Mr. Chrétien. Hockey memorabilia. How Canadian, I thought. "The Prime Minister will join you here, as soon as the Question Period is finished," Danielle told us. "In the meantime, you can wait on the couches outside in the hall, or you can watch the Scrum from the balcony. It's usually pretty interesting."

Danielle took us to the balcony railing just outside the office, where we could look down on the Foyer of the House of Commons where the Scrum, that traditional encounter between ministers and the press, would take place. Then she excused herself and went off to continue her afternoon's work.

Within a moment, Charles, the Prime Minister's Executive Assistant, came over to greet us. Charles welcomed each of us with a warm handshake, and explained again what was about to happen. "The Prime Minister will be joining you soon," he concluded. "Let me know if there is anything else we can do." Then he left us to enjoy the Scrum.

We looked down from the balcony to a beehive of activity. Reporters and technicians swarmed the floor below. Some were positioning floodlights; others were carrying television cameras, and more Parliamentary reporters than I knew existed were hovering around expectantly, microphones in hand, waiting for the Question Period to end and for their prey to emerge from the Commons.

"Look!" Anne exclaimed, drawing our attention to one corner of the Foyer. "There is the staircase we see on television that the Prime Minister runs up after the Scrum."

My eye followed the staircase upwards but my attention was sidetracked by a series of magnificent sculptured stone friezes on the outside of the balcony railing all around the Foyer. They seemed to depict historical events, but there was far too much to take in all at once. My eye drifted upwards to a second band of sculpture at the level of the Foyer ceiling, supported by a series of graceful stone arches reaching up from the balcony railing. I recognized a number of provincial flowers and coats of arms, interspersed with scenes of Canadian industrial activity. Before I had time to identify all the industries, my eyes were drawn to the ceiling, where dozens of magnificent lighted glass panels bathed the Foyer in a gentle glow. The larger panels were octagonal, decorated with roses and *fleurs-de-lis*. The smaller panels, oval, contained maple leaves and a number of other motifs of trade and industry. I tried to take in the whole Foyer at a glance, to get an impression. It was as though Canada was spread out before me, in stone and glass. It was overwhelming.

I turned my attention back to the Foyer floor. The reporters were still waiting for the politicians. I glanced at my watch. It was almost 3:15. The Question Period had gone into overtime, and was still not finished. I wondered what this would mean for our meeting with the Prime Minister. It was going to be rushed for sure, and he had two other events already set up and waiting in his office and in the boardroom. "I hope he still has time for the Brajshoris," Anne opined.

In an instant the Foyer was a blaze of floodlights and the buzzing below us ratcheted up to a pulsating chatter, as ministers were cornered and questions hurled at them from several sources at once. We were too removed to hear the answers, but we knew the government had been under attack on its decision to send soldiers to Afghanistan, on Canada's lack of transport planes for troop airlift, on the adequacy of its ageing Sea King Helicopters, on its new anti-terrorist legislation, on international aid, and on employment insurance, to name but a few of the many issues that we heard about on the news every day. There were several ministers participating in the Scrum that day, so presumably many of these issues were being raised. It was interesting to watch some of the ministers shoot through the Foyer at breakneck speed. Presumably they were not in the mood to field questions from the press.

I was wondering to myself why we had not seen the Prime Minister in the Scrum. By my watch, it was already 3:25. A commotion on the balcony on the far side of the Foyer distracted my attention. I glanced up and saw a man, hustling along behind the arcade with a bevy of handlers in tow. He was walking fast—a man with a purpose—and he was heading our way. "Come on!" I called out. "The Prime Minister is coming. We have to get back to the office right away, or he will beat us to it."

We scurried back to our designated meeting place, and slipped through the door about twenty feet ahead of the Prime Minister.

Hajji stayed outside in the hall to greet him personally. He gave Mr. Chrétien one of his characteristic, robust hugs, and Mr. Chrétien returned it with equal sincerity.

The Prime Minister came into the room and greeted each one of us personally. He started to organize us into a line for a picture, a job which Hajji quickly completed, placing Nazife and Anne beside Mr. Chrétien, then himself at one end of the line, and Dani and me at the other. Mr. Chrétien was bristling with energy, and very focused on the Brajshoris. Anne told him that the Brajshoris were from Kosovo, and he replied, "I know that." He recalled that he had met Mr. Brajshori during the basketball game at Camp Borden, and that Mr. Brajshori had helped him up. He asked if they now lived in Ottawa, and if they liked it here. Anne affirmed that they did. Then he asked if the Brajshoris intended to stay in Canada. Anne said they did, and Mr. Chrétien responded, "Good!"

All this while, as we chatted, the photographer was reeling off shots at a great pace. After six or seven flashes Mr. Chtrétien looked at the photographer and the photographer nodded. Mr. Chrétien prepared to leave, and started shaking our hands. Hajji grasped Mr. Chrétien's hand in both of his, and the two men stood there momentarily, looking each other straight in the eye. Their eyes locked, and I could see that they had truly connected. Then they embraced in a long and sincere hug. The camera flashed again. "He wants to thank you for all you have done for the Kosovar refugees," I heard Anne say. Then Mr. Chrétien was out the door and his aides disappeared down the hall behind him.

We were alone for a moment. Hajji was radiant. His goal had been achieved. We were all glad to see him so happy. I suddenly realized he had not even had time to give the Prime Minister his little gold charm. The reunion had been fast and short, much shorter, I think, than any of us had anticipated. Then Danielle rejoined us, apologizing for the rush, and explained that the photos would be sent to us, enabling us to choose one to be autographed by the Prime Minister.

When we arrived back at the Brajshoris' apartment, they invited us in. Our conversation turned to the events of the day. All of us had been somewhat shocked by the speed of the meeting. Hajji was sorry he had not had time to make his speech or give his gift, but he was quick to understand and accept the special circumstances that had squeezed our visit down to the bare essentials. "The Prime Minister is a busy man," Hajji reasoned. "Anyway," he said, turning to Anne, "I am glad you told him that I liked Canada, and that I wanted to see him and thank him. I heard you tell him that." Then Hajji reached into his pocket and pulled out the heart-shaped charm he had intended to give the Prime Minister. He held it out to Anne. "I would like you to have this. It will remind you of this very special day."

The Prime Minister had made a lasting impression on all of us in a very short a time. We were struck by the man's "presence", by the aura of power around him, by the speed with which he moved, and by his ability to be so focused and present in the moment, when he was rushing from one event to another. The Prime Minister was taller than we expected, a bigger man than we had imagined from watching him on TV. We had all felt very comfortable in his presence, and our chat with him had been easy and informal. We were impressed at how he had been able to establish contact with us, and how he had instantly accepted and returned Hajji's very personal and physical initial greeting in the hallway.

The excitement of being so close to the heart of Parliamentary action had also left its impression. The events and places we had seen – the Scrum, Ministers being interviewed, the Prime Minister with his entourage, the Foyer and its balcony, the stairs used by the Prime Minister and the exit used by Ministers wishing to avoid the Scrum – were all familiar to us, as we had seen them on television hundreds of times. But nothing can quite describe the liveliness, the vitality, and the electric quality of Parliamentary action seen close up, in person. It was absolutely fascinating.

After we left the Brajshoris, Anne and I mulled over all that had transpired. It was obvious that the two men had really connected, a moment of personal feeling and communication achieved largely without words. We thought of the many similarities between these two remarkable men. Both were dynamic, animated individuals, who believed in helping others and in the greater good of the community. Both had a fundamental belief in democratic values and rights. Both had spent their whole life, in very different circumstances and in very different worlds, putting these fundamental beliefs into day-to-day practice.

The photographs arrived a few days later. We had four to choose from. Two were group shots. The others showed the two men saying goodbye. In one, Hajji's face was visible, and his expression epitomized his emotions in that moment of connectedness—a warm expansive smile, a twinkle in the eye, his head cocked playfully to one side, and his hands outstretched and firmly clasping the Prime Minister's hand. It was obvious that he was thrilled to be there. Unfortunately, Mr. Chrétien's back was towards the camera and there was no way of clearly identifying him. We chose one of the group shots instead, and arranged to have it autographed and framed. The caption read: "To the Brajshoris, with my best wishes, Jean Chrétien."

A photograph of the Brajshoris' meeting with Dr. Rugova arrived at about the same time. Hajji and Nazife were standing with Dr. Rugova, Nusret and Shano, behind the table in the Chateau Laurier where they had just had coffee together. We put it in a frame to match the photo with Canada's Prime Minister. Hajji hung the two photographs together in a place of honour over the dining room table.

The two photos are clearly visible from the seating arrangement in the living room. When friends or visitors come to the Brajshoris' apartment, and sit in the place of honour on the long sofa, they are directly facing the cherished pictures. Sooner or later the conversation turns to the photographs. Sometimes a visitor seems perplexed. How did it happen, he asks, that the Brajshoris, in Canada such a short time, have met both the Prime Minister of Canada and the President of Kosovo?

Well, you know Hajji, we respond. Who but him could manage to get such invitations? And then we tell the story.

ten

MECCA

Hajji introduced us to the hajj one day when he saw us looking at a poster-sized photo of the Sacred Mosque in Mecca that was unrolled on his bed. The photo showed the courtyard of the Mosque, with the huge, square structure called the Kaba in the middle and thousands of pilgrims all around. The Kaba, Hajji told us, was originally built by Abraham and his son Ishmael. All Muslims turned toward it when they prayed.

Hajji pointed to the Kaba and described the *tawaf*, an important rite of the hajj in which pilgrims circled the Kaba seven times. Seven was a symbolic number in the Muslim faith, signifying infinity. By passing around the Kaba seven times, the pilgrims confirmed that Allah was at the centre of everything. "*Shtatë, shtatë*, seven, seven," Hajji intoned, tracing out the seven wide circles on the photo.

Hajji drew our attention to a statue in the courtyard a little off to one side. "*Ibrahim*," he told us, and then broke into the story of the sacred water, *zemzem*, that pilgrims cherished and brought back from the hajj.

In the story, Abraham and Hagar, his wife, had found themselves in the middle of a desert wasteland. They were in desperate need of water for their little son, Ishmael. Hagar ran seven times between two hillocks, searching fruitlessly, when the *zemzem* broke forth as an artesian well from beneath the feet of Ishmael.

"*Zemzem, zemzem*," Hajji repeated, demonstrating the benefits of the sacred water by pretending to drink and emitting a satisfied sigh. "Very, very good. One, two, five, seven glasses, no problem. Not too much."

It was at the site of the artesian well that Allah commanded Abraham to build the Kaba, and that Abraham instituted the rites of the hajj, the annual pilgrimage to Mecca for the Muslim faithful. The rites were later confirmed and augmented by Muhammad.

A few days later we noticed that Hajji had taped the photo of the Sacred Mosque to the wall above the spot where he prayed. The photo stayed there a few days and then the tape gave way. "I'll fix that," Anne said as she gathered up the fallen photo and removed the remnants of tape from the wall. The next day we returned with the photo framed and under glass, and hung it permanently in place. That, along with Hajji's prayer beads and a symbolic representation of Allah's name hung centrally on the living room wall, left no doubts that we were in a Muslim home.

As the summer progressed, Hajji talked more and more about the hajj. It became evident that he wanted to go.

Very early on, we had learned from Hajji's neighbour, Ahmed, that Hajji had already been once to Mecca for the hajj. This, indeed, had given him the right to wear the Muslim skull cap and adopt the title "Hajji." As we learned more about Islam, we grew curious about Hajji's trip to Mecca. One day, when Dani was there to translate, we asked Hajji about his experience.

"It was a long trip," he began. "We went by bus, overland. I was 60. It was the year I really learned to read the Koran properly, in Arabic. I had retired, so I had more time. I also had a pension, so my family was supported while I was gone. Even so, it took me a lifetime of savings to provide for the trip. We were gone for a long time, over a month.

"There was a problem with the papers. I had never signed saying I was a communist, so I couldn't get the proper papers. I went anyway, but I had to sneak across some of the borders."

Hajji took a piece of paper and began to trace a trajectory along an imaginary road. "We went through Macedonia, Bulgaria, Turkey, Syria, and Jordan. Most of the time there was no problem at the borders. The officials knew we were pilgrims and just let us through. But one border was very tightly controlled. The brothers knew I did not have the right papers, and they hid me in the back of the bus, underneath some luggage. I was very fortunate not to get caught. We made it through. After that there was no problem.

"We finally entered Saudi Arabia, but we still had a long way to go. We stopped in Medina to see where Muhammad was buried under the green dome of the Prophet's Mosque. Then we carried on to Mecca.

"The high point of my trip was climbing the Mount of Mercy at Arafat, near Mecca, where Muhammad gave his final sermon. There were people all around. Many, many people. We prayed shoulder to shoulder for the forgiveness of our sins. This is called the *wuquf* in Arabic, the standing. I had waited all my life for this moment, and now it was finally happening. I could not believe it, yet I knew it was true."

Hajji paused. His eyes had a far away look, as though he were reliving the moment at Arafat. Then he gathered himself up, took a deep breath, and looked straight at us. When he had done this before, it meant he was going to explain an important religious point.

"Allah watches us throughout our lives. Everything we do is written down." Hajji made writing motions on the palm of his hand, moving from right to left as they do in Arabic, recording the data of day-to-day life. "When our body dies, Allah must weigh the balance of what is written." He cupped both hands and raised them in front of him as though they were the two sides of a balance, and pretended to weigh them carefully to see whether the good actions outweighed the bad.

"If the balance is good, we join Allah in heaven. There we will be reunited with members of our family who have gone before us. There will be no work and no pain. We will eat syrup, milk, and honey. There will be no conflict. Everyone in heaven is equal, and we will all be 33 years old."

Hajji stopped, savouring the peace and beauty of heaven. "Do you think you will go to heaven?" I ventured.

Hajji shrugged his shoulders, raised his eyebrows, and tightened his lips. He pointed upwards. "Allah," he said. "Allah will decide."

When Hajji started talking again, it was about going back to Mecca. He wanted to do the hajj again. This time it would be for his father, who had never in his long life been able to go himself.

Dani explained that this was not unusual, that a pilgrim could dedicate his hajj to a deceased loved one. The loved one would be post-humously blessed and forgiven, as if he had done the hajj himself. He would become a Hajji.

For several weeks we mulled over Hajji's desire for a second hajj. We could not fault his motivation, as he kept repeating that this hajj would be for his father. But how would an elderly man, even one of Hajji's robust stature, survive the rigours of the hajj? We had heard stories of people being injured in the crush of humanity, even killed. And for a man who spoke neither English nor Arabic to go to the hajj alone–? We had a hard time imagining that he would ever find his way. The hajj involved many risks.

In Hajji's mind, however, it became more and more real as the summer wore on. Every time he saw us he mentioned it. He was eager for us to help him with the paperwork, and he pooh-poohed any ques-tions we raised about his getting lost or injured in the crowds. After all, he had been there already, and knew the ropes.

We noticed his bank account was rapidly building up. The Brajshoris were obviously in a saving mode. At this rate, maybe he would have enough money saved by the time of the upcoming hajj in February to fund his trip. At least we could look into it, to see if it was feasible.

We had no idea how to proceed. We made a few phone calls, but were unable to get any leads. We decided to pay a visit to the city's main Mosque. Maybe someone there could help us.

We had often wondered about the Mosque, ever since it had been constructed just to the west of Centretown some years before. It was a substantial, imposing building of red brick, built in a square with a massive central dome. A slim, pointed minaret adorned one of the front corners, but we had never seen or heard anyone calling from it. Perhaps we had just never been there at the right time. On the other hand, maybe it was not used to call people to prayer, out of respect for the neighbours.

We parked in the lot beside the Mosque. Anne waited in the car. We had never seen women go in the front door, and we were not sure that it was allowed. There was another entrance around at the other side, leading to the balcony. That was where the women prayed.

I went up the wide steps and through the door, and found myself in a large vestibule. Shoe racks lined one side, a series of closed doors the other. I instinctively took off my shoes and placed them in one of the little cubby-holes, even though I did not intend to enter the prayer room. My eye fell on a table to one side of the vestibule supporting a carousel full of flyers and brochures. Perhaps I would find some information on the hajj. I spun the carousel and stopped it as soon as I spied the word "hajj." Sure enough, there was a guided pilgrimage being planned for the hajj, leaving from and returning to Ottawa, all expenses included. I folded the flyer and slipped it into my pocket.

Before leaving, I glanced through the open door leading to the main body of the Mosque. To my eye it looked almost empty. There was no one praying at the moment. The floor was covered with dozens of beautiful Persian carpets. At the front were a few straight chairs and what looked like a lectern. I did not go in.

"Hello. Can I help you?" said a voice, right behind me. I spun around, and found myself face to face with a bearded young man in a long white robe, similar to the one Hajji's friend, Ahmed, had often worn. "Oh," I replied, "I was looking at the Mosque and didn't hear you come in. Actually, I am looking for information on the hajj. I took a flyer on the guided pilgrimage. It's for a friend of mine who comes to this Mosque, but who does not speak English."

"You are welcome to the flyer. I believe it is a good guided tour. There is a group that goes from the Mosque every year. It is well organized."

I noticed the young man had a book in one hand. That is probably a Koran, I thought. The young man saw me looking at his book. "Are you a Muslim?"

I replied in the negative.

"Well, it is a good religion. An important feature of Islam is that everyone relates directly to God. There are no priests or other intermediaries. You must find God yourself and listen directly to his word." The man paused to see my reaction, and when I did not react he carried on. "The brothers and I could help you learn about Islam if you wish. I think you will find it very interesting."

I agreed that it was very interesting, and that I was gradually learning about it from my friend. I thanked him for his interest and his offer, and told him I would think about it. Then I excused myself, put on my shoes, and went to join Anne in the car.

We looked over the flyer together in the car. We were encouraged. It was an all-inclusive guided tour, going direct from Ottawa. For the first time, we were beginning to feel that Hajji's dream of going to the hajj for his father might be feasible.

As soon as we got home, I phoned Abdul, the tour organizer. I explained that we were trying to help Mr. Brajshori achieve his wish of going to the hajj, but that since he was an older man who did not speak English, we were concerned about him going alone and wondered if the guided tour would be more suitable.

"I am sure it will be all right," Abdul responded. "The group will leave from Ottawa and come back to Ottawa. There will be someone with him all the time. The brothers are very good about helping older pilgrims, and I will be accompanying the group. We will take care that he does not get lost."

"Should I bring him to see you?" I enquired.

"Wait until next winter, after Ramadan. You can bring him to my office and I will introduce him to some of the brothers. We will help him prepare his visa application for entry to Saudi Arabia, but you will have to ensure he has a valid travel document, proof of immunization, and passport-sized photographs. We will look after everything else: visa, insurance, plane tickets, hotel and bus reservations. It is all part of the package. All Mr. Brajshori will have to do is show up at the airport."

"What about payment?" I asked.

"A small down payment will reserve his place. He can pay the balance when we apply for his visa."

I told Abdul we would send in the down payment to reserve Mr. Brajshori's place, and thanked him for his offer to look after him on the pilgrimage. That offer made all the difference to the feasibility of his going.

When Anne and I gave the Brajshoris the news later that week, Hajji was overwhelmed. He thanked us right then and there with an extra special handshake and hug. We do not know exactly what he said, but it was effusive, and it came from the bottom of his heart.

The autumn went by quickly for us, but for Hajji it must have seemed an eternity. He diligently built up his bank account, taking care to economize wherever possible. Someone from the Mosque heard about his plan to go to the hajj, and gave him a cheque to help fund the trip. Then it was the month of Ramadan, followed shortly by our Christmas. The New Year came and went. I took Hajji for his immunization at the travel medicine clinic, renewed his travel document, and printed up some passport-sized pictures on the computer. It was time to visit Abdul.

Hajji and I had no idea what to expect, as we pulled up in front of a suburban town house. Abdul's office was in the basement of his home. We knocked on the door, and were eventually ushered in by a short, bearded man with a swarthy complexion.

"This is Mr. Brajshori," I said, introducing Hajji, "and I am Dave. Are you Abdul?"

"No, I am his assistant. Abdul is downstairs. Please come down and join us."

Hajji and I took off our shoes and placed them at the end of two rows of shoes already crowding the small vestibule. We followed Abdul's assistant down the stairs, and into Abdul's office. It was a large room, I guessed almost the size of the entire basement. A number of area rugs gave the impression of wall-to-wall carpeting, and I could feel them thick and soft underfoot. At one end of the room, the subdued light of a floor lamp revealed a grouping of easy chairs around a glass coffee table. On the table was a large bowl of apples, oranges, grapes and bananas. Two men were seated there, talking in low tones and sipping coffee from small expresso cups. The other end of the room contained a more traditional grouping of office furniture, awash in bright light from overhead neon lights, and almost hidden under a layer of files and papers. A man sat at a computer monitor entering data that another man read from a file in his hand.

Abdul's assistant motioned us to two wooden chairs on the other side of the computer monitor, and then went to a table where he appeared to be searching out the next file to be processed. We waited. There was a slight lull in the tapping of computer keys and the man entering the data, whom I guessed to be Abdul, told us he would be with us in a moment. Finally the tapping stopped completely and Abdul got up and introduced himself.

I shook Abdul's hand and presented Hajji. The two men embraced in what I had come to assume was a typical Muslim greeting between men, although I never really knew. Maybe it was just Hajji's way. I thought I detected an immediate rapport between the two, and I was pleased. If they got off to a good start, it would make for a more pleasant pilgrimage for Hajji.

Then Abdul presented Hajji to the other men in the room. They spoke to him in a language I did not know, but which I assumed was Arabic. They seemed to be welcoming him. Hajji spoke back in Albanian. I could see they did not understand his words, but his body language as usual was friendly, outgoing, and accepting. Then they all went back to their respective activities, and Abdul handed me a blank visa application. "Please fill this out," he asked, "and we will enter Mr. Brajshori's particulars into the computer from the completed form."

I completed the form, and handed it back to Abdul. He perused it carefully, and checked the other documentation we had brought with us. "This is fine," he said. "There is no need for you to stay. We can finalize this now ourselves, and we will arrange for Mr. Brajshori's visa to Saudi Arabia along with all the others."

These words were music to my ears. I had been dreading the possibility that I would have to get the visa myself. My cousin had been on contract to work in Saudi Arabia, and I knew that the administrative procedures at the Saudi Embassy were demanding and time consuming for individual travellers. Having Hajji go on the guided pilgrimage was turning out to have all kinds of advantages.

Abdul took Hajji by the shoulder and started to chat with him. Surprisingly, Hajji was nodding and seemed to understand. Abdul turned to me. "I told him we will give him his *ihram* on the plane. The *ihram* is the special garment that all men must wear at the hajj. Come, I will show you." He led us to the side of the room, where there were several cartons piled one on top of the other. He took what looked like a shirt box from the top carton, and opened it. Inside were what looked like two pieces of white cotton cloth. I made the linkage immediately. It was the same garment that all the pilgrims were wearing in Hajji's large photo of the Sacred Mosque in Mecca.

Now it was Hajji who was questioning Abdul. Abdul was having a hard time understanding, and I was unable to help. Then Hajji used the word Arafat, and pretended he was climbing. Abdul caught on immediately. "We will be going to the plains of Arafat," he explained. "There we will do the *wuquf*, the standing. But we will not be climbing the Mount of Mercy. There will be too many people. It will be too crowded."

Hajji looked disappointed. Abdul saw the look and tried to be encouraging. "We will be doing all the rites of the hajj. After Arafat, we will go to Mina, where we will cast pebbles at the white pillars. We will be sacrificing a goat. Then we will go to Mecca for the *tawaf*, where we will circle the Kaba seven times. And we will pray at the Station of Abraham and drink the *zemzem*."

Hajji seemed to cheer up a little at the sound of some of the well known hajj names. Abdul turned to me. "The rites of the hajj all have meaning. Casting the pebbles is symbolic of our attempts to cast away evil. The sacrificing of the goat, which is then given to the poor, is symbolic of our willingness to obey God's wishes, in the same way that Abraham was willing to sacrifice his son. The circling of the Kaba implies that all our actions must have God at their centre. The *zemzem*, the miraculous water, is healing and purifying."

It was time to go. Abdul accompanied us upstairs, telling me again not to worry, that they would look after Hajji on the pilgrimage. He shook my hand and embraced Hajji. The two exchanged words in Arabic. Hajji and I went outside, back into the snow.

The few weeks remaining before the departure passed quickly. There was little for us to do, as Abdul was looking after all the travel details. Hajji had his bags prepared well in advance this time. He proudly showed us how he had put all the necessities into one small suitcase and one carry-on bag. He left his carry-on bag half empty. This would give him a place to put his street clothes when the pilgrims put on their *ihram* before landing in Mecca.

On departure day we took Hajji to the airport, giving ourselves plenty of time in case there were unforeseen delays. As we waited outside the security gates, little knots of pilgrims and their families started to form around us. There was much happy talking and laughing as the pilgrims began to introduce themselves to each other. This was a special occasion for everyone. Then it was time to go through security. We said goodbye, and watched Hajji disappear through the security gate with a group of other pilgrims. He would be well looked after.

Nazife, Dani, Anne and I were at the airport two weeks later with many of the same families to welcome the pilgrims home. Some in the welcome parties were carrying flowers or other gifts to give to the returning travellers. Traditionally, the return from the hajj has always been a joyous occasion. The pilgrims began to come out the gate in dribs and drabs, as they all had to pass through customs. We thought that Hajji, who always liked to be in the lead and did everything with exuberance, would be among the first to emerge, but he was not. We witnessed dozens of happy family reunions as the other pilgrims came through the door. After about three-quarters of an hour, the flow of returnees diminished to a trickle, and then there were no more. Hajji was no where to be seen.

Trying to suppress a sinking feeling, I went to the customs office beside the gate to make an enquiry after Hajji. The customs officer told me to wait there, that he would go and investigate. A few minutes later he returned. Yes, there was a tall gentleman of Hajji's description still in the customs area. His suitcase had been lost, and he was trying to make a claim. By this time Dani had joined me, and asked if the officials would like someone to translate. The officer immediately took him up on it, and Dani disappeared into the customs area to help his father make the lost baggage claim.

Minutes later Dani re-emerged triumphantly with his father. Hajji was on a high. He did not even look tired, and after a round of emotional greetings immediately launched into some of his most vivid impressions of the hajj. His life had been in danger two times, he told us, from the crush of the crowds. It was especially at the Black Stone, a relic of the original Kaba built by Abraham, that the relentless push of humanity was the worst. Hajji demonstrated against the airport wall how he had to brace himself and use the immense power of his shoulders and arms to fend off the crush and avoid falling beneath all those people. It was an exciting tale, but not one we had particularly been wanting to hear. We had heard of people dying in the crush before, and in fact the news had told of about thirty deaths earlier in the week, during the throwing of the pebbles. We were all the more grateful that our Hajji was back safe and sound.

Hajji entertained Nazife and Dani with stories all the way home in the car. When we arrived at their apartment, Hajji invited us in. He had just completed a twenty hour flight, but there was no way he wanted to rest. As we went upstairs, I noticed he had two carry-on bags, not just the one he had left with. Immediately on entering the apartment, he unzipped the second bag and pulled out two large plastic bottles of water. *"Zemzem,"* he told us gleefully, and rushed into the kitchen to search for glasses. He poured everyone a drink. *"Zemzem, zemzem,"* he intoned as we all sipped the water. "Very, very good water." It was true. It was refreshingly clean and pure, and had no taste at all. Hajji smiled and nodded at our positive reactions, and eagerly poured us a second glass. I could tell from his body language that sharing this sacred water with us was very important to him. It had been provided miraculously to Hagar and Ishmael by God, and now by bringing us this water Hajji was allowing us to participate in the miracle.

Of all the tales Hajji told us that afternoon, the one that fixed itself most indelibly in my mind was his visit to the tomb of Muhammad in Medina. Apparently, access to the area around the tomb in the Prophet's Mosque is strictly controlled; there is a cordon beyond which pilgrims cannot go. Somehow Hajji convinced the guard to lift the rope to let him enter the sacred ground. There he prayed, I am sure, a prayer he will never forget. If prayers are answered, his father must surely now be in heaven.

We stayed for quite some time that day, but we could see that Hajji's energy was beginning to falter. It was time for us to leave, and for him to get some rest. As we were preparing to go, Hajji had a sudden thought. Groping through the items left in his carry-on, he produced a coloured Polaroid photo. It was himself, standing on the desert plain outside Medina with tents and busses behind him, and mountains in the distance. He was clothed in the simple, white *ihram*, and his hands were clasped in front of his stomach, as though in prayer. "Medina," he said simply. "Medina." His lips parted in a smile. The photo obviously meant a lot to him. One of his dreams had just been realized, and he had a photo that would help him relive his memories as the years passed by.

We went home happy that this man, who had come to mean so much to us, and done so much for so many other people, had been blessed with the opportunity of a second hajj. After a lifetime working and caring for others, one of his personal dreams had been realized. It was telling that even this one personal dream had another person, his father, as its central beneficiary.

eleven

NAZIFE

Nazife's shy, quiet demeanour made her hard to get to know, especially in comparison to her ebullient, outgoing husband.

We reasoned that her quiet way was partly cultural. When she first arrived in Ottawa she would greet us at the door, but then retreat silently into the background, busying herself with cleaning the apartment or preparing food. If men she did not know had entered the room, she would serve them a drink and something to eat, and then leave the room. Business, or socializing with strangers, was Hajji's role.

She was much more relaxed with women. She related well to the female sponsors, and obviously appreciated their attention and companionship. She loved cooking and it was not long before she was teaching her new Canadian friends how to prepare Albanian specialities, by rolling out pasta for a *pite*, or mixing the batter for a *fli*. Her apartment was always spotless. She scrubbed so hard and so often she even began to wear the finish off her coffee table. We often thought how happy we were to have prepared their apartment so diligently before they arrived.

As time went on it became clear she loved to talk, and she would sit beside Anne for long periods of time, telling stories in Albanian. Her voice was soft and gentle, and had a pleasant lilt to it, even though I understood nothing. "What do you and Nazife talk about?" I asked Anne after one particularly long conversation between the two of them, as they sat on a park bench enjoying the splendour of the autumn leaves.

"I haven't the slightest idea," Anne responded, her tone reflecting equal amounts of sadness and frustration. "Nazife goes on and on, explaining things to me in Albanian. But she doesn't use gestures or facial expressions to help get her meaning across, and makes no attempt at charade. Mostly I think she talks about Kosovo and about her children, because I recognize their names. However, she doesn't repeat herself the way Hajji does, to try to make herself understood. She just carries on, as though she were talking to another Kosovar. I wish I knew what she was saying. It would be so nice to get to know her better. But for now, all I can do is smile and nod."

Anne explained to me later that she felt it was good for Nazife to talk, and for her to be there with a listening ear, even if she could not understand. Anne was, in effect, playing the role of a counsellor, listening without offering solutions or passing judgement. It was obvious that Nazife had been through a lot of distress. Having Nazife talk about Kosovo and her children might help to defuse some of her anxiety.

As their first few months in Canada went by, it seemed to us that Nazife was gradually starting to enjoy life again. She had a mischievous, playful sense of humour. We would watch Hajji intentionally provoke her, by spilling tea on the coffee table or dropping crumbs on her clean carpet. Nazife would dutifully clean up the mess, but we could see a smile forming on her lips, and watch as she glided silently behind him, pretending as she passed to swat him over the head. We would laugh, and Hajji would pretend not to notice her playful rebuke. All the while, Nazife would be the consummate hostess, in the time-honoured custom of putting guests first and meeting their every need.

Nazife seemed to live for her outings, and was especially content when we would drive through the countryside. She missed nothing as we drove along past farms and forests, and would engage Hajji in a lively discussion while feeding us a stream of Albanian words for the names of trees, crops, flowers and animals. She seemed to know them all. Nazife loved the outdoors.

In spite of the moments of relaxation and frivolity that we were able to spend with the Brajshoris, we felt a certain unease at the difficulty

Nazife appeared to be experiencing, even after many months, in relating to her new environment. She did not seem to be adapting. She was isolated in her apartment most of the time, and was not trying to learn English. Always talking about Kosovo, her children, and her grandchildren, her voice stressed, she was obviously missing her family. She often looked sad. Dani's arrival provided temporary reprieve. She was happy to cook for him and have him around, but he alone could not fill the void. We began to speculate that Nazife's heart and mind were still in Kosovo, and that her inner desire was to return to live there, with her friends and children, at the earliest possible time.

Nazife's predicament became more and more obvious to us as we watched the experience of her Kosovar friends. They had been attending language school, and were starting to speak English and find jobs. They were "Canadianizing" themselves as fast as possible. Nazife was being left behind.

Nazife's discomfort in her Canadian environment stood in sharp relief to her husband's well-being. By the time the Brajshoris' second summer in Canada had rolled around, Hajji was adapting well. He liked Canada. He was integrating well into his neighbourhood, was trying to learn English, and was acting as though Canada was now his permanent home.

During that second summer, Nazife started to talk constantly about the fact that two of her sons in Germany, Ali and Sabri, would soon be repatriated to Kosovo. Her mood took a turn for the worse. She looked anxious most of the time, was often morose, and complained frequently of headaches and stomach problems. Although she was under doctor's care, and being treated, the symptoms persisted. She began to look pale and lifeless most of the time.

When we asked her what was wrong, she would invariably talk about her grandchildren returning to Kosovo, and her fear that they would not get enough to eat. She seemed to worry incessantly. We watched as Hajji cracked jokes and made efforts to cheer her up, but it was all in vain. If she talked at all, it was about Kosovo, her brothers and sisters, her children, and her grandchildren.

In the autumn, Ali and Sabri and their families were repatriated to Kosovo. It was a gruelling experience. Kosovo was full of shelled and burned out buildings. The impact of the war could still be seen everywhere. "It looks like Chechnya," one of the sons lamented, in disbelief, after he arrived back in Prishtina. It was difficult for them to find a place to live; there was no money for food; there were no jobs. The sons repeatedly called their parents in Canada, complaining of conditions and asking for money to buy food for the children. Hajji and Nazife sent a little, but any spare money they had soon ran out. The parents fretted and agonized, feeling helpless. There was nothing they could do.

Anne and I watched Nazife's mood darken and her health deteriorate. "You know," Anne said to me one day, "Nazife's mind is in constant turmoil. She was thrown out of her home, and was witness directly or indirectly to all kinds of violence and cruelty. She followed her husband to Canada in desperation, not because she wanted to come. Before leaving Kosovo she didn't even have time to say goodbye to her brothers and sisters. She has not even spoken to most of them since the war because they have no telephone. Nazife still thinks one of her sisters is dead, even though in fact she is alive. She reasons that people are telling her the sister is alive just to make her feel better. Now Ali and Sabri have been sent with their families back to Kosovo and are complaining they don't have enough food for their children. Nazife is constantly trying to deal with everything that has happened."

"Yes, and right now most of her anxiety seems to flow from her fear that her grandchildren don't have enough to eat," I observed.

"Any mother would be in agony if she thought her grandchildren were starving and she could do nothing about it. Nazife has simply been subject to too much anxiety, and there are too many unresolved issues. I think she needs closure on these issues. And she can probably get closure only by going back to Kosovo where she can see for herself."

I reflected on Anne's analysis and on Nazife's need for closure. It made sense. Nazife needed to get so many things resolved in her mind, one way or the other, before she could be at peace again. Travel to Kosovo was possible now, and many refugees had already been back on scouting expeditions to see whether it was feasible to take their families back. Some had returned for good, but most, on seeing the dire situation in Kosovo, had opted for a permanent new life in Canada.

"It sounds like a good idea," I told Anne. "But how would she get to Kosovo and back? She can't travel alone."

"I know. But I have an idea. Dani has been talking for a while now about visiting Kosovo. Maybe he would take his mother back for a visit. It could be just what she needs."

After our discussion, we both felt that a trip to Kosovo could help to put some of Nazife's demons to rest, and we were eager to talk to Dani. We did not have to wait long. The next time we visited the Brajshoris, Dani was at home. Nazife had a long, sad face, and eventually started to talk about her children in Kosovo.

"Nazife, would you like to visit your children in Kosovo?" Anne asked. Dani translated.

Nazife's smile just at the thought of seeing her children touched us to the bottoms of our hearts. Anne wasted no time, asking Dani if he would take his mother with him on this trip, if she could arrange it.

Dani saw the tear in his mother's eye and said immediately, "Of course I would take her with me." The project was off the ground.

We knew the Brajshoris had no money to send Nazife to Kosovo. Anne felt the trip was important to Nazife's well-being, and decided to pay for her trip. Dani would pay for his trip out of his own earnings.

The finances were arranged, but we still had to organize the trip and do all the necessary paperwork. We filled out the forms for travel documents and hand-carried them over to the Passport Office. Anne explained the circumstances and the urgency. The official explained that the normal waiting period for a travel document was four months. Given the circumstances, however, and the fact that we had included an explanatory letter, he would put our application on the fast track. Everything should be ready in about one month. He did need approval from Citizenship and Immigration Canada, CIC, but did not expect any problem.

The official's assurances lulled us into a false sense of security. We were not in the least prepared for the phone call Anne got from CIC a few weeks later. It was John, our old friend from the CIC Regional Office. "We're not approving any more return visits to Kosovo by Kosovar refugees," John informed her. "Word has come down from the top. The policy has been reversed on grounds that it is not safe for Kosovar refugees to go to Kosovo."

Anne was completely devastated and told John so. She told John about Nazife and how she would receive the news. We had prepared her for a four month wait to get the papers, but not for this. We had no warning that this could even happen. Nazife had been counting the days and had been knitting night and day, making socks, vests, and toques for her grandchildren. Anne could not imagine what the news would do to Nazife's stress level and her precarious state of health.

John was sympathetic but was holding fast to the new policy. He told Anne that the chances of any change to the new policy were virtually nil.

When Anne got off the phone, she was shocked and in a state of disbelief. The new policy was cruel to Nazife for no valid reason. Surely someone would see the soundness of Nazife's case and would realize that the reversal in policy made no sense. Why was it safe right after the war for refugees to go to Kosovo when Kosovo had no airport and the refugees had to go through Macedonia to get home? Now they could fly directly to Prishtina, so if anything it was safer now than before.

The next day Anne telephoned the responsible officials in the Passport Office and in CIC and went over the case in detail. Then she sent a follow-up letter. Her letter outlined Nazife's bouts of severe stress and stated that her doctor was prepared to confirm this in writing if needed. It explained about Nazife's needing closure on war trauma, seeing for herself who in her family was still alive and having an opportunity to say proper goodbyes. She needed to see where her children, recently returned from Germany, were living, and whether they had enough food. She needed to see her daughter, Xhevrie, who had remained in Kosovo throughout the war, and whom she could not contact because there was no telephone.

Anne agonized for another day over what to do, and decided to call again and speak to more senior officials. She spoke again to officials in CIC, stating that many Kosovars had gone to Kosovo and made it back safely. Why had government officials considered it safe for them to go back for exploratory visits, and now all of a sudden it was considered no longer safe? This made no sense, and she wanted to speak to the person responsible for reversing the policy.

Anne was told it was impossible for her to speak to the responsible person, so she asked to be put in touch with the supervisor. She repeated her questions to the supervisor and made her case again. The supervisor listened but did not budge. Anne said she could not accept the government's negative decision, and would do whatever she had to do to change it. Her next step would probably be to speak to her Member of Parliament.

The next day Anne received another call from John. He had been asked to phone and was doing his best to explain the decision that Nazife could not go to Kosovo. Anne could not believe what was happening. "This is unacceptable and not an option," she told John. "I am not giving up on this."

The following morning the phone rang again. It was the supervisor from CIC. She explained that some of these decisions were very difficult to make, and that there were sometimes exceptions and extenuating circumstances. She had discussed Nazife's case with her boss, and they had reversed their decision. CIC would authorize the travel documents. Nazife could go! The papers could probably be processed in a day or two. There was just one catch. It was already the end of the first week in March, and Nazife and Dani would have to be back in Canada by April 26. We had no time to lose.

The next few days were a flurry of unending activity. Anne put flights on hold for March 15, but prudence dictated that we get the travel documents before confirming and paying for the flights. On Monday, March 12, we literally sat in the Passport Office and waited while they processed the travel documents. With the documents finally in hand, we rushed over to the Brajshoris' apartment and could hardly contain ourselves as we told Dani and Nazife to pack. They would be flying to Kosovo on Thursday. This gave them, and us, just three days to get ready!

We shuttled between the travel agency, the bank, the Austrian Embassy, and the British High Commission. Nazife and Dani's flight to Kosovo included a stop in England, for which they needed a special document. The High Commission faxed it to us. Their return trip to Canada included an overnight stop in Austria. This was more complicated. They would need a visa, but time was short. We personally delivered the application and photographs to the Austrian Embassy, were promised a one-day turn around, and went back the next morning to pick up the visa. Anne's co-ordinating skills were put to the test, as we went right down to the wire, getting all the required authorizations, insurance, tickets and foreign exchange just hours before their departure.

Two days before the flight, we had dropped by the Brajshoris' apartment to bring Dani and Nazife up to date on our progress. To our surprise, there was a party going on. It was a going-away celebration for Dani and Nazife. The apartment was full of Kosovars and a huge meal was in preparation. Dani was fielding telephone calls on his cell phone, while typing an e-mail to his brother in Germany. There was no way we could talk to either Dani or Nazife about trip details. We were just in the way. "Come over to our place tomorrow at 11:00AM," Anne arranged with Dani. "We'll take you through all the plans for the trip in detail, without interruption. You can tell your mother about it later."

The next morning we met Dani and took him through the documents and itinerary. Anne had written everything down clearly for Dani as she knew the amount of information would be overwhelming. She handed him the paper to take with him. "It's a good thing I came over here," Dani joked. "My mother has another house full of guests today. It is an even bigger party than yesterday. Usually these things go on all day and late into the night. And my mother hasn't packed yet. I don't think she will get much sleep tonight."

Sure enough, when we went over on the day of the flight to pick them up, we learned that the party had gone on until 1:00AM Nazife had got up at 5:00AM to pray. Maybe that is when she packed. Anyway her bag – a huge duffle bag that even Dani could hardly manage – was packed. "She has a lot of things in here to take to her family," he commented as he hefted the bag into the car.

We took pictures of our smiling travellers and saw them off at the airport. Then we came back with Hajji alone, kidding him that he would have to survive on his own cooking for six weeks. We knew he was not used to cooking for himself. "No problem. I'll just eat whatever is around," Hajji laughed. "And I can always go to the store and buy things I don't need to cook."

A few weeks later Dani called from Kosovo to let us know how things were going. "We are doing well," he reported. "We have seen all the relatives. Things are difficult here, but everyone has a place to stay and no one is starving. My mother is very happy. She was thrilled to see her sister that she thought was dead. We have spent time with Ali, Sabri, and Xhevrie. The grandchildren are fine, and have enough food. That was a huge relief to my mother. One day I was joking with her. I said, 'You are so happy here, I think I will leave you here and go back alone.' She looked right back at me and said without hesitating, 'I am coming back with you to Canada. And if you go without me, that doesn't matter. I will just get the next plane.'"

When Nazife and Dani came back to Canada a few weeks later, Nazife was a changed person. We could see it in her step, her look, and her voice. Gone were the sad, downcast eyes and the shuffling, tired movements. Nazife had energy in her gestures and life came back into her face. She was happy to have seen her family in Kosovo, but she was also happy to be back in Canada. She began to take an interest in things Canadian. Her health improved, too, and the complaints of stomach problems and headaches were relegated to the past. Shortly after coming home, she began to express interest in learning English. We were thrilled to see her renewed zest for life. Her trip to Kosovo had been everything we had hoped for, and more. It looked like the gremlins of the war had been left behind.

The following winter we held English sessions for Hajji and Nazife, three times a week. Nazife soon began to make progress in English, learning the alphabet, discovering how to print, and mastering words of English vocabulary associated with her day-to-day life in Canada. She was, of course, still unable to talk to us in English. This in no way inhibited her from sharing her thoughts with us in Albanian, and her conversation was becoming lively and animated. She began to regale us with stories, a little like Hajji had been doing right from the beginning.

It was a joy for us to see Nazife start to enjoy life more, but, apart from the few times Dani was available to translate for us, we were none the wiser about what she was saying. Our own progress in Albanian had been slower than the Brajshoris' progress in English! One day Anne and I were musing about our inability to understand Nazife. Several months had gone by, and although we were spending a lot of time with our adopted couple, we really knew very little about Nazife. We suspected that she had told us a lot about herself, her family, her life growing up in Kosovo, her likes and dislikes, and her feelings about being in Canada, but we were totally unable to understand. We could see that Nazife wanted to connect more, and so did we. We were frustrated.

This stood in sharp contrast to our experience with Hajji. Even before he mastered simple English, he had held us spellbound with stories of his early life in Kosovo, punctuated by sounds and gestures and acted out in charade. As he learned English words, he began to throw them into the mix, helping us to understand even better. We loved his stories, and we had quizzed him thoroughly over the years, often using Dani as an interpreter. We felt we really knew Hajji, and wished we could get to know Nazife as well.

"I've got an idea!" Anne proclaimed, as we sifted through our various options. "I'll ask Nazife if she will sit down with me for an interview, and I'll ask Dani if he will translate. I'll organize my questions ahead of time, and I will just encourage Nazife to talk. I'll ask her about her parents, about her childhood in Kosovo, about her wedding, and about raising her family on the farm in Sharban. There are so many things I would like to know, and I feel sure Nazife will be happy to share."

"That's a great idea," I responded. "Could you ask her if she would mind having me sit in? I would love to hear her stories, too." I was as eager as Anne to know Nazife better.

The next time we visited the Brajshoris, we could hardly wait for Dani to come home. When he was there, Anne explained her idea to him and he quickly agreed. Then she put her proposition to Nazife. She agreed, too, without hesitation. We set a date for the interview, and went home, bubbling with anticipation, to prepare the questionnaire.

The day of the interview finally arrived. Anne began the questions. "Where were you born and raised?"

"I was born in Koliq, a little village not far from Sharban," Nazife began. "I had three brothers and three sisters. I was the second child. Only my sister, Hanife, was older. We lived on a farm, much like everybody else, and had an average standard of living."

"Tell me about your father and mother."

"My father was a kind, gentle man. He was very caring, and not at all strict. He was religious, and fulfilled a special function in the community that we called a *Hoxh*, a prayer caller. He used to go to people's houses to lead them in prayer. He also prepared people's bodies after they died, washing them. People used to ask for him before they died. He was well respected by everyone.

"My father died when I was twelve years old. It all started when my uncle ordered my sister, Hanife, to marry a man my father did not like. My father was afraid my uncle would get into trouble if he did not agree to the marriage, and anyway in those days you had to respect the decisions of your older brother. Hanife was beautiful and mature for her age, but she was still very young to marry. I remember my mother finding out that Hanife had to marry. My mother went to the window where she could see Hanife playing with my younger brothers and sisters. She had tears in her eyes and she said, 'How will Hanife survive this marriage? She is so young.'

"The marriage lasted three years. Hanife suffered and was unhappy. Her husband was a thief, and would steal cows, goats and sheep, then cut them up and bring the meat back to Hanife to cook. She would say, 'No, I will not prepare that food, because you stole it. I will not shame my family and my father by cooking that stolen meat.' So her husband would become enraged, and beat her up. It was a terrible way to live.

"After three years Hanife went to my father and told him of the beatings. There were no laws to protect her, so my father told her, 'You don't have to stay with him any more. You can come back home.' So that is what she did.

"When the husband found out where she was, he came over, full of rage, to pick her up. My father just said, 'Go away. She is not here.' The husband was furious with my father for protecting Hanife, and yelled out, 'You won't get away with this. You will see.'

"A few days later my father was called to pray at a neighbour's house. It was summer and he took me and my brother, Ahmet, with him. We were all sitting in the courtyard eating when Hanife's husband suddenly appeared. He pointed a gun at my father and said, 'This is your last meal with your friends.' Then he shot my father right there in front of everybody. My father collapsed in a heap, and I went and threw myself on him and said, 'You can't die. Who will take care of us if you die?' My father pointed a finger upwards, showing Allah. It was the last thing he did. He died in my arms. He was 39 years old."

Nazife paused for a moment, her mind transported back to that appalling event. She seemed to be thinking, but was remarkably composed. Maybe time had helped to heal this wound. Anne broke the silence. "Nazife, can you tell us what life was like for you and your family, after your father died?"

"Hanife never went back to her husband. People were afraid to marry her because of the husband, but years passed, and finally someone did marry her. She had a happier life with her new husband.

"My mother was a tall, strong woman, well respected in the village. She was left with the seven of us to raise all by herself. She never remarried. She was very strict with us, but fair. I was already staying at home, working on the farm, even before my father died. I was responsible for the animals, letting them out to the pasture and then bringing them back. After my father died the work became even harder. With my father gone, my mother needed me at home even more, so I never went to school. All my younger brothers and sisters went, but I was the oldest unmarried child, so my mother asked me to stay home.

"I was never afraid of work. My mother and father never had to ask twice to have a job done, and my work was always done on time. After my father died, I did everything on the farm except cut hay. Sometimes I went to the forest to cut down trees, and then I had to chop the wood. I worked hard and the hours were long. On winter days, I would have to knock the ice off my shoes. I did not have time to go inside to warm up. There were many bright days, but for me they were always dark. Our cousins offered to look after us, but I said no, because we would have had to give them our land. I wanted to keep the land for my brothers. I said to them, 'Even if you were a fire, you would not get me out of this house. We are keeping this land.'

"I would often walk to other villages to buy flour and other basic food. One day in late fall I walked to a village that was a little farther away. The day had started off warm and sunny but at noon the weather changed. It got very cold and windy, and started to snow. I was not dressed for it, but somehow struggled back. When I was just outside the door, I could hear my mother crying and telling my brothers and sisters that I would probably never make it home."

Nazife paused again, her face grim with determination. Growing up on the farm had not been easy. She had done what she had to do, what she felt was right, and she had not shrunk from responsibility. "Sometimes I think I tortured my spirit." The words hung in the air for a few seconds like the toll of a bell in mourning, encapsulating the agony of those far-away days.

Anne broke the silence. "Can you tell us, Nazife, how it was that you got married to Hajji?"

Nazife broke into a big smile. As she started to talk about Hajji, she became animated and energized. These were good memories.

"Hajji's mother went to see one of her relatives who lived right next door to us. I knew she was looking for a wife for her son, because she looked at me and said I was too young. She came back two years later, and this time she asked my mother for permission to marry me to Hajji. My mother said no, that she did not want me to marry into a big family because there would be too much work. I thought the issue was closed, but Hajji's mother did not give up. She went to my mother's nephew, a nephew that my mother really loved. The nephew came and asked my mother, and she at last said yes.

"I never saw Hajji until the wedding day, but I had heard a lot about him. My mother and brothers respected Hajji a lot. One day we were working in the field, and my best friend said to me, 'That guy they are talking about–. I think they will marry you to him.' When someone from Hajji's family came to our house to set the date, I felt embarrassed and shy. I went to my uncle's place, but it didn't help, I still felt embarrassed, so I went back home."

"What was your wedding ceremony like?" Anne queried.

Nazife eagerly recounted her wedding, becoming ever more lively with gestures and demonstrations as the story went on. This had been a happy, exciting event.

"We had a traditional Albanian wedding. Four days before the wedding, the women of the neighbourhood came over to begin the preparations. While they worked they sang songs, laughed and teased me, telling me what I was getting into. The neighbour who was baking the cake wore a man's hat. This is the tradition. Then she put the hat on me. We had a lot of fun, but everyone cried at the end. I cried because I was leaving my family, and the neighbour women cried to see me go. That was normal. An Albanian girl never marries a man from her own village, so a wedding always means that the bride will be leaving her family and friends.

"The day before the wedding all the men of Hajji's village got together with him to celebrate. On the day of the wedding, there was no official marriage ceremony. The verbal agreement to marry and the fact that I went over to Hajji's house meant that we were married. The neighbours all gathered at my house and sang songs and had fun while they waited for me to leave. Meanwhile, Hajji's male relatives came with a beautifully decorated cart to pick me up. The cart was pulled by two oxen, fixed up really nice. On arrival, the lead man in the groom's cortege gave an Albanian flag to my uncle, and he held the flag until we left. I rode in the cart with five or six of my girl friends, and one little boy about five years old. Everyone else walked beside the cart back to the groom's house, where Hajji was waiting for me."

Nazife stood up and started to describe her wedding dress, showing with flowing gestures how it cascaded down around her. She was having fun reminiscing.

"I hand-made my entire wedding outfit myself, in the traditional Albanian style. I made my dress from four metres of white material. It was a full skirt with a big flair and pink needlework decorations. I also made a white blouse and a flashy white vest with needlework in dark pink designs. I had a special gold sash around my waist, and I wore my hair up, circled, with a wide wire headpiece full of flowers at the back.

"My wedding lasted three days. On the first day, only the people we invited were there. They sang, talked, and danced all day. I showed off my work – my knitting and embroidery, all the things I brought to the groom's house. In my case I had a lot: about sixty shirts, bed sheets, long red and black aprons, and head scarves. I made them all myself. Such a collection would be very expensive now.

"On the second day everyone from the neighbourhood came. They brought gifts and wished us good luck. Then they partied for the rest of the day. The third day was just for the family. The celebration was more or less finished.

"For our honeymoon all our friends and neighbours invited us to dinner. It took about three weeks for us to visit everybody. It was a wonderful experience.

"I had fun at my wedding, and was very happy to be married to Hajji. My family made a good choice. In all the surrounding villages there was no one who was more handsome, stronger, or healthier than Hajji. After we were married we were relatively well off. I was able to dress nicely. When people in the village saw us together, they would call us 'Tito and his wife,' because we looked so prosperous and were so well dressed."

Nazife had finished her description of the wedding. She sat quietly for a moment, still beaming. Anne picked up the interview again. "Where did you live after you got married?"

"I moved in with Hajji's family. There were sixteen of us, but not all in the same house. The houses in the Brajshori family compound were arranged in a circle. Each of Hajji's brothers had his own house, and Hajji's mother had a house. I moved in with Hajji and his mother. She took me into a small room, and I expected to open a door and find another large room, but that was it. I was shocked, and thought, 'I have to live and sleep in this small room?'"

Nazife laughed as she recalled the event. It must have been upsetting at the time, but now it just seemed funny. The joke had been on her.

"When I first arrived at the Brajshori compound, I was not sure what to do. So I just got up every morning and worked. Hajji's mother looked after the animals and milked the cows, but after one year she became too old and weak, so I had to take over. My sister-in-law, Shaban's wife, was older and supposed to help, but she refused. I spent the days minding the animals, cleaning the houses, and cooking. I would bake fourteen or fifteen loaves of bread every day. My mother was right. It was a big family and I was working all the time. My sister-in-law was lazy and did hardly any work. She would often go and visit her mother, and I would clean her room while she was away. She was not respected by the family.

"Hajji and his brother took me to see my mother every week. They would stay and help with the farm work. I know my mother was lonely, too. I was glad to have those visits."

"What were the highlights of your child-raising years?"

"I had fun raising my children. That was not work. I made all their clothes, diapers, little outfits, socks and shirts. It was not hard to raise the kids. It was the farm work that was hard. It was hard to take care of the kids and the farm at the same time.

"Sometimes I had to do jobs that were reserved for men. Hajji was working in Prishtina, so he was not around to do them. When I was pregnant with Sabri, I was in the field, ploughing. A neighbour saw me and said, 'Why are you ploughing? That is a man's job.' I was embarrassed, but I did not feel I had a choice.

"One year was full of tragedy. Both Hajji's brothers died, one month apart. In between, my second child, Ramadan, also died. He was just a baby. He was always very healthy, but I was so busy on the farm I did not have time to be always nearby. Some neighbours came when I was not there. They stared at him and cast a spell. I think that is why he died. In Kosovo they say that if a baby is really beautiful he will die. Perhaps that is also why he died. He was truly beautiful.

"Hajji's brother, Shaban, had a dispute with the neighbour over our property line. They could not resolve it peacefully, so the neighbour came up to Shaban while he was chopping wood, and shot him. The shot injured Shaban, but did not kill him. Shaban was a strong man. He grappled with the neighbour, took the gun from him, and shot him in the head, killing him instantly. Shaban died anyway, about one week later, from his injuries.

"Hajji and I took in Shaban's seven children, and raised them as our own. Hajji had to leave his job in Prishtina, and come back to help on the farm. We bought Shaban's children better clothes than the clothes we bought for our own children, to show them they were being treated fairly. When the boys were about twenty years old, they took their share of the land and left us. Hajji was disappointed. He was hoping the boys would stay, help him with the farm, and expand it. Instead they broke the farm up, and left Hajji alone. It was not fair.

After that, Hajji went back to work in Prishtina. The farm by itself was not enough for us to live on."

"What was life like for you under the communists?"

"Because Hajji would not sign that he was a communist, neither Hajji nor I could vote. We were often bothered by the police, even the Albanian police, who were always looking for Hajji. Hajji would escape through the window and run into the forest. He would say, 'They can shoot me and kill me, but they will never take me alive.'"

"When the Serbs took over, what was life like for you then?"

"Because of the Serbs, all my sons had to leave. Eventually only Hajji and I were left. I was very lonely. Only my spirit did not leave me. Sometimes I forgot to eat for three days. Even a new day did not seem like a new day."

The memories welling up inside Nazife were too much for her to bear. She started to sob quietly. Anne sat beside Nazife to comfort her, and then suggested to her that they stop the interview. Nazife shook her head, and would have none of it. She wanted to continue, to get the story out.

"The first to go were Ali and Avdi. A Serb was given Ali's job. The Serbs were taking over all the jobs. Ali had a wife and three children and no way to support them, so he went to Germany to look for work. Avdi helped Ali move to Germany, to help with the children and the luggage. Then when he got there he decided it would be better just to stay there. He had earlier been drafted for the army in Yugoslavia, but had managed to stay out because he was a student. Maybe he thought he had a better chance of finishing medical school in Germany than in Kosovo. I have not seen him now for almost ten years."

Nazife paused, looking thoughtful and sad. Then she continued.

"Dani left later without saying goodbye. The police were beating the students, and his life was in danger. Hajji helped him leave, and then told me. I could not bear to go in Dani's room or make his bed. I worried constantly until he got through the checkpoints, and I knew he was safe in Germany.

"Sabri was the last to go. Sabri and Lujlia and the baby were going to get on the bus, but the police were chasing them and they did not make it. We heard later that the bus crashed en route to Germany, and several people died. We were glad they did not get on that bus. Finally, they did go. Hajji and I were left alone.

"Every time someone left, I couldn't sleep. I would stay close to the phone, to hear if they were all right. When they finally phoned from Germany, I was relieved. I still missed them but I knew they were better off. In Kosovo, they would have been beaten or put in jail. At least I did not have to worry about that.

"My sons had no choice except to leave. People were being forced out of their jobs, schools were being closed, and young men were being taken into the army or killed. They had to leave to survive. Each time one would go, we helped them financially as much as we could."

Nazife had finished the story of her sons' departure, but I could see it had been hard on her. We all sat quietly for a moment. Then Anne began again, reluctantly. "Nazife, is it too difficult for you to talk about the events leading up to your departure from Kosovo? We can stop the interview now, if you like."

Nazife again shook her head. She would go on. When she started speaking again, it was almost with relief, that she could at last tell us her story.

"They were difficult times. Food was hard to find. The police would be in the street and they would tell us, 'Say the Serbs are the greatest and the best in the world.' We had to say it, or we would have had nothing to eat or drink. It was hard for the Serbs, too. One day our Serb neighbour came to me. He had not had food for a few days, and he asked for food for his kids. I gave him some.

"There was a village just outside Prishtina where one of my cousins lived. The village was half Albanian and half Serb. One day my cousin came to visit me, and I asked her why she did not leave that village, since it was half Serb? She said, 'I feel safe in our village. The Serbs told us they would protect us. They told us not to worry.'

"Later when I was in Macedonia, I met someone from that village. All the Albanians had been driven from the village. Several had been killed, including my cousin's son and daughter-in-law. Her son was shot. His wife jumped from the window to help him and she was shot, too. They had been married for only two weeks."

"What were your feelings when you had to leave Prishtina?"

"I did not think we would make it. I was sure we would be killed. Each time we got farther, I did not believe it.

"We left our apartment with only a few clothes, two loaves of bread, a bag of roasted beef, and a bag of milk. When we were in the street, headed for the train station, we met an old friend, a Serb who was now a policeman. He told us how to reach the station safely. He said, 'Don't go that way. You will be stopped by the militia. It is too dangerous. Go the long way, by the railroad tracks. There is no militia down there.' So we went down on the railroad tracks. It was two levels, with us down below and the city above us. We could see people running and soldiers with machine guns, shooting. We saw tanks going by, and we heard explosions. We could see the smoke. Buildings were on fire. We had to hide, to stay out of sight. We finally made it to the station. We caught the last train. We somehow managed to squeeze in.

"When they told us to get off the train, they said, 'Walk that way and watch out for the mines.' We crossed into Macedonia. The first night, we slept under a tree. The next day we stayed in a town. I found a stroller and put our things in it. It was raining, but we had a piece of plastic to put over our heads. Then I met a distant relative, who had a baby. I gave her the stroller so the baby would have somewhere to sleep. By then we had run out of food. When the UN finally came with food, people went crazy, and pushed too much. The police beat them back. Some small or old people were crushed or trampled, but we were all right. Hajji had seen the danger and said, 'We will not go into that crowd.' Finally someone saw us sitting there with no food, and brought us bread.

"We stayed in that town for three or four days. Then a young couple who had been watching us from their house came to help us. They took us in a car to Skopje, where their relatives looked after us. The lady gave us water to wash our hands and face. She had coffee ready for us. She made us feel comfortable, and we were able to forget our problems for a while. I did not have to do any work, or even make my bed.

"Many Macedonians helped the refugees. Many emptied their stores to give us food. But there were too many refugees.

"From Skopje we went to the refugee camp, hoping to go from there to Germany. But when we got there, the German stand was closed. I hated the camp. It was dirty, messy, and smelly. Disgusting. Better than dying, but terrible.

"If I had known what I was going to go through in this world, I would have stayed inside my mother's womb. This world is not for people.

"I was praying to go anywhere, just to get out of that camp. Hajji chose Canada. Even though the Red Cross came three or four times to offer Turkey, Hajji refused. We were headed for Canada."

"Well," Anne asked, "now that you are in Canada, are you happy to be here, or would you have preferred somewhere else?"

"We were offered Turkey, Sweden, Switzerland, and Portugal. Some cousins tried to talk us into going to England. Wherever we would have gone, I am sure we would never have found a place better than here. No one would have taken such care of us. Right from the beginning, I was thankful for the air flight attendants, and for the people who cared for us in Trenton and Borden. These people cooked food for us every day, and they always had a smile on their faces and never made us feel uncomfortable or unwanted. We were also thankful for the sponsors. We did not have to look for an apartment, and the sponsors had food ready for us. We just had to settle in. I did not know about Canada before. I did not think that such a place existed."

"What were your first impressions of Canada?"

"The first thing I noticed was that people were calm. I never saw any conflict. Everything was peaceful. A country is a reflection of its people. Here, people are peaceful and work together. It is much better than in Kosovo.

"In Kosovo, anyone who had a different political belief was killed. One Kosovar we knew studied political science in the United States and went back to Kosovo. Because he had different opinions on politics, he was shot.

"People here were nice to me when I arrived. Even though I was dressed differently, people did not give dirty looks or stare. Instead, they seemed interested in me and where I was from. I am pretty old, so that is why I dress this way. In Kosovo, my kids wanted me to change my style of clothes. Nowadays, even in Kosovo, women wear clothes like the women in Canada. My sister, Hanife, wears normal pants. But

I said to my kids, 'I am going to stick to what I know.'

"When we came here we had only our clothes. Now we have everything we could possibly expect to have. When we went into the apartment it was clean. It looked like no one had lived there before. The fridge was full of food. The salad was all cut up and ready to eat. We had dessert and anything we could think of. When we were in Borden we had our own room, but we had to share the bathroom. When we got to Ottawa, we had our own apartment and our own bathroom. I thought I was in heaven.

"I noticed that in Canada women are different. There are enough jobs here for women to work. They are educated and dressed up and many wear glasses. A lot of women drive.

"I would love to speak English. When I answer the phone, I feel badly. I do not want people to think I am ignoring them, but I cannot speak to them. I feel alone and lonely. Even if I visit the neighbour, I cannot speak to her. I wish I had had a chance to go to school in Kosovo. My youngest brother went to school, finished university, and taught English."

"How do you feel about your day-to-day life here in Canada?"

"Here, life is much better. You can do what you want, when you want. Since I can't speak English, I do not like to go outside by myself. If I got lost or needed to know something, I could not ask anyone. But with someone with me, I am fine. I cannot write, but people are kind. When I first had to write my name, they told me, 'Just make scribbles,' and they would always say it was fine. Now I know how to write my name and it is much easier for me to get by.

"In the apartment everything is different. Here we have all the electricity we need and we never get cut off. I have been in Canada almost four years, and I have never been cut off. In Kosovo, we were always getting cut off. Here we always have hot water. We just have to turn on the tap. Even in the morning there is hot water. In Kosovo the water is very cold in the morning. If we want hot water there we have to heat it. Here we have elevators in every building. Prishtina had hardly any elevators. In Kosovo we cooked with gas. At first it was hard to cook with electricity here in Canada, but I am used to it now. I never got used to the washing machines. They are very different here. Dani does the laundry now, but sometimes I wash things by hand."

"What did your trip to Kosovo mean to you?"

"Before I went, I worried about my kids, my grandchildren and my brothers and sisters. I thought my sister and her family were dead, even though people told me they were alive. I could not make myself believe it, and I could not reach them on the telephone. My thoughts made my days heavy. I always wondered if people in my family had a decent place to live and food to eat.

"When I saw that my sister was alive, and that my grandchildren had food to eat, I was relieved. I felt so much better. That trip took my worries away. It was a whole load off my back.

"People in Kosovo changed a lot. They looked tired and thin. People lost everything and had to start over again. They were so busy. Some were traumatized. My cousin's family was still sad. They had lost their twenty-two year old son, and were having a hard time accepting that he and his wife were no longer there.

"My younger brother, the teacher, could not get out of Kosovo during the war. His whole family was in the forest for weeks. The three kids almost died. They did not know if the kids would survive, but they are better now. His wife was in hospital because she almost went crazy. She couldn't take staying in the forest in the rain.

"Everything was different over there. Our house in Sharban no longer existed. My sister, Emine, saw it being blown up by the Serbs during the war. One minute it was there, and the next minute it was rubble. Even my mother's house was gone. My oldest brother's house was gone, too. He died before the war, and that was the last time I saw his house.

"During the war my brother's son was trying to escape to Macedonia with his father-in-law. They had no identification papers. The police caught them and beat them, and then made them dig their own graves. Luckily, someone came along and said, 'How could you do this?' He gave money to the police and so their lives were saved. The guy that saved them is now in Ottawa.

"When I returned to Kosovo I noticed one thing that was much better than before the war. When we lived there before the war, each time we went out we did not know if we would have a gun at our head. When

I went back for a visit, we knew there would be no gun at our head.

"After our visit, it was hard to leave my family to come back to Canada. I felt down and sad. Everyone cried when I left. Emine, the youngest of my sisters, cried a lot. She always said I was like a mother to her.

"When I came back to Canada, I got over my sadness. I knew my place was in Canada. My health was better, too. The stomach pains went away, and my blood pressure stabilized. My health has been good ever since."

Nazife had been talking for a long time. Now she paused. Dani went into the bedroom and came back with the family photos taken the day they had left Kosovo to come back to Canada. When Nazife saw the photos again she broke into tears. It had been hard to leave her family behind. When she composed herself, she started again. She wanted to talk about Canada.

"I like the way we are here in Canada. I can even accept now that my son will marry someone from here. The only thing missing is my family. Before the war, we lived all right in Kosovo, but here it is even better. For four years we never missed a single thing. In Kosovo, even if we had the money we often missed things because of shortages.

"When we first came here we thought we would some day go back to Kosovo, but we never thought we would feel so welcome. We did not know much about Canadians. We met them, and even though we had different food, clothes, language and religion, nothing was taken away. We were allowed to carry on. We were free to do whatever we wanted. We were accepted for who we were, as we were.

"I would say, just to compare, that it was like coming from there to heaven. Everything seems to be perfect. I was not expecting this to be the case. If someone had said, 'When you go there someone will care for you,' I would not have believed them, because I did not think that kind of care existed. It proves there are all kinds of people. God bless Canada. God bless them for sure."

Nazife had finished her story. The story had left us moved. We felt close to her, and to her family. All the events of her life, and all the episodes of her long marriage to Hajji had been brought together, woven into a beautiful tapestry of human joy and suffering. Anne was sitting beside Nazife now, her arm around Nazife's shoulders, comforting her. We were all exhausted. Even Dani, who had been translating the whole time with care and attention, was beginning to fade. Hajji came home, wafting in like a breath of fresh air, bringing us back to the reality of the present. He made us some tea, providing a running commentary all the while. Then we sat and joked about trivialities.

It was the same as many previous occasions we had shared tea. But it was also different. We were family now. We were accepted and we knew it, feeling a deeper bond that had come to encompass the totality of the Brajshoris' family life.

After the interview we finally knew who Nazife was. Like Hajji, she was a truly amazing person. Deceptively small and gentle, she had been a rock, keeping together her mother's family and then doing the same for Hajji's extended family. She had raised her own children with love and devotion, all the while running a farm that required the hard physical effort we associate with the life of our own Canadian pioneers. After years and years of effort, and just as she was entering her golden years, all that she had worked for was wrenched from her grasp, unmercifully and irrevocably. Deposited in a new land, she had to start from scratch, to put it all together again. Somehow, her strength had seen her through. She had knitted her life together again. She was becoming a Canadian.

It gave us pleasure to see Nazife becoming relaxed and happy in her new land. We watched as the habits, attitudes and little rituals of Canadian culture began to seep slowly into her life. More and more English words were finding their way into her stories. More importantly, she now seemed comfortable. Her eyes sparkled, she moved with energy and confidence, and her little infectious grin always lay lurking just below the surface, waiting to be provoked. It was always a pleasure to visit her. When she had arrived in Canada, Canadians had welcomed her, and now they could be proud to count her as one of their own.

twelve

CITIZENS AT LAST

"*Faleminderit, faleminderit.*" Nazife was thanking us as we helped her on with a freshly ironed chef's jacket and scarf and placed a floppy baker's hat on her head, but her face was looking puzzled.

"I really don't think she has any idea why we are doing this," Anne mused. "We'll have to get Dani to explain."

Dani gently adjusted the baker's hat, straightened the scarf, and spoke in quiet tones to his mother. "We want you to look your best today, *Nëna*. We are dressing you as a chef because today you will be teaching us how to make *fli*. Since you will be in charge, we thought it would be fun if you wore the chef's uniform. Besides, we are going to film the event, and we want you to look like the *professeur*."

Nazife accepted the explanation and was going to respond, but a knock at the door distracted her attention. It was Valerie. Nazife welcomed her warmly, and Hajji leapt up from the sofa to do the same. Valerie had been Dani's steady girlfriend now for three years, and had become one of the family. Valerie was keen to learn how to prepare traditional Albanian dishes, and her expression reflected excited anticipation. "I see you are ready for us this morning," she said as she held Nazife's hand and made a show of looking her up and down. "Let's get started."

Nazife herded her flock into the tiny kitchen while Hajji and I observed from the door, curious as to how the lesson would unfold.

Anne went over the procedures with Dani. "If your mother could explain to us what to do, Valerie and I will do exactly what she says. I will write the recipe down in English as we go. If you have any spare time it would also be nice if you could film the lesson on the video camera. I think your parents would enjoy seeing this later on the TV. This should be a lot of fun."

Nazife bristled with energy as she slipped between bodies from one side of the kitchen to the other, collecting pots, pans, and various ingredients. She had a continuous smile, that disappeared momentarily as she delivered her instructions, and then returned. I could see that she was in her element, and was certainly enjoying her role as chef.

Before I realized what was happening, Nazife had poured flour and milk and a few other ingredients into a saucepan, and Valerie was meticulously stirring them together. Dani was already filming, and could not avoid some good-natured ribbing. "That's not how you stir, Valerie," he teased. "You have to go faster."

Hajji saw his opening. He somehow squeezed his bulky frame into the kitchen and asked Valerie for the spoon. Then he started beating the mixture with a rhythmic wrist action, happy to show off his culinary skills. This amused me, because I knew Hajji prided himself on never doing any cooking. Now in the excitement of the moment, the chef in him was itching to come out. He continued to beat until the mixture was smooth and flowing, like a pancake batter. When he showed no sign of wanting to relinquish the spoon or the space in front of the saucepan, Nazife said something to him affectionately in Albanian and easily pushed him to the side. This was her show, and the lesson was for Anne and Valerie, not for him. Hajji mumbled something about it being time to get ready for prayers, anyway. The other men would soon be waiting for him to issue the call to prayer down in the mosque on the first floor of their building, and he had to go and wash in preparation.

The lesson continued, and soon the women were ready to begin the cooking, the batter for the *fli* in one saucepan, and a mixture of oil and yoghurt in another. Nazife covered the bottom of a large round cake pan with some of the yoghurt mixture, and then demonstrated to her students how to spread the batter in the bottom of the cake pan.

When she had finished, the result looked like a giant daisy with half the petals missing. She whisked the pan away and placed it under the broiler in the oven. In a few minutes it had turned a golden brown.

Nazife retrieved the pan from the oven. Now it was time for Anne to try her skills. Her job was to spread a thin layer of yoghurt mixture over the whole pan, and then to make another daisy-shaped layer of batter, filling in all the spaces that Nazife had left between the petals of the initial layer. But first she had to re-mix the oil and yoghurt emulsion, from which the oil was already starting to separate. As she mixed she hummed a little tune and moved her shoulders up and down in accompaniment. Nazife, seeing her student so obviously enjoying herself, went over to her and gave her a big hug. Then it was time for Anne to lay out the batter. Dani was ready with more ribbing.

"That's not the way to do it, Anne. You're not supposed to move the spoon back and forth. The correct motion is drag and release. Drag and release. Drag and release – ."

"OK Dani, we get it," Valerie interrupted. She was used to Dani's teasing and had developed her own method of retaliation, which she now used in Anne's favour. The pan went quickly back under the broiler, and in a few minutes it was Valerie's turn to make a daisy-shaped pattern, filling in the spaces Anne had left behind so that Nazife's initial daisy would be completely covered.

"You are dripping batter on the counter," Dani chided with a certain amount of satisfaction that he was able to find something wrong with everyone's efforts in turn. "You have to wipe the excess off the spoon on the edge of the saucepan, before you lay out the batter."

"Yes, Dani, you are right," Valerie conceded as she adjusted her technique. "But wait until its your turn. Then we will all get to criticize you."

Soon it was Dani's turn, and then mine. The critiques flew thick and fast around the room, everyone enjoying the light-hearted kidding and no one escaping corrective comments of one kind or another. Nazife joined in the banter, offsetting the negative comments with positive praise and encouragement at every turn. The layers of *fli* gradually built up in the pan, until there were six complete layers, topped off with an ample spreading of the yoghurt mixture. Then the whole concoction went back in the oven for a final bake.

By the time the *fli* was ready, Hajji had returned from prayers. We all sat down to eat. "This is one of the best *fli* I have ever eaten," Dani commented. Valerie and I concurred. It was tender, slightly salty, and tasted of yoghurt. Maybe it tasted so good because we had all worked hard to make it. Hajji started to laugh.

"It took five of you over two hours to make one *fli*," he chortled. "I came back from prayers and made four teas in ten minutes." He was obviously pleased with himself for this deft display of one-upmanship. I could see where Dani got his love of teasing.

As we sat there chatting, Hajji inquired as to the status of their citizenship applications. The three Brajshoris were eager to become Canadians, and it was over a year since we had helped them fill out their application forms. Dani had now been in Canada for over four years, his parents almost five. They were all loving Canada, and they wanted to belong.

"You should be receiving notification of the date of Dani's citizenship test in the mail any day now," Anne offered. "Once Dani has written the text, the three of you will be invited to a ceremony to receive your citizenship cards and certificates all together as a family. It won't be long now."

As seniors, Hajji and Nazife were exempt from the test. Everyone, however, had the same residency requirements. Hajji seemed reassured. I turned to Dani. "Have you started to study for the test, Dani? You will have to know all about Canadian history, the founding peoples, the regions of Canada, levels of government and the procedures for voting in elections."

"Yes, I have started," Dani replied. "I think I already know the required material fairly well."

"If you would like to come over to our apartment some day soon, I would be happy to quiz you on the material," Anne offered. Anne was very familiar with the designated topics. She had already prepared a scrapbook on Canada for the senior Brajshoris, so they could learn about the country and its culture even though they did not have to write the test.

"Yes, I will come over."

"Don't wait too long," Anne cautioned. "You should be receiving your letter from the government any time now."

Given our expectations, we were not too surprised when, a few days later, the phone rang in our apartment.

"Hi, Anne!" It was Dani's voice. "I got the letter. My test is on March 6 at 8:00AM If I pass the test, the citizenship ceremony will be on March 8. We are going to be Canadians!"

"That's wonderful!" Anne shared in Dani's enthusiasm. "Where are you now, at home?"

"No, I picked the mail up on the way out the door, and I'm phoning from school. Now I am going to phone my father, to give him the good news."

We were not surprised to get Dani's call from school. On week days Dani was a full time student at Algonquin College, in his first year of studies in computers and business administration. He was loving it, and working hard. On Sunday, he also found time to work in a bistro as assistant manager and *maître d'* for the brunch.

About ten minutes after Dani's call, the phone rang again.

"Hello, how are you?" It was Hajji's deep, booming voice, and today it was even more upbeat and positive than usual. "Canada citizen!" he went on. "No more *refugjat*! Refugee finish. Come here after for pizza. All sponsors. *Crete*. Food, tea, laughing."

Reading between the lines, I realized that Hajji was inviting all the sponsors to go to his apartment after the citizenship ceremony to celebrate. How in keeping with Hajji's character, I thought. He is always wanting to thank the sponsors for helping him adjust to Canada, and he is always wanting to be with people, to talk and to laugh. He is a consummate extrovert.

"Yes, Hajji," I replied. "Very good. Thank you for the invitation. You are becoming a Canadian. Congratulations!"

A few days later I dropped in unannounced on the Brajshoris. I wanted to see what their thoughts were on Canadian citizenship, now that the date of the ceremony was so close. Luckily, Dani was there, too. He would be able to translate precisely. Without Dani, I would be able to grasp only the gist of what they were saying.

Dani showed me the letter from the government. It was just as he had said. The citizenship ceremony was scheduled for March 8, following successful completion of the test on March 6. Only Dani was convened to the citizenship test. His parents were excused on account of their advancing age. I tried to explain this to Hajji. "Because you are pensioners and over 65, you and Nazife do not have to write the test," I told him.

"It's because we are old and useless," Hajji snorted, and made an exaggerated throwing-away motion with his arm. "We are only good at this point in life to be ignored and left to the side."

"Not at all," I rejoined. "At your age you are experienced and mature and will make excellent citizens. The government gives you the special privilege of going directly to the ceremony, without writing the test."

Hajji did not look convinced, but talk of old age had triggered an idea. He launched into a discourse. "When you get old like we are, there are only two possible paths, the path to heaven and the path to hell." His hands formed an imaginary balance and he weighed the two possibilities, moving one hand up and then the other, and shrugging his shoulders indecisively. "I am still not sure which path I will be taking."

"There is no doubt in my mind, Hajji. You are a good man and will surely go to heaven," I suggested.

Nazife laughed. She had heard all this before. Her eyes sparkled and her lips curled up in a half smile. She had some advice for her husband. "If you want to go to heaven, you had better start to make amends right now," she joked. "Try to think of all the excuses you can."

I could see that Hajji appreciated the humour, but he resumed anyway in a serious tone. "I may have hurt some people in my lifetime. But I never hurt anybody intentionally. Whenever I was challenged, I tried to avoid conflict. If someone shouted at me, I told them I would be happy to discuss their problem if they would be civil. If they persisted, I would just turn and walk away."

This man will make a good Canadian, I thought to myself. I turned to Nazife. "What about you, Nazife, which path will you be taking?"

"In all my life, wherever I was, whatever I had to do, I never hurt anyone." Nazife replied with a seriousness and conviction that left no doubts.

"Yes, that is true," Hajji said softly.

Hajji and Nazife sat quietly for a moment, and then Hajji offered an assessment of his life, in solemn, measured tones. "Maybe I am a good man. If I were not, would God have brought me to Canada? Probably not. I cannot imagine anywhere else that could be as good as Canada. I don't know how I got here, unless God willed it."

It moved me to hear someone talk so highly of my country. Somehow, though, I felt it only fair to suppose that there were many other countries which would be as good. "But Hajji, there are other countries, like Turkey for example, which would have welcomed you. They would have been good, too."

"Yes, maybe," he admitted, "but not this good. My friends who have visited Kosovo recently, and my sons who live there, told me that some Kosovars who went to Turkey did not have a good place to live. It was very difficult for them there."

"It's true," Dani joined in the conversation. "In fact we hear that nowhere in the world were people treated better than in Canada. Refugees who went back to Kosovo exchanged notes about their experiences. That is what they told us."

Hajji stood up and excused himself. It was time for him to call the faithful to prayer. I had been touched to the core by this couple's wisdom and respect for others, and by their kind words for Canadians. I followed Hajji downstairs in the elevator and said goodbye at the mosque door. His eyes reflected the sincerity of his voice as he hugged me and thanked me for coming to visit. "You are very welcome," I responded, not knowing what else to say. "Thank you for having me."

I went home, eager to tell Anne of my encounter.

The weeks flew by, and we drew ever closer to the day of Dani's test. He came to our apartment one day for Anne to help him with his review of the material. He was feeling anxious.

"I don't know how I would tell you if I failed the exam," Dani confided in Anne. "My parents are depending on me to pass, so that we can all get our citizenship on March 8. And the sponsors are depending on me, too, because they are all planning to come over on the 8th to celebrate. What if I fail?"

"You won't fail," Anne concluded when she had taken him over all the topics likely to be on the test. "You know this material cold. Just review it once more the evening before the test, and relax."

From where I was working down the hall, I could hear the review session winding up, so I went out to join them. I had been working on Canadian passport applications for Dani and his parents, and I needed Dani's help to fill them out.

We turned to Dani's first, and I mechanically began to fill in the blanks on the first page. "Single, married, or divorced," I mumbled under my breath, as I automatically checked off "single."

"I can't say that I am single," Dani gulped. "Valerie will be furious. I am not single. I am taken."

"Taken," Anne chuckled. "Cute. I think I like that better than the latest term, partner."

"There is no doubt at all about that, Dani," I replied, smiling, but I could see Dani was confused. "You are definitely taken, but you are not yet married. Until you get married, you are officially single for all the papers you have to fill out. There is no separate category for taken."

With that little confusion cleared up, we breezed through the rest of the forms. We wanted to send them in to the Passport Office as soon as the Brajshoris received their citizenship cards on the day of the ceremony. The passports would be one of the main tangible and practical benefits of Canadian citizenship, and we wanted to have them as soon as possible after they became citizens. Besides, Anne and I were planning a surprise trip for Hajji and Nazife to visit family in Kosovo, and we wanted them to be able to go in the spring, should they so choose.

When March 6 finally arrived, we could hardly wait for Dani to phone us with the results of his test. The telephone rang at 9:35AM Anne pounced on it.

"Anne, I don't know what to do," Dani was saying. "I slept right through the test. Should I go now anyway?"

"You can't fool me with that," Anne countered. "I know you too well to bite. Is the test over? How did you do?"

"I passed. I had all the correct answers except for one. I was not sure of the date that Nunavut became a territory. I put July 1999, and it should have been April 1999. Other than that, I got them all."

"Good. Congratulations! Can you bring your parents and Valerie over here for lunch at 1:00PM? We will celebrate your passing of the exam, and to make it a special occasion. I will be serving Albanian food. I was preparing the *pite* when you called."

Everyone arrived as planned at 1:00PM, and they were in a festive mood. The last hurdle before the citizenship had been successfully cleared. We feasted on Anne's *pite*, along with soup and salad. The *pite*, Anne's first, was a great success. What a mixture of cultures, I thought, as we later sat around the coffee table and poured tea, Albanian style, into little glasses. Sometimes I wondered who had been doing the cultural integration, us or them.

The day of the citizenship ceremony finally arrived. At 10:30AM Dani called. "I am just back from my classes," he said, and I could hear the anticipation in his voice. "What time will you be picking us up?"

"We will come and get you at 12:30," I replied. "Better to be there a little early, rather than a little late."

"Very good. We will be ready."

They were ready. In fact, when we drew up at 12:30, Dani and Nazife were waiting outside their apartment building. They greeted us, and then we all got into the car. I inquired after Hajji.

"He is inside praying, but he will be with us in a moment," Dani explained. Then he handed me a satchel of files. "My parents will need identification at the ceremony, but I am not sure which ones."

We reviewed the letter of invitation to the ceremony, and selected the right papers from the files. Hajji joined us, and immediately the air became charged with excitement. This was a great day for Hajji, and he could not stop talking.

Anne decided to channel some of that energy into preparations for the ceremony. "You will have to take the oath of allegiance," she told him. "Would you read it out loud for us now?"

Hajji read out the oath in his loud, resonating voice, proud to show that he could read. Then it was Nazife's turn. Anne asked her to repeat the oath after her. Nazife's soft little voice was hesitant, but she was determined and stuck with it to the end. We congratulated her. Those were a lot of English words to string together one after the other.

We set off in the car for the ten-minute drive to the citizenship court where they would be sworn in as citizens. I commented that this was a happy day, and that the days of sponsorship were gone forever. Nazife seemed perplexed, and replied with consternation, "If our becoming citizens means you will no longer be our sponsors, we will turn around and go home. We will forget citizenship."

We hastily explained the difference between sponsorship and friendship. This was not the first time the Brajshoris had confused the two, but we hoped it would be the last. Reassured, Nazife laughed. "I just want to be sure you will still come to visit us," she explained.

We arrived at the Regional Office of Citizenship and Immigration Canada and went up the short flight of stairs to the citizenship court's anteroom. It was in fact the very same place we had gathered as sponsors almost five years earlier to hear about the impending arrival of refugees from Kosovo. As we entered the room I had a sense of satisfaction at having come full circle, and having helped three eager new Canadians achieve their dream.

Hajji and Nazife's eyes lighted up as they scanned the room. Theresa, Don and Claire were already there. They all received a heartfelt greeting from our three Canadians-to-be. Theresa explained that Anne M. was waiting outside in her car while her little grandson had a nap. She and Travis would come in just in time for the ceremony. Rose-Aline was the only sponsor not able to be present. She was on a winter holiday in Florida. This had all been carefully explained to the Brajshoris, as we knew they would be looking for her, too.

As we waited, the room gradually filled up, and soon there was standing room only. There was a lot of excited chatter as people waited in anticipation. Finally two officials came and explained what was about to happen: citizenship applicants would be registered, family by family, and would take a seat in the court room. When everyone had been registered, guests would be invited to join them, and the ceremony would begin.

It seemed a serious affair. People were processed quietly and took their seats in the court. When guests were finally invited in, we were directed to sit in the two side sections. Citizenship applicants were waiting quietly, almost apprehensively, in their places in the centre section. A kind of hush enveloped the room, broken only by whispers and muffled talk. No one knew quite what to expect, and the hush was even more pronounced as the judge entered the room.

The judge, an attractive woman with stylish, light brown hair, did her best to put her charges at ease by flashing a welcoming smile around the room. The formality of the occasion, however, combined with her fulsome black judge's gown and the imposing lectern on her desk, had an overall intimidating effect, and the room remained hushed, people waiting for the judge to speak. "Hello, *bonjour!*" she chimed, but her friendly greeting was met with only a few indistinct "hellos." She looked at us with an expression of mock disbelief, and then said encouragingly, "Let's try that again! Hello, *bonjour!*"

"Hello, *bonjour!*" The greeting resounded this time with energy and conviction, amid a certain amount of laughter at the overall awkwardness of the moment. The ice was broken, and the room relaxed. The judge leaned forward, as if to confide in us, and began her discourse.

"I want to welcome all of you to this very special ceremony of Canadian citizenship," the judge intoned, in a manner so personal it was as though she was addressing each of us individually across the kitchen table. "It is a particular pleasure to welcome those of you who will shortly become new Canadian citizens, and I do feel extremely privileged and honoured to have the opportunity to share this moment with you. Today is a special day for you, your family and your friends. With this ceremony we are strengthening Canada."

The judge was specifically addressing her remarks to the new Canadians, and her message was spoken with conviction and came from the heart: "This is an important milestone in your lives. Canadian citizenship is a right you had to work to earn. You are embracing a wonderful country and we are all the richer for it. From the beginning, this country was built by the First Nations and by immigrants. Let me thank you for choosing Canada.

"The road to this ceremony has not always been easy. You made the agonizing decision to leave your home. When you got here, you faced many challenges: adapting to a new way of living, to a new culture, to an ever-changing climate, and perhaps to a new language. Some of you had to leave family members behind, and most of you left close friends. When you came you had to start from scratch, all over again.

We admire your courage. You are an example for all of us. Your perseverance is outstanding."

The judge shifted gears, moving on to address the rights and responsibilities of being Canadian, but always speaking in the same emotive, personal tones, gesturing constantly with her hands to make her point. She reflected on the real meaning of being Canadian, enumerating a number of fundamental Canadian rights: the right to be free from discrimination and persecution, the right to live and work in any province, the right to vote, the right to practise our own religion, and freedom to express our own opinions. Then she reminded everyone of the responsibilities of being Canadian, in particular the responsibility to give something back to Canada by participating in the community through volunteering, sharing and helping others. It was important for all Canadians to become involved.

Soon it was time for everyone to stand, and for the new Canadians to raise their right hands and take the oath of allegiance. We were all invited to join in. I looked over at the Brajshoris. Hajji's hand was held high, at the level of his head. I could see his lips moving in synchronization with the words, and I could feel the strength and conviction of his voice, even though I could not hear his words.

After the oath the judge moved down off the stage to present the individual certificates of citizenship and the accompanying citizenship cards. People were called up by family, and the Brajshoris, being near the beginning of the alphabet, were first to be called. The room had become quiet again, and I sensed that people were a little wary and uncertain of just how the certificate ceremony would proceed. Hajji set the tone. Beaming, he accepted his certificate from the judge, and immediately enveloped her in one of his traditional hugs. The room responded with a gasp, and then erupted in applause. The judge, smiling, responded graciously. Hajji had helped her set the informal, personal tone, I guessed, that she had been striving from the beginning to achieve.

When he arrived back at his place among the new citizens, Hajji looked over at us, his face filled with pride. Raising his thumb, he displayed his certificate for us to see. I am sure it was a moment he will never forget. Nor will we.

Following the certificate ceremony, the judge led everyone in sing-ing the national anthem, and then she posed with each family in turn for photographs. As Dani shook the judge's hand, he said, "We would like to have a picture with you. Every time I look at it I will remem-ber the beautiful words you said about being a Canadian. I am very proud to be a part of this country. I will treasure the memory of this day forever."

The proceedings over, we retired to the anteroom to retrieve our coats. I saw Hajji fumbling in one of his pockets, from which he drew a small package of dates. Hajji rushed back into the court room to find the judge before she left. Her face was to me and I saw her accepting the gift and engaging in light banter with Hajji. I suspected that she understood scarcely a word he said, given his thick accent and halting English, but there was no doubt in my mind that his message of pride and gratitude would be loud and clear.

After the ceremony the sponsors all joined the Brajshoris at their apartment to celebrate their citizenship. Nazife went into her hostess mode, serving coke, followed by a full Albanian meal and tea. "I cannot have a single guest come here and go away hungry," she informed us, when we chided her for doing so much work on this her special day.

We took advantage of the moment to have the Brajshoris sign their passport applications, which we would take to the Passport Office as soon as possible, along with their proof of citizenship. Now that they were citizens and could travel freely, Anne and I would be sending them on holiday to Kosovo. We asked them when they wanted to go, and they both replied eagerly, "As soon as possible!" We considered the options together. May was the best month for good weather. They also wanted to visit their old farm in Sharban at cherry-picking time in late May or early June. They had often talked over the years about these big, red, juicy cherries. In addition, they hoped they would be able to visit their son, Avdi, in Kosovo, and he could travel there from Germany to see them there if they went early in April. This became the deciding factor. They would go to Kosovo in early April, stay for two months, and come back in early June.

As promised by the Passport Office, the passports arrived promptly ten working days after we hand-delivered the applications to the Office in downtown Ottawa. Anne decided to throw a party as an occasion to formally present the passports to the Brajshoris. It would be a family affair—the senior couple, Dani and Valerie, and the two of us would gather at our apartment to eat and celebrate. Anne decided to make Albanian *fli*, a project that took her over two hours the morning of the party.

"It was worth the time," Dani pronounced as he took his first bite. Nazife was quick to agree. "This is really good," she effused. "You are a success as an Albanian cook."

The party continued with laughter and merriment as we finished the *fli* and moved on to fruit and dessert. Then it took on a more serious tone as we questioned them about their feelings on becoming Canadian citizens.

Nazife was first to respond. She was relaxed, eyes shining, and gestured rhythmically with both hands as she spoke. This was a new Nazife, so different from the quiet, retiring woman with sad, downcast eyes who had sat in the same chair almost five years earlier.

"I was looking forward to the ceremony. It was good to know I would become a part of this place. The only thing is I was hoping they would not ask me any questions, because I knew I could not respond in English. When they gave me papers to hold with the oath written on them, I was afraid I would have to say the oath by myself. I was relieved when everyone said it together. I saw that the people around me were happy, even if I did not know what was being said. I like to be a Canadian because people here are so nice. No matter where I go, people are never rude or angry.

"I know I have changed a lot. I have changed in every respect. Many of the old traditions are gone. I have seen so many things that we never saw back home. If you see something often enough, you will accept it. For example, I used to sit and wait to be called to the telephone. Now I jump on it when it rings, like everyone else. In the old country, men and women used to sit apart. Here, no one cares where they sit, so I don't either, and we all sit together. At home, when I would go out to a wedding, I used to take my food and go off somewhere quietly by myself or with a few women. Now I go and sit with everyone else. I like the new way."

It was Hajji's turn to share his feelings about being a Canadian.

He considered the issue carefully, his eyes lost in thought. He licked the outside of a cigarette, a ritual learned long ago in smoky rooms of family and friends. Then he peeled a tangerine and ate it, still contemplating. The long hesitation was quite unlike Hajji, and we all waited patiently. Finally he spoke.

"I am happy I can vote. I never had a chance to vote before. I worked a long time in Kosovo for democracy, for the right to vote. Now I have it. It is for me the realization of a lifelong dream.

"The Canadian passport is also very important to me. Now I have a country. Now I belong. If I go back to Kosovo and somebody threatens me or tells me I am wanted for something that happened in the past, I will just show my Canadian passport. All the problems and conflicts of the past can be forgotten. I can walk away from them. I am a Canadian now."

Hajji's lips curled up into a smile. He had remembered an anecdote from the past that was amusing him, and wanted to share it with us. He launched into his story.

"When I was back in Kosovo preparing my first pilgrimage to Mecca, the officials told me I needed a visa for Saudi Arabia, but they would not give me one. I went anyway. When I came back, they asked me where I had been. I told them honestly that I had been to Saudi Arabia. They said, 'How can that be? You need a visa to go there.' I said, 'Yes, but I do not need a visa to come home.' They said, 'That doesn't matter. You went illegally. You will be charged with this crime, and the fine will be 4000 German marks.' My case was waiting in the courts when war broke out in Kosovo. The building where the court records were held was bombed and burned. I was laughing and making jokes with my friends as we watched the building go up in smoke. They did not see it funny that the court was burning, and they asked me why I was laughing. I said, 'I am laughing because the trumped-up charges against me are burning. With that fire, my debts are being paid.'"

We all joined in the laughter, as I tried to imagine the special qualities of this man who could find delight in the irony of a situation which in all other respects was frightening and horrible, if not completely tragic.

Hajji wanted to make another point. He raised his hand to indicate that he was about to speak.

"I have always been against conflict and violence. Now that I am a Canadian I can leave violence behind for good. But when I was in Kosovo I worked for non-violent solutions, too. In fact my mind was so attuned to non-violence that I missed opportunities. You know that in Kosovo before the war I was a security guard. The president of my company gave me the key to the security vault where all of security's guns were kept. He told me my job was to clean the guns. I did not realize it at the time, but he knew I was one of the leaders of the protest movement, and he was giving me a chance to steal the guns. As it was I did not think of stealing them. Now, in retrospect, I am glad I did not steal them. It would have led to violence and bloodshed. I am glad I did not provoke violence.

"Later on, the president was fired and a new one came in. He knew I was marching with the protesters because he saw me on TV with them in the marches. As soon as he saw that, he transferred me out of security. He thought I was a threat. He told me I could retire. But I kept going in to work until my first pension check arrived. I did not trust him to give me my pension."

Now it was Dani's turn. "I am happy to be a citizen," he began, "because I feel as though I finally belong somewhere. I have a country. I was tired of being an immigrant. Now I have the proper papers when applying for a job, and I can work anywhere, including the government. Also, it is great to have a passport, instead of a travel document that always had to be updated and would not even let me travel to Kosovo. More than anything it is a new feeling of belonging. I cannot really describe it but if you had no country you would know better what I mean. I am now a full-fledged member of Canadian society. I like the "philosophy" in Canada. It is a good place to live. For example, here people think, reason and discuss when they have disagreements, rather than becoming violent. In Canada you have to work hard for what you get, but at least there is opportunity to advance."

We all moved over to the living room, where we would later share tea. The time had come for the presentation of the passports. Without fanfare, I handed out the treasured documents. Hajji, Nazife and Dani all beamed as we captured the moment on video. Hajji made a big show by holding his passport high, then kissing it and tucking it carefully in his suit coat pocket, which he then patted proudly.

"We are so grateful to you all," he said as he jabbed the air with his index finger to emphasize his meaning. "Thank you, thank you, thank you all – Davi, Anna, Valerie, and all the sponsors. We have never received a treat like this before."

Nazife added her words of thanks. "We have never been taken care of the way you and the other sponsors took care of us. Some people look after others out of obligation, but you did it from your heart. Parents sometimes have disputes and problems with their children. That is normal. But we never had disputes with you or the other sponsors. Sometimes, we wonder if you look after yourselves as well as you look after us. If there is another world, as we all hope there is, you will be there."

"If it was not for you," Dani added, "I would not even be here."

"The last five years have been the best years of our lives," Nazife summed it up. "We have had no problems. We have felt safe. We have had everything that we needed."

Speaking calmly and in a serious tone that that we had come to know always revealed his true inner feelings, Hajji echoed his wife's sentiment, "In Kosovo we have an expression, *flej shlir*. It means 'sleep with no worries.' Since we arrived in Canada we have been able to sleep with no worries. That's what Canada means for us – *flej shlir*."

"Given the centuries of problems in the Balkans, it has not always been possible to sleep with no worries," Dani explained. "In fact, sleeping with no worries has been the exception to the rule. That is why we value it so highly."

Dani's explanation struck a chord. *Flej shlir* encapsulated in so many ways how the Brajshoris' lives had changed over the past five years, and what Canada meant for these three proud new Canadians. But it was only half the story. What had the Brajshoris meant to us? I thought back over the good times, the tears, and the hard work that we had shared with this family. Both Anne and I marvelled at what they had accomplished, and we were proud to have been a part of it. Little did we know when we chose to become sponsors that it would affect us so profoundly. We had been inalterably changed, and for the better. Our lives had been enriched.

Flej shlir, I repeated to myself as I watched the Brajshoris' smiling faces and listened to Hajji launch into yet another anecdote. In my mind I could see three separate threads – peace, freedom, and democracy – threads that came together in *flej shlir*. The Brajshoris had spent all their lives pursuing these threads, sometimes grasping one, sometimes another, only to have them pulled away. Now in their new country the threads had all come together. Their journey was over. They were home.

ISBN 142514377-6